EU Values in Investment Law and Policy

OXFORD STUDIES IN EUROPEAN LAW

Series Editors:
Paul Craig, Professor of English Law at St John's College, Oxford and
Gráinne de Búrca, Professor of Law at New York University School of Law

The aim of this series is to publish important and original research on EU law. The focus is on scholarly monographs, with a particular emphasis on those which are interdisciplinary in nature. Edited collections of essays will also be included where they are appropriate. The series is wide in scope and aims to cover studies of particular areas of substantive and of institutional law, historical works, theoretical studies, and analyses of current debates, as well as questions of perennial interest such as the relationship between national and EU law and the novel forms of governance emerging in and beyond Europe. The fact that many of the works are interdisciplinary will make the series of interest to all those concerned with the governance and operation of the EU.

OTHER TITLES IN THIS SERIES

Saving the European Union from its Illiberal Member States
András Jakab and Lando Kirchmair

Constitutional Disintegration and Disruption
Withdrawal and Opt-Outs from the European Union
Oliver Garner

Business Freedoms and Fundamental Rights in European Union Law
Niall O'Connor

Compliance with European Consumer Law
The Case of E-Commerce
Felix Pflücke

Legislative Authority and Interpretation in the European Union
Martijn van den Brink

Secession and European Union Law
The Deferential Attitude
Núria González Campañá

Fiscal State Aid Law and Harmful Tax Competition in the European Union
Dimitrios Kyriazis

The Abuse of Constitutional Identity in the European Union
Julian Scholtes

Judging European Democracy
The Role and Legitimacy of National Constitutional Courts in the EU
Nik de Boer

EU Values Before the Court of Justice
Foundations, Potential, Risks
Luke Dimitrios Spieker

Postnational Constitutionalism
Europe and the Time of Law
Paul Linden-Retek

The Legislative Priority Rule and the EU Internal Market for Goods
A Constitutional Approach
Eadaoin Ní Chaoimh

The Jurisprudence of Constitutional Conflict in the European Union
Ana Bobić

Reflexive Governance in EU Equality Law
Emma Lantschner

Enhanced Cooperation and European Tax Law
Caroline Heber

EU Values in Investment Law and Policy

Promises of Democracy and Rule of Law?

Maria Laura Marceddu

OXFORD
UNIVERSITY PRESS

OXFORD
UNIVERSITY PRESS

Great Clarendon Street, Oxford, OX2 6DP,
United Kingdom

Oxford University Press is a department of the University of Oxford.
It furthers the University's objective of excellence in research, scholarship,
and education by publishing worldwide. Oxford is a registered trade mark of
Oxford University Press in the UK and in certain other countries.

Published in the United States of America by Oxford University Press
198 Madison Avenue, New York, NY 10016, United States of America.

British Library Cataloguing in Publication Data
Data available

Library of Congress Control Number: 2025934327

ISBN 9780192899576

DOI: 10.1093/9780191986208.001.0001

Printed and bound by
CPI Group (UK) Ltd., Croydon, CR0 4YY

MIX
Paper | Supporting responsible forestry
FSC® C013604

The manufacturer's authorised representative in the EU for product safety is
Oxford University Press España S.A., Parque Empresarial San Fernando de Henares,
Avenida de Castilla, 2 – 28830 Madrid (www.oup.es/en or product.safety@oup.com).
OUP España S.A. also acts as importer into Spain of products made by the manufacturer.

To those who never give up, like my Mum and Dad

Series Editors' Preface

This book deals with the important issue as to whether the EU is able to apply values that are central to its internal ordering when it engages in external action. The book pursues this inquiry in relation to the values of democracy and the rule of law, and the extent to which those EU values have been expanded into the international investments' regime. The EU's new competence in relation to international investments post-Lisbon raises the question as to whether the EU can align its external actions in a manner that is consistent with its internal principles.

This study is not predicated on an 'EU model', which is to be imposed or transplanted from the EU legal order to the regime of international investments. The focus is rather on the extent to which there is evidence to suggest a projection of the EU values of democracy and the rule of law into international investment law and policy. This is more especially so given that there have been calls for reform within the regime of international investments, what the author terms 'demand for adjustment'. The thrust of the ensuing argument is as to whether the EU is able to capitalize on this need for adjustment as an opportunity to reaffirm its core values concerning democracy and the rule of law.

The book is structured into three parts. Part I considers the EU value of democracy and examines how democracy is incorporated into the international investment regime. This includes discussion of the way in which transparency and public participation have become the EU's channels for projecting democracy in this regime. Part II is concerned with the EU value of the rule of law. The EU's conception of the rule of law embodies both formal and substantive dimensions of the concept. There is analysis as to how far the rule of law thus conceived is applied within the international investment regime at both a micro and a macro level. Part III of the book reflects on the limitations of the EU project in this area, the internal and external rationales for such limitations and the prospects for further developments in the future.

The book deals with a topic that is important and that has not hitherto been considered in depth. It will be of interest to scholars of commercial policy and international investment, and also more broadly to those interested in EU values and their influence in different substantive areas.

Paul Craig and Gráinne de Búrca

Acknowledgements

This book is my opportunity to share my ideas about the EU's promises of democracy and the rule of law within one of the most chaotic and evolving systems of international law: the regime of foreign investments. It is the culmination of a journey that began in London and was inspired by my doctoral research project. At King's College London, my supervisor Federico Ortino provided invaluable guidance, profound knowledge, and immense generosity. He has been a mentor and a role model, embodying the kind of scholar and human being I aspire to become. I am deeply indebted to him. During my time at King's, I had the pleasure of collaborating with Andrea Biondi (now also Advocate General at the Court of Justice of the European Union) and Holger Hestermeyer (now at the Diplomatische Akademie Wien); to them I express my sincere gratitude.

I am particularly grateful to Gráinne de Búrca and Paul Craig, the Oxford Studies in European Law (OSEL) Editors, for believing in my project; to Kathryn Plunkett, and Jacqueline Ridberg Larabee for their invaluable editorial assistance; to Kiruthiga and her team at Newgen for the publication management.

The various stages of this book were completed in different places, and I am grateful to the institutions and individuals who made this possible. The Law School of the University of Edinburgh was a nurturing place and I owe my gratitude to both my students and colleagues. I am particularly thankful to Andrew Lang, Nehal Bhuta, Filippo Fontanelli, and Ana María Daza Vargas. The hills of the European University Institute (EUI) provide new sources of inspiration for the journey. This would not have been possible without the help of the Working Group of International Economic Law. I am particularly grateful to my mentor Jürgen Kurtz, as well as Ernst-Ulrich Petersmann, Dorian-Ciprian Grumaz, and Tobias Traxler for their challenging questions and detailed comments on specific chapters. Many scholars, colleagues, and friends have provided comments on drafts related to this book or posed thought-provoking questions along the way. In particular, I would like to thank Lorand Bartels, Colin Brown, Mary Footer, Moshe Hirsch, Clara Lopez Rodriguez, Tibisay Morgandi, Pietro Ortolani, Lauge Poulsen, Christopher Vadjia KC, and Joseph H. H. Weiler for their insightful contribution. Thank you also to others who helped through friendly conversation, good advice, or both: Pinar Artiran, Elisa Baroncini, Laurence Boisson de Chazournes, Maria Beatrice Deli (to whom I owe the merit of introducing me to international investment law), Ilaria Espa, Ignacio García Bercero, Claudio Gasperini, Gabrielle Marceau, Gracia Marín Durán, Sergio Puig, Cécile Rapoport, Peter-Tobias Stoll, Christos Tassis, and Marina Trunk-Fedorova.

Some friends had little, if any, idea that I was writing a book. Yet they believed in me anyway especially when I did not. Their encouragement and support kept me from giving up. Special thanks go to D. Francesco, Gabriele, Franziska, Louise, and Rebecca.

My deepest thanks go to my parents for the gift of life, their support, and their unwavering belief in me—never giving up on life or on me. This book is dedicated with love to them and to all those, like myself, who strive not to give up.

Contents

Detailed Contents

Tables

Table of Cases

Court of Justice of the EU and Court of first Instance/ General Court

Opinions

Investment arbitrations

Abbreviations

Abbreviation	Meaning
AB	Appellate Body
ASEAN	Association of South-East Asian Nations
BIT	Bilateral Investment Treaty
CAFTA	Central America Free Trade Agreement
CAI	EU–China Comprehensive Agreement on Investment
CCP	Common Commercial Policy
CETA	Comprehensive Economic and Trade Agreement between Canada and the European Union (and its Member States)
CJEU	Court of Justice of the European Union
EC	European Community
ECT	Energy Charter Treaty
EEC	European Economic Community
ERT	European Round Table of Industrialists
EU	European Union
FDI	Foreign Direct Investment
FET	Fair and Equitable Treatment
FTC	Free Trade Commission
FTA	Free Trade Agreement
GATS	The General Agreement on Trade in Services
GATT	General Agreement on Tariffs and Trade
GDPR	General Data Protection Regulation
ICJ	International Court of Justice
ICS	Investment Court System
ICSID	International Centre for Settlement of Investment Disputes
IGC	Intergovernmental conference
IIA	International Investment Agreement
ILO	International Labour Organization
IPA	Investment Protection Agreement
ISDS	Investor-State Dispute Settlement
MERCOSUR	Mercado Comùn del Sur (Southern Common Market)
MIC	Multilateral Investment Court
MFN	Most-Favoured Nation

MST	Minimum Standard of Treatment
NAFTA	North American Free Trade Agreement
NGO	Non-governmental organization
OECD	Organisation for Economic Co-operation and Development
PO	Procedural Order
QMV	Qualified majority voting
SIA	Sustainable impact assessment
SOE	State-owned enterprises
TEU	Treaty on European Union
TFEU	Treaty on the Functioning of the European Union
TRIMS	Agreement on Trade-Related Investment Measures
TSD	Trade and Sustainable Development
TTIP	Transatlantic Trade and Investment Partnership
UNCITRAL	United Nations Commission on International Trade Law
UNCTAD	United Nations Conference on Trade and Development
VCLT	Vienna Convention on the Law of Treaties
WG	Working Group
WTO	World Trade Organization

1
Introduction

A. Overview

Is it possible that values like democracy and the rule of law can expand from EU borders to the realm of international investments? No matter how fascinating the idea that values (be they legal, social, or economic) know no borders and transcend geographical boundaries, the most honest answer is likely to be 'perhaps, perhaps, perhaps'. Like the song[1] where a man wishes that a woman would declare her love definitely, yet she never does, so it is with the values the EU holds dear—democracy and the rule of law (Article 2 of the Treaty on European Union (TEU)). However sound and promising these EU values appear on paper, their way into the regime of international investments is fraught with uncertainties. EU aficionados would view the international investment regime as a new political opportunity for the EU to shape the world according to the rules established in Brussels. The most sceptical observers might view the EU's ambition to promote and export normative values such as democracy and the rule of law as overly ambitious, or even unrealistic, given its evident internal flaws. This scepticism is particularly pertinent given that the investment regime already embodies these principles to some degree, and that the EU may not be in a position to provide exemplary guidance on matters such as democracy, the rule of law, or human rights. Nevertheless, more idealistic perspectives—such as that of the author—find it compelling to explore whether elements of the visionary ethos that have defined the EU's narrative since its inception can be discerned within the regime of foreign investment, arguably one of the most controversial frameworks in global governance.

It is this visionary component that piqued my curiosity and coalesced into a book to 'carry the fire'[2] and continues to tell precisely that story of vision—albeit in a fairly downsized and less idealized form. Inspired by premises that have become promises of democracy and the rule of law, the book is concerned

[1] Day, Doris (1965), *Perhaps, Perhaps, Perhaps*.
[2] McCarthy, Cormac (2006), *The Road*.

EU Values in Investment Law And Policy. Maria Laura Marceddu, Oxford University Press.
 DOI: 10.1093/9780191986208.003.0001

with how, and to what extent, these EU values expanded into the international investments regime. While the book is not an ode to the EU, there is potential for the EU to leave an imprint on the international investment dynamics. It is this potential that this book unravels to explain how the international investment regime problems are turned into an opportunity for the EU to extend its normative values in a new field. The story of thriving in critical times sounds quite familiar to the EU but is often vested with more rhetoric than being taken at face value. The regime of international investment is no exception to this unfortunate trend, albeit it displays some moments of sparks in its unfolding.

The expansion of laws and values across geographical boundaries has long captivated both political and legal scholars. The EU, in particular, has demonstrated remarkable creativity in extending its economic and normative influence beyond its borders. Beyond imposing its preferred model of economic integration and political cooperation on prospective members through accession and neighbourhood policies, the EU has increasingly relied on political and economic conditionality—such as sanctions—as a favoured modus operandi. In addition, the EU's regulatory capacity to create market-based incentives for global compliance with its rules has drawn significant attention. Yet the question of whether investment agreements[3] and the policies underpinning their negotiations could be vectors for transmitting EU values has remained largely unexplored. After the Lisbon Treaty bestowed upon the Union exclusive competence over foreign direct investments (FDIs), attention has been shed on the EU as a new golden standard setter, on the constraints of its new competence, and on the ambiguity that permeates investment agreements as proper instruments to ensure development. The question of whether the EU vision of democracy and rule of law is fulfilled or defective with respect to the regime of international investments, however, remained largely disregarded.

Truth be told, the Lisbon Treaty and the consequent entry of the EU into the regime of international investments most likely codify an expansion of the Union's (read the Commission's) exclusive competence rather than a promise for a better future. As often the case with EU law, the simple addition of the phrase 'Foreign Direct Investment' among the exclusive competences[4] was

[3] It appears that trade and finance treaties show consistent effectiveness. Agreements like the North American Free Trade Agreement (NAFTA), the World Trade Organization (WTO), and Mercosur have boosted trade, investment, and market access, especially for developing nations. Mercosur also improved competitiveness and human rights observance among members. However, most international treaties fail to achieve their intended goals. Trade and finance stand out as notable exceptions. See on this point Hoffman, Steven J and Others (2022), 'International Treaties Have Mostly Failed to Produce Their Intended Effects', Proceedings of the National Academy of Sciences USA.

[4] Among the novelties introduced by the Lisbon Treaty, the Common Commercial Policy includes trade-related aspects of intellectual property as well.

more a combination of political chance and stealth[5] rather than a politically rational choice. It radically altered the multilayered situation governing international investments, however, and, by shifting competence from Member States to the Commission, it increased the EU's international role significantly. The new competence enhanced the EU's ability to project its norms, values, and rules on a global scale, following the precedent set by other countries, such as the North American Free Trade Agreement (NAFTA) members, which had long established themselves in this arena. However, it also challenged the EU's capacity to ensure that its external actions align consistently with its internal principles, particularly within the regime of international investments.

Just like in marriage, where one hardly knows the person until they are together, when the EU gained competence over FDI it probably had a vague idea of the storm that was about to hit the legitimacy of the regime of international investments. The EU's gradual placing on the international investment chessboard, in fact, coincides with an escalation of events that started at the end of the 1990s with a wave of lawsuits in the ambit of NAFTA, reached a peak around the 2010s,[6] and have become somewhat chronic since. While it is challenging to pinpoint the exact moment when the malaise first arose, it is clear that since the early 2000s, the system has faced unprecedented levels of contestation. This backlash has been driven by the increasing discretion afforded to arbitral tribunals, the marginalization of states in the decision-making process,[7] and the structural inability of the regime to adequately address concerns that extend beyond the purely economic sphere, such as health, environmental, social, and labour issues.

It is at this yet unsettling moment that the EU gained formal recognition of its exclusive competence over FDIs and, as frequently happens with the EU's history, a crisis provided opportunities. My intuition is that the EU intruded on a moment of investment regime disquiet and sought to introduce a new *EU way* of shaping the global rules of the game. The intuition is simple, but,

[5] Meunier, Sophie (2014), 'Integration by Stealth: How the European Union Gained Competence over Foreign Direct Investment', European University Institute Robert Schuman Centre for Advanced Studies (EUI RSCAS) Global Governance.

[6] Bolivia, Ecuador, and Venezuela withdrew from the International Centre for Settlement of Investment Disputes (ICSID) convention in 2007, 2009, and 2012 respectively, and Ecuador rejoined in 2021. In 2014, Indonesia announced its intention to terminate its Bilateral Investment Treaties (BITs). South Africa has begun a similar programme of termination. India followed suit and issued a new model BIT in 2016.

[7] As Pelc observes, although the Investor-State Dispute Settlement (ISDS) regime has been in existence for over fifty years, the majority of cases in its history have been initiated within the past decade. Effectively, states and investors are navigating what is, in practice, a relatively new legal recourse mechanism. Pelc, Krzysztof (2017), 'What Explains the Low Success Rate of Investor–State Disputes?', International Organization.

as I hope to show, also very illuminating: some systemic issues affecting the investment regime functioning (i.e. the inputs) triggered an EU response. The EU attempted to address these issues by delivering outputs modelled on what the EU stands for—at least on paper—and diffusing its values, as spelled out in the Treaties. The framework builds on the promise and premise that, in the EU's eyes, its values could, or at least promise to provide, effective responses to the problems affecting the investment regime.[8] Whether this holds true or not is for the book to uncover.

From this standpoint, the regime of international investment presents new political and legal opportunities to extend the influence of the rules established in Brussels. Should this be the case, the EU could demonstrate the resilience of its visionary approach, which has been integral to its identity, despite frequent challenges to its efficacy. Prior to addressing the core issues, this chapter will outline the EU's concepts of democracy and the rule of law (Section B), clarify the research methodology (Section C), describe the research approach (Section D), and explain the structure of the book (Section E).

B. The EU concepts of democracy and the rule of law

The EU is often depicted as a common space for democracy and the rule of law. This section briefly attends to key definitional matters and delineates the EU values categories of democracy and rule of law in a manner that is sound for international investment law scholars as well. A complementary and more pointed explanation of each key concept is offered at the beginning of Part I (democracy) and Part II (rule of law) respectively. Although the values of democracy and rule of law possess different interpretative nuances and do not necessarily mean the same for EU and investment law scholars, there are a few points on which both systems of interpretation tend to converge. The challenge, therefore, is to identify the points that distinguish and characterize the EU concepts of democracy and the rule of law and, at the same time, resonate within the international investment regime.[9]

[8] For example, albeit formulated in a different context but still very much in line with this approach, the EU believed that its proposal of a two-tier mechanism 'is the only type of reform which can effectively respond to all the concerns identified'. UNCITRAL Working Group III (24 January 2019), 'Possible Reform of Investor-State Dispute Settlement (ISDS) Submission from the European Union and its Member States', UN Doc A/CN.9/WG.III/WP.159/Add 1, 40.

[9] See Section D, and Parts I and II.

The Lisbon Treaty expressively refers to democracy and the rule of law as the principles that have inspired the creation of the EU and should guide the EU in its external relations. Article 21 TEU includes a list of foundational values like human rights, fundamental freedoms, human dignity, equality, and solidarity, along with respect for the principles of the UN Charter and international law. Amidst this list of options, the choice of this book to focus on democracy and rule of law appears rather straightforward. One first reason is that these two values/principles constitute the essential foundations, the core, that build up the Union and have gradually evolved into EU primary law. Though the original Treaties did not offer many anchors to the rule of law or democracy, they gradually became a 'given', up to the point of becoming requirements for joining the Union. While there is no hierarchy among EU values, rather intuitively, respect for the rule of law is essential for the respect of all other values.[10] In this respect, Habermas argues for an internal normative connection and also a practical one between public rights anchored in popular sovereignty and democracy, and private rights protected by the rule of law.[11] A second reason behind this choice is the congruence of these two values from an investment law perspective as well. While manifestations of democracy and the rule of law are subtle yet discernible within the investment system, other values such as human dignity, equality, and human rights may be present to some extent only. However, their interaction with investment protection is complex and remains nebulous at best.[12] This issue is not immune to criticism even within the EU, particularly given that the EU itself is not a member of the European Convention on Human Rights, although all its Member States are.

Democracy and the rule of law are abstract concepts. It would be naïve to talk of a comprehensible rule of law or democracy—or liberty or peace—that adequately reflects an unequivocal position, especially in the absence of explicit definitions within the EU Treaties. However, as has often become the unintentional practice of the EU, the Court of Justice of the European Union (CJEU) has, even in this context, taken on the role of putting flesh on the bones of these values, thereby shaping and defining their contours with greater precision. Rather reluctantly, the Court has provided its normative imprimatur to these values, often mediating between economic considerations (good for the market) and moral (good for all) considerations. For example,

[10] Case C-156/21, *Hungary v Parliament and Council*, EU:C:2022:97.

[11] Habermas, Jürgen (1995), 'On the Internal Relations between the Rule of Law and Democracy', European Journal of Philosophy.

[12] Scheu, Julian and Others (2022), *Investment Protection, Human Rights, and International Arbitration in Extraordinary Times*.

in *Van Gend en Loos*—one of the first cases that indirectly touched upon the value of democracy—the Court called for cooperation between 'nationals of the states brought together in the Community' for its functioning 'through the intermediary of the European Parliament and the Economic and Social Committee'.[13] In one of its earliest landmark rulings, *Les Verts*, the Court described the European Community as a Community founded on the rule of law, emphasizing that neither its Member States nor its institutions are above the law. It asserted that they cannot evade judicial scrutiny regarding whether the measures they adopt conform to the Community's basic constitutional charter—the Treaty—thereby underscoring the centrality of judicial review in upholding the rule of law.[14]

While putting some flesh on treaty bones, the Court was and has consistently remained prudent in interpreting the treaties teleologically. After all, some would argue, and rightly so, that it was not the Court's prerogative or mission to give meaning to treaty drafters' intentions, especially with morally intricate issues like the value of democracy or the rule of law. It would be too naïve, however, to dismiss the Court's implication in the democratic deficit and legitimacy crisis that affects the EU. Truth be told, the *Van Gend en Loos*'s cooperation link was rather weak, with the European Parliament often left out of the Commission and Council travails. The Court did not, rightly or wrongly (depending on where one stands), denounce a highly problematic decision-making process but interpreted the treaty in light of a predominantly, if not exclusive, economic spirit, in some measures at the expense of democratic legitimation.[15] The 'general scheme' remained the Single Market where nationals of states are called to cooperate through the Parliament, which, however, problematically sat in the decision-making process. The Court did not rectify this uncomfortable situation and contributed to maintaining the status quo. Although the role of the Parliament has expanded since then, the consequences of these birth deficits have not vanished and citizens are still far from influencing the outcomes of any political choices, hence maintaining the image of the EU as a democracy of means rather than ends.[16]

[13] Case 26/62, *van Gend & Loos v Netherlands*, EU:C:1963:1.

[14] Case 294/83, *Les Verts v European Parliament*, EU:C:1986:166.

[15] Weiler Joseph (2012), 'Deciphering the Political and Legal DNA of European Integration: An Exploratory Essay.' In *Philosophical Foundations of European Union Law*, edited by Julie Dickson and Pavlos Eleftheriadis, 153–5.

[16] Kochenov, Dimitry (2004), 'Behind the Copenhagen Facade. The Meaning and Structure of the Copenhagen Political Criterion of Democracy and the Rule of Law', European Integration Online Papers.

When it comes to the rule of law, the picture is slightly different. The preliminary ruling procedure gave individuals the chance to enforce their Community rights vis-à-vis the Member States. Interestingly, preliminary rulings frequently created scenarios where personal and private interests were upheld against the Community itself, ensuring that its actions remained firmly within the boundaries of the law. This dynamic underscored the role of judicial oversight in safeguarding individual rights while holding the Community accountable to its own legal framework. In these stances, the Court was more assertive than in the context of democracy and mitigated possible distortions deriving from these (private) vindications imposing respect for human rights as an unquestionable condition, thus reinforcing what was already very much in line with the Member States' constitutional traditions.

More recently, the Court has exhibited audacity in engaging with democracy and the rule of law. It has begun interpreting Article 2 TEU in operational terms, granting it judicial application. A significant starting point for this reorientation is the *Associação Sindical dos Juízes Portugueses* case, which represents a departure from the Court's traditional scarce reference to democracy and the rule of law. As Spieker argues, this reorientation has expanded in three main directions since. First, Article 2 TEU values are considered justiciable for individuals. Second, the Court has been interpreting other provisions in a way that gives expression to these values.[17] Lastly, Article 2 TEU has evolved from merely being part of a constitutional content, though its precise contours can be narrowed or expanded. The extent of this expansion or narrowing positions Article 2 TEU values as benchmarks for the judiciary, endowing the legal with a powerful political tool. While these developments can be viewed as positive advances, they are unlikely to bridge the gap between the ideals preached by the EU and the reality in which it operates, particularly concerning democracy and the rule of law.

International investment agreements (IIAs), on their part, say very little about the definition of democracy and rule of law. They contain a set of general obligations for the states hosting the investment to protect the foreign investor and its assets, and accord them fairly and non-discriminatory treatment as if they were domestic investors. Democracy and the rule of law might occasionally feature the preamble's commitments of an investment agreement but no definitions are attached to these concepts, possibly because the expectation that they had to ensure at least some adherence to them took time to emerge.

[17] Spieker, Luke Dimitrios (2023), *EU Values Before the Court of Justice: Foundations, Potential, Risks*, 22–28.

Investment treaties remained dormant for a long time since the first bilateral investment treaty (BIT) was signed off in 1959 between Germany and Pakistan. Often driven by the enthusiasm and need to attract foreign investments, states voluntarily bound themselves to broad commitments of 'promotion and protection of investment', even if the reach and implication of these commitments were not entirely foreseeable at the time of treaty ratification. This was particularly true for developing countries,[18] whereas developed countries, with Member States at the forefront, sought to capitalize on violations of the rights accorded to their private investors investing abroad, while eventually seeking remedies when IIA's substantial protections impinged on their own regulatory capacity.[19]

This seemed to be further exacerbated by the broad authority granted to arbitral tribunals to review matters of public interest and award compensation from public funds when certain public policy choices amounted to treaty violations. The 'side effects' of investment arbitration at the domestic level suddenly became noticeable to a larger audience, especially when highly publicized cases like *Vattenfall v Germany* and *Philip Morris v Uruguay* demonstrated that investment tribunal decisions could hinder domestic policy goals and infringe upon domestic sensitivities. The more these investment claims arise, the greater the need to justify the accountability and fairness of the judicial review powers bestowed upon arbitrators reviewing matters of domestic public interest. Unlike the EU, where democracy and the rule of law were at least theoretically foundational principles, within the investment regime, democracy and the rule of law had to emerge as aspirational benchmarks[20] to address systemic legitimacy and foster acceptance.

To understand how the EU promises and the investment regime's expectations meet, the most promising angle for this research is to concentrate on the core manifestations that have shaped the contours of democracy and the rule of law in both legal systems. Investment tribunals have seldom dealt with issues like the rule of law and democracy. The former, however, has often been

[18] For example, Pakistan's Attorney-General described investment treaties as 'a piece of paper, something for the press, a good photo opportunity and that was the end of it'. 'Reflections on Pakistan's Investment Treaty Program after 50 Years: An Interview with the former Attorney-General of Pakistan, Makhdoom Ali Khan', *Investment Treaty News* (16 March 2009) http://www.investmenttreatynews.org.

[19] While it remains difficult to pinpoint the exact moment when dissatisfaction within the investment regime first surfaced, it is reasonable to trace its origins to the initial wave of NAFTA lawsuits in the late 1990s. Additionally, United Nations Conference on Trade and Development (UNCTAD) identified 2008 as the onset of a reorientation era for the investment regime, likely to have been spurred by the growing number of lawsuits during that period. See Sornarajah, Muthucumaraswamy (2015), *Resistance and Change in the International Law on Foreign Investment*.

[20] See Section D.

interpreted as a procedural condition for the respect of investors' rights.[21] Unsurprisingly, the EU—the CJEU and the Commission in particular—has been more prominent in unpacking these two principles into a non-exhaustive set of 'measurable' manifestations.

Under EU law, the rule of law encompasses several fundamental principles: the principle of legality; a transparent, accountable, democratic, and pluralistic process for enacting laws; legal certainty; the prohibition of arbitrariness in executive power; effective judicial protection; access to independent and impartial courts; the separation of powers; and equality before the law.[22] The concept of democracy, central to the EU's values, is closely tied to the aspiration of fostering 'an ever closer union among the peoples of Europe, in which decisions are taken as openly as possible and as closely as possible to the citizen' (Article 1 TEU). To enhance the legitimacy and accountability of EU institutions in the eyes of its citizens, certain recurring principles and practices are emphasized. These include: ensuring the legitimacy of the legislative process as a whole; upholding the principle of transparency; guaranteeing access to documents; promoting fairness, justice, and openness; encouraging the participation of civil society; and safeguarding the lawfulness of individual legislative measures.[23]

Although all these manifestations are somehow linked to one another, I found that some aspects like legal certainty, the impartiality of the adjudication system, judicial protection's effectiveness, transparency, access to documents, and civil society participation emerged as EU distinguishing traits in the regime of international investments. For this book, it is not necessary to have a strict definition of democracy and the rule of law (and anyway, one that is universally accepted does not exist). It is enough to concentrate on these traits as indications of the spillover of EU values into the investment system. This, however, is not to agree with the neo-functionalism argument, according to which integration in one sphere placed pressure to achieve functional and political integration in other areas. Rather, it is to emphasize how democracy and the rule of law *à la* EU offered grounds to address certain structural problems of the investment regime.

[21] *Petrobart v Kyrgyzstan* (Award, 29 March 2005).

[22] *Hungary v Parliament and Council* (n 10); Craig, Paul and De Búrca, Gráinne (2020), *EU Law: Text, Cases, and Materials*.

[23] Articles 1, 10, and 11 Consolidated version of the Treaty on European Union, OJ C 326, 26 October 2012 (TEU); Article 15 Consolidated version of the Treaty on the Functioning of the European Union, OJ C 326, 26 October 2012 (TFEU). Case C-157/21, *Poland v Parliament and Council*, EU:C:2022:98; joined cases C-106/19 and C-232/19, *Italy, Comune di Milano v Commission*, EU:C:2022:568; case C-57/16 P, *ClientEarth v Commission*, EU:C:2018:660.

C. Can normative values be spread from one regime to another?

Having delineated the concepts of democracy and the rule of law, the next step in studying the influence of EU values on the investment regime is to conceptualize the mechanisms of their diffusion. Given that nearly all legal traditions are in continuous contact with one or more other traditions, and that regulations overlap across countries, the question of legal transplants has garnered significant interest from both legal and political scholars. A substantial and intricate body of norm export theories has emerged to explain the occurrence of these legal transplants. However, as this section will elucidate, none of these theories appear particularly suitable for the current investigation.

Before addressing the shortcomings of these theories in Section 2, Section 1 offers clarifications regarding the terminology adopted throughout this book.

1. Setting the scene: the meaning of 'value' in the EU context

What does 'value' mean? Value is an abstract concept representing something regarded as worthy, important, or useful, often closely associated with desirable ideals. From a normative perspective, the notion of value transcends mere compliance with legal rules, instead reflecting a deeper connection to the vision of justice upheld by a legal system.[24]

When it comes to the EU context, the book you are holding is acutely aware of the confusion caused by the terminology introduced by the Lisbon Treaty. The TEU Preamble describes values as the product of Europe's cultural, religious, and humanist heritage, serving as the foundations upon which the Union is built. These values are vested with symbolic significance that must be expressed in legal norms. The values listed under Article 2 TEU[25] constitute both a source of and index for cross-national differentiation and assimilation of the most important aspects of the political culture and identity of European societies. These values provide the overarching point of reference that outlines the basic tenets of the Union's constitutional foundation.[26] They are more significant than the general concept of values in constitutional contexts, reaching as deep as the very foundation of the European legal order. These values

[24] Kingsbury, Benedict (1998), 'The Concept of Compliance as a Function of Competing Conceptions of International Law', Michigan Journal of International Law.

[25] These values are respect for human dignity, freedom, democracy, equality, the rule of law and respect for human rights, including the rights of persons belonging to minorities.

[26] Spieker (n 17).

constitute the EU's DNA, the core components on which both the Union and its Member States are built, and they contribute to the identity constitutive dimension of the EU.[27] Article 2 TEU is not merely a statement of policy guidelines or intentions; it contains values that are integral to 'the very identity of the European Union as a common legal order'. These values are given concrete expression in principles that impose legally binding obligations on the Member States.[28]

The confusion arises from the fact that these values are tautological givens: the Lisbon Treaty refers to 'foundational values' multiple times, yet these values are nowhere properly defined, and a meaningful appreciation of their systemic role remains defective, if not confusing, despite the Court's recent engagement with them. Nonetheless, these values are regarded as the foundational pillars of the EU project. In practice, they seem to align with the codification of legal principles, as the general principles of EU law serve as expressions of these underlying values. For instance, the rule of law has always been recognized as a binding principle; Article 2 TEU does not diminish its normative essence but rather bestows it with an additional layer of 'constitutional virtue' by framing it as an EU value.[29] While it is undeniable that the principles in Article 2 possess a legal connotation (i.e. they are legal norms), conceiving them as values implies an expansion beyond an exclusively legal dimension, particularly one that encompasses an EU vision of justice.

Herein lies the confusion. The law has served as the engine of integration, providing certainty and order for a system as complex as the EU institutions, the Member States, and their citizens. Although values have been rhetorically espoused since the inception of the EU, their depth, scope, and role have constantly remained ambiguous. Values such as democracy, liberty, and the rule of law were invoked as foundational but their meaning appeared ambiguous and their application has often been incoherent. This ambiguity arises because the process of juridification of rights, reluctantly undertaken by the CJEU, occurred without a coherent political determination of their ideal meaning. In the absence of a comprehensive vision of justice articulated by political institutions, the CJEU has cautiously interpreted values through the lens of a common economic—rather than legal—denominator: the preservation and maintenance of the Common Market. This approach aimed to avoid, or at least

[27] Cremona, Marise (2011), 'Values in EU Foreign Policy.' In *Beyond the Established Orders: Policy Interconnections between the EU and the Rest of the World*, edited by Malcom Evand and Panos Koutrakos.

[28] *Hungary v Parliament and Council* (n 10).

[29] *Les Verts* (n 14).

mitigate, political disagreement. Without political confrontation at a supranational level, community market rules extended into other areas of law, further promoting integration through law. From this standpoint, freedom, and subsequently other values, became ancillary to market integration. Broadly speaking, it was the economic Union that provided the foundation for numerous decisions; the economic body of values constituted the inspirational bedrock for the Union.[30] I found William's argument—and, to a lesser extent, Maduro's—of a predominantly economic-oriented justice in the EU convincing, albeit it comes at a high cost in terms of legitimacy, as demonstrated in Chapters 4, 5, and 6.

Without denying its economic orientation and the impact the Common Market rules had on the development of the entire EU system, it would be a disservice to ignore the ideological component underpinning EU values, even if these values are not organically structured and often procedurally weak on many fronts. The Common Market rules approach might explain the lack of legitimacy and the EU democratic deficit, but they cannot alone account for the success of European integration. As Weiler posits, expecting legitimacy from an economic outcome/process framework is unlikely to yield desirable explanations for the EU context. Rather, he argued, a new conceptual type of legitimacy anchored on political messianism is more suitable to explain the mobilizing drivers underpinning the EU action.[31] From this angle, it is the ideal pursued—the destiny to be achieved—that explains the EU's successful process of integration and, at a later stage, the story of its decline as well. Political messianism precedes institutional structures and decision-making processes; it constitutes the fibre or the DNA, as Weiler put it, of the EU political and legal culture that existed before the pursuit of the Common Market. It is the 'humanistic inheritance of Europe', as the Lisbon Treaty labels it. While it is undeniable that European integration has been realized through an economic programme—such as the European Coal and Steal Community, the European Economic Community—it is guided by the principles that have inspired its creation (Article 21(1) TEU) and geared to messianic, symbolic, and idealistic aspirations.

From this standpoint, Habermas's definition of values appears particularly suitable. Values are ends worth pursuing. While norms deontologically possess a sense of obligation, values are teleological. They are aspirational, provide a sense of '*telos*' and fill gaps when normative principles fail to provide guidance.

[30] Maduro, Miguel Poiares (1995), *We the Court.*
[31] Weiler (n 15).

Leaning on this definition, the term 'value' is here intended to depict the optimal realization of certain legal principles, the achievement of which is the result of often unintentional interactions of law and politics. In a teleological fashion,[32] the selection of values to be pursued shapes the legal and political mechanisms used to achieve these goals. Simultaneously, the political and legal culture influences and defines specific values, creating a continuous cycle of mutual interaction.[33]

This is all good and inspiring in theory; however, an underlying issue exists that cannot be overlooked. The idealistic veneer that characterizes EU actions, both internally and externally, is further compromised by a reality that significantly diverges from the EU's prescribed values, undermining its 'lead by example' approach. Without delving into the controversies surrounding Poland, Hungary, or other contentious power dynamics, it is worth highlighting the contradictions in the behaviour of EU Member States in the realm of international investment. While they have long relied on investment arbitration to protect their investors abroad, they have recently begun emphasizing its flaws—particularly regarding rule of law concerns such as independence and impartiality—once these mechanisms started being invoked against European Member States by foreign investors. This inconsistency reveals deeper problems of incoherence in the EU's external relations, especially where the promotion of certain values abroad conflicts with internal practices. Such contradictions undermine the EU's credibility and weaken its stance as a normative power on the global stage. These issue will not be dismissed in the book, rather they will be critically examined to provide a better understanding of whether, and to what extent, the EU is indeed in a position to lure other into its values' orbit.

At this juncture, it is plausible to scrutinize the foundation for the values considered here. It would be too naïve and overly simplistic to dismiss the notion that the very idea of values has universal worth. More realistically, the concept of values has developed under the auspices of Western hegemony,[34] which has demonstrated a significant degree of convergence and acceptance regarding the meanings of democracy and the rule of law as its distinguishing traits—primarily among Western democracies, of which the EU Member States are epitomes. The principles underpinning this form of hegemony materialized, for example, in enforcement mechanisms that allow the use of vetoes by

[32] See in Section D.
[33] ibid.
[34] Pollack, Mark and Shaffer, Gregory (2001), *Transatlantic Governance in the Global Economy.*

members (as seen in the UN system), or in decision-making processes that operate on consensus, where each participant retains the capacity to object (as exemplified by the General Agreement on Tariffs and Trade (GATT) system). These principles were compelling and widely pursued because they offered a rule-based coordinated approach to handling (though not necessarily solving) collective tasks without infringing on States' sovereignty and decision-making capacities, and, perhaps more importantly, without divesting American preeminence. Simply put, the increasingly legalistic nature of international relations since the end of the Cold War has facilitated a process in which multilateral legitimacy is grounded in respect for the rule of law (rule-based coordination) and democracy (non-infringement of state sovereignty). This legitimacy stems from state consent (input) and state satisfaction (output), without necessarily accounting for other variables in the equation. Eurocentric inclinations align well with this characterization, as the EU continues to function as an influential supranational power, promoting its values through discourses of 'normality'—that is, the perceived desirability of its norms—even in the absence of multilateral cooperation.

Having defined what value means, it is necessary to clarify the terminology used for the diffusion of values from the EU system to others. Terms such as 'spreading', 'selling', 'promotion', 'shaping', 'diffusion', and 'infiltration' do not necessarily describe the same phenomena and may generate confusion. I operate on the assumption that the influence the EU values of democracy and the rule of law on the investment regime results from a combination of factors. On one hand, the diffusion of EU value is instrumental in ensuring that external actions are compatible with internal principles (as per Article 21 TEU), and serves to keep a united front among Member States. Terms like 'promotion' and 'diffusion' are particularly apt for this purpose. On the other hand, the EU possesses an inherent inclination toward the promotion and projection of EU values abroad—a 'messianic vocation'—to contribute to the achievement of global objectives (as per Article 3(5)TEU). This inclination, however, does not always correspond to a deliberate effort by the EU to propagate its principles and values as '*the*' values. There have been instances where the influence of the EU on other systems qualifies as a by-product of its external actions.[35] For example, Bradford contended that the General Data Protection Regulation (GDPR) was not intended to export the EU approach abroad, but the costs of non-compliance with these rules have nonetheless made them a key reference for global regulations concerning data.

[35] This is one of the arguments developed in Bradford, Anu (2020), *The Brussels Effect.*

When examining other systems, the EU's conscious efforts to persuade third countries to accept its values become more discernible. For instance, in the WTO, the EU as a litigator has strategically contributed to rule development by advocating for an overarching vision of what the rules should encompass, including its strong endorsement of a hierarchically superior position for the Appellate Body. In the international environmental regime, the EU has often taken the lead in environmental protection measures.[36] The use of the precautionary principle exemplifies the EU's influence on the environmental agenda.[37] From this standpoint, one might be tempted to use terms like 'imitation', 'cross-fertilization', and 'reception'. Although these terms all focus on the desirability to emulate and transfer values and norms from the EU to foreign countries, they emphasize the EU's appeal to third countries, thereby diminishing the sovereignty equally conferred on each party. 'Assimilation' and 'integration' align more closely with the EU standard-setting aspirations and shift the focus to the source providing the norm/value, yet they seem too extreme to describe the EU's approach to the investment regime. Terms like 'spread', 'sell', 'shape', and 'infiltration' are more nuanced and capture rather better the EU's messianic attitude. 'Diffusion' suits this goal even better, as it is the broadest and most general term that encompasses contagion, mimicry, organized dissemination, natural spread, and planned change.[38] I shall use 'diffusion' and 'expansion' as generic terms to describe the abstract process carried out by the EU within the investment regime. Terms such as 'spread', 'sell', 'shape', and 'infiltration' will be used to emphasize the EU's deliberate intention to export its legal values abroad.

A further point to clarify is some terminology for the regime of international investments. I rely on the work of Bonnitcha, Poulsen, and Waibel, and consider investment agreements, treaty arbitrations, and the involved actors as parts of a broad 'regime':

> A regime is traditionally understood as the 'principles, norms, rules and decision-making procedures around which actors' expectations converge in a given area of international relations' (Krasner 2009, 113). This broad

[36] Herlin-Karnell, Ester (2012), 'The EU as a Promoter of Values and the European Global Project', German Law Journal.

[37] In Case C-366/10, *Air Transport Association of America v Secretary of State for Energy and Climate Change*, EU:C:2011:864 the Court used the environmental provisions to enforce a spillover of EU law into the external sphere. See on this Karnell (n 36).

[38] Strang, David and Soule, Sarah A (1998), 'Diffusion in Organizations and Social Movements: From Hybrid Corn to Poison Pills', Annual Review of Sociology; Twining, William (2004), 'Diffusion of Law: A Global Perspective', The Journal of Legal Pluralism and Unofficial Law.

> definition ranges from formal arrangements (e.g. international organizations and treaties) to more informal arrangements (e.g. shared norms and principles among tribunals and arbitrators), and actors include states as well as non-state actors, including foreign investors.[39]

Hence, I shall use the term 'regime' instead of 'system' to encompass the frameworks of relationships among instruments (the treaties, the norms), institutions (arbitral tribunals), and actors (states, foreign investors, third parties) that structure the politics of the application of investment legal rules and their social effects,[40] as well as the international investment policies. Whenever referring to the norms (rights and obligations), I will use the term 'international investment law', whereas 'investment treaty arbitration' or 'ISDS' will be used interchangeably to indicate arbitral claims and, more generally, the system of adjudication.

One last aspect to clarify concerns the meaning of 'EU' used throughout the book. The book frequently refers to the EU/the Union as the main subject and to the main actors involved in the negotiation and ratification process of IIAs. Unless otherwise specified, this often implicitly means the Commission, whereas reference to the Council and the Parliament will be explicit. The issue is discussed in more detail in Chapter 2.

2. Legal transplants

From a legal standpoint, scholars have predominantly focused on how legal transplants and norms takeovers occur. The term 'legal transplant', coined by its founding father the legal scholar Alan Watson, refers to the modality of diffusion and adoption of certain laws from one country to a foreign other ever since.[41] Inevitably, the term 'transplant' conjures up the image of a complicated surgical operation by which part of a human body is transferred from one person to another. Legal transplants have been conceptualized as predominantly horizontal transplants of a precise rule from one country to another, often driven by cost-saving considerations, societal changes, or legitimacy

[39] Bonnitcha, Jonathan, Poulsen, Lauge, Waibel, Michael (2017), *The Political Economy of the Investment Treaty Regime*, 2–3.

[40] Hurst, William (2018), *Ruling before the Law: The Politics of Legal Regimes in China and Indonesia*, 24.

[41] Watson, Alan (1974), *Legal Transplants—An Approach to Comparative Law*; Watson, Alan (1995), 'From Legal Transplants to Legal Formants', The American Journal of Comparative Law; Twining (n 38).

aspirations. In terms of outcomes, transplanted rules often survive without any close connection to a particular group of people, moment in time or place.[42] This outcome was particularly criticized for the inevitable, yet overlooked, contamination introduced by legal transplants throughout the process.

Over time, the scope of the term has become more nuanced, encompassing various phenomena depending on the type of law in question. For example, a legal transplant might be understood as the transfer of general ideas (e.g. the ideal of a Western model of human rights) or specific elements of a country's legal system (e.g. the transplant of the legal education system). Furthermore, the incorporation of these elements occurs in a differentiated manner, resembling the process of language assimilation.

The socio-legal approach is more focused on normative comparison, where laws are 'borrowed' from one country to another, and norms are adopted in foreign jurisdictions. The term 'borrowing' implies a somewhat active stance by the transplant country, but other elements are seldom considered in the process. The primary condition for this process is the ideological political compatibility around basic objectives and values between the country of origin and the transplant country. Despite acknowledging a differentiated degree of integration of laws from the origin country into the recipient country, these theories appeared trapped in 'fixed binaries': the country of origin, the recipient country, and the transplanted law.[43]

As they stand, these scholarships have limited value for this book. Values are left out of the equation, despite their significant impact on law-making and societies. Questions of adjustment or rejection, and the factors influencing the transferability process are either not considered or only partially addressed. One of the main limitations of these theories is their strict focus on one object—a precise codified legal rule—disregarding what Montesquieu elegantly described as '*l'esprit de loi*'. The spirit of the law is a compound of ingredients that transcend the purely normative sphere, encompassing a more comprehensive vision of justice:

> Plusieurs choses gouvernent les hommes: le climat, la religion, les lois, les maximes du gouvernement, les exemples des choses passées, les mœurs, les manières; d'où il se forme un esprit général qui en résulte.

[42] Watson, Alan (1976), 'Legal Transplants and Law Reform', Law Quarterly Review.

[43] Harding, Andrew (2019), 'The Legal Transplants Debate: Getting Beyond the Impasse?' In *Legal Transplants in East Asia and Oceania*, edited by Vito Breda.

One might suggest that to investigate the full panoply of the legal structures, political and economic processes underpinning the EU values' transmission into the investment system, more insightful contributions might be found examining the theories of legal convergence. Fukuyama posits that this convergence gravitates around the universalization of Western liberal democracy and its aspirational values: the rule of law and accountability of state powers. This convergence towards the Western model reflects the power imbalances among countries and results from factors such as internationalization, growing economic interdependence across societies, and their constant exposure to the influence of the international and regional organizations to which they often belong. Unlike legal transplants, convergence is driven by the accelerated pace of globalization in recent decades. The need for common solutions to global problems (e.g. the pandemic and climate change), the avoidance of conflicts of laws, and the resulting transaction costs are all epitome of the reasons why state laws are converging. This convergence, however, is less about the direct adoption of specific legal rules and more about the alignment of broader legal and normative frameworks to address shared challenges effectively.

In today's interconnected world, the overlap of multiple legal systems is almost unavoidable. Regardless of their success, attempts at convergence are necessary to ensure that common rules are applied uniformly and that differences among applicable rules do not prejudice legal certainty. Amid these numerous attempts stands out the so-called Brussels effect as particularly remarkable, albeit unintended. The Brussels effect[44] refers to the EU's unilateral power to regulate global markets both *de jure*—when law-makers follow EU law—and de facto—when companies voluntarily follow EU regulation. The Brussels effect is seminal in highlighting the EU's capability to generate rules even in the absence of multilateral cooperation. However, it remains focused on the 'EU regulator' role and it is quite dismissive, if not sceptical, about the effectiveness of treaties in exporting norms and standards. While the Brussels effect acknowledges the EU's ideational power in shaping international relations, it does not account for the EU's influence outside its regulatory framework. This limitation underscores the EU's broader role in promoting legal and normative convergence beyond mere regulatory authority.

Despite their notable contributions, none of these theories adequately serve the purpose of this book. Transplant theories, some of which have been labelled as the worst ever academic debate,[45] provide an explanation—albeit

[44] Bradford (n 35).

[45] The reference is to the debate between Watson and Legrand on legal transplants, often described as full of logical fallacies that lead nowhere.

superficial—for the phenomenon of transplanted law's incorporation into a foreign country. These theories remain predominantly focused on a specific object (the transplanted rule) and the outcome in the transplant country. Theories on convergence are broader in scope but tend to underscore the economic factor as the primary driver toward the internationalization of norms. The Brussels effect aligns with convergence theories to some extent but relies more emphatically on a market-driven explanation, which undermines the importance of treaty-driven harmonization, especially in the absence of states' agreement. This emphasis on market forces over treaty frameworks reveals limitations in addressing the complexities of international norm diffusion and the nuanced role of EU values.

As they stand, none of these theories convincingly account for how, and to what extent, the EU values of democracy and the rule of law are projected into the investment regime. Even if an attempt were made to utilize these norm export theories, a system as compound as the EU would, at best, qualify as a peculiar 'transplanter', given that its values extends beyond the mere legal sphere. As values enshrined in the Lisbon Treaty, democracy and the rule of law must be treated in a way that acknowledges their complex, multifaceted nature. They should not be reduced solely to the objectifying logic of legal transplants, which, when embedded in law, are often detached from political debate.[46] Within the EU, law and politics always stand in a particular tension.[47] The concept of 'integration through law' identifies the law as both the object and motor of integration, which cannot unfold without the emergence of a specific legal *culture*. While virtually all norm export frameworks (including the Brussels effect) can explain how laws are incorporated into foreign legal systems, none adequately account for the translatability of EU normative values or their expansion and influence on other policy systems. The aforementioned theories might explain why law-makers copy another country's law or why companies are inclined to converge toward the EU regulation. However, this transplant/convergence remains disconnected from the cultural environment[48] and is likely to disregard the EU idealistic and visionary connotation of its identity. To understand whether and how values like democracy and the rule of law

[46] On the point see Eckes, albeit she referred to the EU: 'Law refers to a solidified and formalized expression of political will (constitutional law; legislation) or a judicial decision (case law) of the past, adopted pursuant to specific procedural rules and expressing a particular normative claim. Politics refer to political struggle. . . . Law adopted in the past has a framing and constraining force on present politics, including law-making.' Eckes, Christina (2019), *EU Powers Under External Pressure—How the EU's External Actions Alter its Internal Structures*.

[47] ibid.

[48] Legrand, Pierre (1997), 'The Impossibility of "Legal Transplants"', Maastricht Journal of European and Comparative Law.

diffuse from the EU to the international investment regime, it is necessary to devise a different conceptual approach. The work of Alexy, Sartor, and Weiler has been particularly suitable to provide the foundational design for my framework, as I elaborate in the following section.

D. The research approach

Having conceptualized the meaning of 'values' and their potential diffusion from one system to another, it is necessary to turn to the conceptual framework devised for this book. Given the peculiarities of the EU system, the most convincing approach to reaching these goals rests on a framework that conceives values in a normative fashion while simultaneously understanding norms in an idealistic manner. The framework must be flexible enough to accommodate political questions that require judicial answers and judicial questions that would benefit from a political stance. It should, therefore, provide the analytical foundations to account for the factors and the instruments underpinning the diffusion of the EU values of democracy and rule of law into the international investment regime, though it could also be applicable to other systems. Once established, the framework will facilitate addressing questions such as: what manifestations of the EU's promises of democracy and rule of law can be observed outside the EU borders? To what extent do these manifestations exist? How are EU values utilized in the process of investment law-making? What conditions must be met to make it desirable or even possible for legislators to adopt rules or values developed in the EU? What are the implications of the EU's affirmation of its own 'Promethean' vision into the regime of international investments? What are the benefits and challenges associated with these promises?

One of the most compelling perspectives on these questions arises from conceiving teleology as a mode of integration within the EU. In this view, the starting point is a postulated end goal, considered valuable[49] for driving integration efforts. The EU's visionary history has provided ample inspiration, fuelled by the noble idealism that has characterized its development since its inception. The Schuman Declaration (1950), though not highly technical, promised new hopes and opened the door to transformative possibilities, seeking to overcome the lingering horrors of war in people's minds. This

[49] Krygier, Martin (2021), 'Democracy and the Rule of Law.' In *The Cambridge Companion to the Rule of Law*, edited by Jens Meierhenrich and Martin Loughlin.

profound idealism characterized the EU project from its beginning, persisted throughout its development, and has become a fundamental pillar of the EU's entire narrative. This idealism culminated in Articles 3(5) TEU and 21 TEU, which respectively charge the EU with the mission of upholding and promoting its values abroad and serving as an inspiration for the rest of the world.

As is well known, the 'messianic' narrative for European integration was realized through an economic programme and the establishment of a legal order hierarchically superior to and independent from those of its Member States. This result was achieved predominantly through the incessant Commission's use of agenda-setting powers and entrepreneurial inclinations,[50] and, albeit only in part, through the CJEU validation. This program, however, fuelled internal tension between the EU and its Member States, given the increasing influence of the Union's external actions at the expense of the Member States' autonomy. External relations thus put the EU's constitutional connotation to the test,[51] especially when it came to issues particularly sensitive at the domestic (Member State) level, and to dynamics that might drive the Union apart (e.g. Brexit). While these risks have not been entirely eliminated, they have been mitigated through the recognition function performed by the values and principles enshrined in the EU treaties. Normative values have played a key role in identifying Member States,[52] as they express a form of normative cohesion within the EU and provide the criteria that distinguish 'what is European' from the rest. However, the risks of fragmentation persist due to a disconnect between what the Union advocates and the inconsistencies at the decision-making level in upholding those values. In reality, the situation is even more complex and less idealized than the values articulated in Article 2 TEU. The list of instances that exposes the EU's incoherence is longer that the rhetoric of idealism, creating a significant gap between the image presented by Article 2 TEU and the actual lessons the EU is able to impart to the rest of the world.

To understand how and to what extent EU values are diffused into the investment regime, it is essential to develop a theoretical framework that critically conceives these values as drivers of actions and examines their performance in different legal and political settings. Specifically, the framework is design to problematize the EU's responses within the regime of international investments. The goal is to move beyond the idealized image of Article 2 TEU, which takes values at face value, and instead explore whether, and in what

[50] Basedow, Robert (2017), *The EU in the Global Investment Regime: Commission Entrepreneurship, Incremental Institutional Change and Business Lethargy*.

[51] Eckes (n 46).

[52] On the EU values as identity constitutive see Cremona (n 27).

circumstances, the EU's actions are genuinely promising or merely imbued with hypocrisy and rhetoric.

When conceptualizing the EU as a promoter of values, much of the discussion has been framed through constitutional models. For instance, Pernice's framework referred to multilevel constitutionalism to explain the ongoing processes that establish new structures of supranational governance. This approach builds upon, while also transforming, existing forms of self-organizations of people and societies.[53] Kumm and Stone Sweet, on the other hand, have relied more on the concept of cosmopolitan law. From their perspective, a cosmopolitan legal order requires that fundamental rights are respected for every person within a given territory, regardless of their nationality or citizenship, with a 'categorical imperative' serving as the guiding norm. In their view, within the EU cosmopolitan order, the maintenance of peace is the *grundnorm* from which other norms derive, ultimately contributing to a constitutional order.[54] Other scholars, like Teubner, are more sceptical of the notion of a global, unitary constitutional law, particularly in a context as multilayered as the EU. According to him, the EU framework presents at least two main challenges: (i) the difficulty of transferring the EU's internal discourse to external contexts, and (ii) the legitimacy of the EU's actions as a source of political power in non-EU settings. An acceptable compromise, according to Teubner, might be EU's role as a conflict resolver within multilayered systems.[55]

Whichever explanation, the book does not revolve around an 'EU model' to be imposed or transplanted from the EU legal order to the regime of international investments. Instead, my interest lies in gathering the evidence that suggests a projection of the EU values of democracy and the rule of law into international investment law and policy. By assembling these pieces, I am to understand the role the EU is playing in this evolving scenario. Specifically, I seek to determine whether the EU is acting as a power capable of both stabilizing the global order and guiding the way forward for many countries and people,[56] or whether it fulfils one of these roles, or perhaps neither.

Generally speaking, legislative action is primarily guided by norms of action, which mandate specific behaviours, such as prohibiting government

[53] Pernice, Ingolf EA (2009), 'The Treaty of Lisbon: Multilevel Constitutionalism in Action', Columbia Journal of European Law.

[54] Kumm, Mattias (2011), 'How Does European Union Law Fit into the World of Public Law? Costa, Kadi and Three Conceptions of Public Law', NYU School of Law Public Law Research Paper; Stone Sweet, Alec (2007), 'The Juridical Coup D'État and the Problem of Authority', The German Law Journal, 915.

[55] Teubner, Gunther (2012), *Constitutional Fragments: Societal Constitutionalism and Globalization.*

[56] European Council Meeting in Laeken (14–15 December 2001), SN 300/1/01 REV 1.

interference with citizens' freedom of speech. However, there exists, another category of norms that prescribes the pursuit of certain values, goals, and interests. For example, the goal of limiting government's interference has to be balanced with competing objectives like preserving public order, upholding morality, preventing offences to dignity, and curbing the spread of racial and ethnic hatred.[57] Article 2 TEU belongs to the goal norm category, which assumes that the decision-making process should pursue the most appropriate path to achieve the values upon which the EU is founded. From this standpoint, a norm serves as a directive to optimize the realization of certain values,[58] with the goal being achieved through the most effective and appropriate normative means. It is the ultimate value (the goal) that teleologically guides both the action and the norm. This is inevitable, given the impossibility of numerically quantifying the weight of the values at stakes. When dealing with goal norms, evaluating the worth of an outcome in terms of expected utility—a quantifiable economic measure used to assess value—becomes problematic. The challenge with goal norms, and many legal cases, is that there are no straightforward or reasonable ways to measure the weight of values numerically or simply in terms of compliance versus non-compliance.

What appears to be particularly fitting for the investment context, and thus for this investigation, is to begin by viewing goal norms as a response to a problematic situation. According to Sartor, teleological reasoning and goal norms become relevant when a social arrangement is deficient, revealing an unmet need that the legislator believes must be addressed. This concept of deficiency resonates strongly with the EU's modus operandi, where crises often serve as catalysts for change. It is only in the face of a crisis (whether actual or perceived) that alternatives to existing standards and practices are seriously considered.

In the context of international investments, this initial point of deficiency can be identified as the legitimacy crisis affecting the investment regime. The call for reform within this regime of international investments is broad and multidirectional, tacking stock of different types of demand, and leading to various reform paths. I describe this external pressure on the EU system as a 'demand for adjustment'. Such demands influence the behaviour of other systems in multiple ways and are frequently sources of change in political and legal systems. As the environment fluctuates, it generates new types of demand

[57] Sartor, Giovanni (2010), 'Doing Justice to Rights and Values: Teleological Reasoning and Proportionality', Artificial Intelligence and Law, 179.

[58] Alexy, Robert (2003), 'Constitutional Rights, Balancing, and Rationality', Ratio Juris.

input that require systemic responses.[59] The crisis within the investment regime crisis thus provided the EU, along with other actors, an opportunity to respond and address some of its systemic shortcomings.

Once the demand is triggered, it becomes essential to understand the type of answers that are provided. In the book's view, the EU sought to project its values as appropriate and suitable answers to the investment regime's call for adjustment. I refer to this response as the 'supply of EU values'. My argument is as follows: the EU capitalizes on the investment regime's need for adjustment as an opportunity to reaffirm its core values—democracy and the rule of law. By supplying its values as solution sought by the investment system, the EU bolsters its normative, economic, and political influence on a global scale.

This process is inherently teleological, as EU values function as goal norms that aim to optimize the realization of specific values, serving as the definitive response to the investment regime's deficiencies. The use of economic terminology—such as 'demand' for adjustment, 'supply' of values—aligns well with the EU's tendency to address political issues through economic strategies rather than direct confrontation.[60]

A final concern that needs to be addressed is how to measure the diffusion of the values in question. The number of parameters that should be accounted for is staggering and exhibit certain non-linear properties, such as the judicial impact of decisions on policy-making, which complicates the underlying physics even more. Although the concepts of democracy and the rule of law do not necessarily mean the same for EU and investment law scholars and possess different interpretative nuances, there are areas where both systems of interpretation converge. The challenge, therefore, is to identify a set of measurable indicators that reflect these points of convergence, capturing the essence of the EU's concepts of democracy and rule of law while resonating within the investment regime. This categorization is grounded in those aspects where the EU aligns with expectations of the investment regime.[61] For instance, transparency, access to documents, and civil society participation could be used to gauge the diffusion of democratic values, while legal certainty, legitimate expectations, impartiality, and independence of the adjudication system could assess the spread of the rule of law. By evaluating this indicators, I aim to

[59] Easton, David (1957), 'An Approach to the Analysis of Political Systems', World Politics.

[60] For instance, when confronted with war problems, the EU did not directly confront them as such, but indirectly by dealing with them as economic and technical issues, hence potentially solvable. De Baere, Geert (2012), 'European Integration and the Rule of Law in Foreign Policy.' In *Philosophical Foundations of European Union Law*, edited by Julie Dickson and Pavlos Eleftheriadis.

[61] See Section B.

determine whether, and to what extent, the EU's responses suggest structural adjustments or signal a paradigmatic shift within the investment regime.

E. Structure of the book

Moving from these introductory considerations, Chapter 2 lays out the historical background and conditions that coalesced to form the EU investment law and policy.

The book is then structured into three main parts.

Part I focuses on the EU value of democracy and discusses how democracy is incorporated into the international investment regime. It outlines the principle of democracy as specified in the EU treaties and details how transparency (Chapter 3) and public participation (Chapter 4) have become the EU's channels for projecting democracy in the regime of international investments. Although often conflated, participation and transparency are both critical for the EU to ensure systemic legitimacy and accountability, addressing the disconnect felt by citizens increasingly alienated from global economic relations and the complexities of today's multilevel governance systems. While many perspectives on democracy in the EU are possible,[62] transparency and public participation are particularly illustrative of the EU's ambition towards a legal and political project that is not merely *for* the people but also *by* the people.

Part II focuses on the dissemination of the EU value of the rule of law. Despite being one of the founding principles of the EU (Article 6(1) TEU), the rule of law has historically been somewhat amorphous in the realm of international affairs, including investment matters, gradually developing more defined characteristics over time. Despite the relatively superficial and fluctuating nature of definitions, the EU institutions have consistently promoted and reiterated a comprehensive understanding of the rule of law. This understanding encompasses substantive components like non-discrimination, equality before the law, and respect for human rights, along with formal procedural elements, like legal certainty, the independence and impartiality of the judiciary, and the prohibition of arbitrariness. These procedural aspects resonate well with infiltration of EU values into the investment regime and the progressive solidification of an international consensus around these values, more so than in other areas such as human rights. Therefore, this section explores two complementary but

[62] This part does not attempt to reach a conclusion on this matter but remains focused on how the EU value of democracy has been spread in the regime of international investments.

distinct levels of inquiry. At the micro level, Chapter 5 examines the role played by the EU in balancing the principles of conduct imposed on host states by IIAs, and how host States and investors' legitimate expectations have aligned to these principles. At the macro level, Chapter 6 discusses how the overall investment regime has been reshaped according to a certain approach particularly favoured by the EU: judicialization.

Part III wraps up the book by critically acknowledging the limitations of the EU project and the bold rhetoric often present in the EU's external actions. Chapter 7 provides mixed insights regarding the EU's projection of its benchmark values within the international investment regime. Beyond the ontological constraints between the EU and its Member States, one of the most problematic aspects of the EU's action lies in the premises upon which the EU's globalizing promises have been built. The EU has yet to carve out a distinct identity for itself and continues to fluctuate across multiple personalities. This identity crisis has weakened the *Europeanization* of the investment regime and is further exacerbated by the ambivalence that permeates the EU relationship with international law and governance. This ambivalence begs, in turn, the question of whether the EU is genuinely attempting to share its value vision throughout the world, with the associated conditions, in response to the investment regime' challenges or whether the EU is leveraging multilateralism and fidelity to international law as mechanisms to shape the system according to its own interests and needs. Chapter 8 posits that the EU's fascinating journey within the international investment regime is 'an unfinished adventure'. As it stands, it appears unlikely that the EU will achieve its aspiration of a global standard setter, particularly given that not all its commercial partners are willing to adopt EU-specific peculiarities unreservedly. A more audacious approach, which the EU has either dismissed or only lightly pursued, would have embraced systemically radical lines of reform, such as holding investors liable to the state or extending remedies to domestic investors. While nothing is set in stone, for the EU to adopt a more audacious stance would require a decisive understanding of the teleological foundations of its messianic identity within the international investment regime. Is the diffusion of values the raison d'être, the visionary mission, for which the EU was created, or has it gradually become a purpose the EU exploits to fulfil its own interests? It is my hope that the EU will live up to its values and not, in Brecht's words, 'grub first then ethics'.

2

The EU investment law and policy

A. Overview

This chapter surveys the historical background and conditions that were brought together in what constitutes today's European Union (EU) investment law and policy. The process underpinning the EU's international investment policy creation began in the 1980s, but it was only in the Lisbon Treaty that the EU formally acquired exclusive competence over foreign direct investments (FDIs). From a legal perspective, it is hardly questionable that the Lisbon Treaty pushes towards 'more Europe': the Union is vested with legal personality (Article 47 of the Treaty on European Union (TEU)); is the entity behind all external actions (Article 218 Treaty on the Functioning of the European Union (TFEU)); and, most importantly for present purposes, its competences extend to services and FDIs as part of the Common Commercial Policy (CCP) (Article 207 TFEU). Truth be told, however, the birth of the EU policy on FDI matters was more a combination of political chance and stealth[1] rather than a politically rational choice, yet it radically changed the multilayered situation governing foreign investments in Europe. A vibrant academic debate has flourished since the Lisbon Treaty entered into force, but what role the EU would play in the future of international investment law remains a work in progress.

This chapter proceeds as follows. Section B chronicles the moments underpinning the birth of a new international investment policy under the EU aegis. Section C brings to light the effects of EU external actions on the power divisions between the EU and the Member States and among the EU institutions—in particular, the Commission, the Council, the Parliament, and the Court of Justice. In the last step, Section D draws conclusions about how these effects may influence the direction of the EU policy on international investments.

[1] Meunier, Sophie (2014), 'Integration by Stealth: How the European Union Gained Competence over Foreign Direct Investment', EUI RSCAS Global Governance.

EU Values in Investment Law And Policy. Maria Laura Marceddu, Oxford University Press.
 DOI: 10.1093/9780191986208.003.0002

B. The beginning of the EU's international investment policy: The road to Article 207 TFEU

In early years, the investment regime and the EC communities largely ignored one another. Little overlap existed between the two groups, and instances of cross-communication were few and far between. The European integration process remained predominantly focused on the liberalization of trade in goods, and foreign investments played a marginal role under Member States' competence. The EU occasionally negotiated investment liberalization provisions (market access and pre-establishment protection) under free trade agreements (FTAs), but the reins of investment matters remained in the hands of the Member States, as attested by their hundreds of bilateral investment treaties (BITs) providing post-establishment treatment protection.

In light of the growing importance that foreign investment was gradually acquiring, since the mid-1980s the Commission has begun to plead for extending the GATT's, or General Agreement on Tariffs and Trade's, reach to investments, framing them as new trade-related issues. This pleads called for the recognition of the Commission's competences, which in practice were already exercised, to some extent, within the ambit of the CCP and encompassed issues like investment matters. These de facto and fringe competences find justification in the teleological narrative of speaking with 'one single voice', proportionally commensurate to the EU's role in the world.

The Commission's subtle attempts to expand its competences under the pretence of making the EU a meaningful external actor, however, were consistently rejected by the Member States on different occasions. With the liberalization of capital flows, the Commission proposed to include foreign investments and trade in services under the CCP. Initially, it called for a competence shift during the intergovernmental conference (IGC) that led to the Treaty of Maastricht in 1992 but was quickly abandoned. It resurfaced a few years later in the IGC underpinning the 1997 Amsterdam Treaty with the purpose of strengthening the EU's role in bilateral and multilateral negotiations on investment policy. Meanwhile, the Court delivered its Opinion 1/94 that gave Member States a further opportunity to keep the Commission's intrusions at bay. Opinion 1/94 clarified that while the Commission holds competence over trade matters, it cannot override or prejudice the Member States when negotiating and concluding agreements in the field of services. The Court refrained from allocating further treaty-making power to Community institutions to the detriment of the Member States. It rejected the Commission's invitation to recognize its external competences in areas where internal powers were already set forth in the Treaty by reinstating that internal competence can give rise to exclusive external competence only if it is exercised.[2] The Court concluded that the Community holds exclusive competence to conclude multilateral agreements on trade in goods (i.e. the GATT), and on the General Agreement on Trade in Service (GATS) rules governing cross-border provisions of services. Member States, therefore, still retained a key role in the ratification of international agreements and remained jointly competent with the Community in concluding the GATS and Trade-Related Investment Measures (TRIMs).

After the setback of the Amsterdam Treaty, the Commission concluded negotiations for an FTA with Chile (1999–2002), which happened to be the first agreement to include a chapter on investment liberalization and post-establishment treatment provisions. The result galvanized the Commission, which again attempted to acknowledge its extensive legal competences under the CCP to regulate international investments,[3] as reiterated in its opinion for the 2000 IGC that led to the Nice Treaty. The political anti-globalization sentiments levelled against trade and investment, however, derailed the Commission's attempts once again. The failure of the Organisation for Economic Co-operation and Development (OECD) negotiations for a Multilateral Agreement on Investment—which sought to ensure that host governments treated foreign and domestic firms equally to facilitate international investment—created unfavourable conditions for the advancement of the EU's transfer of competences over FDIs. This was the case even though the Treaty extended the EU's competence to most trade in services, including service-related investment.[4]

After failures at the Maastricht, Amsterdam, and Nice IGCs, the Commission asked again that foreign investment regulation be included under the CCP during the IGC that led to the Constitutional Treaty. The Trade Commissioner, Pascal Lamy, specifically asked the Convention's Working Group VII on external relations to include the regulation of investment policy, given the Commission's de facto competence on those matters. John Bruton, the former Prime Minister of Ireland now representing national parliaments in the Praesidium, insisted on the need to remove 'obstacles to foreign direct investment'. This was agreed (Article III-314). He also suggested that the recognition of an EU competence over FDIs was necessary to ensure effective

[2] Eeckhout, Piet (2011), *External Relations Law*; Montanaro, Francesco (2023), *The European Union and International Investment Law—The Two Dimensions of an Uneasy Relationship*.

[3] Basedow, Robert (2017), *The EU in the Global Investment Regime: Commission Entrepreneurship, Incremental Institutional Change and Business Lethargy*.

[4] Meunier (n 1).

representation of the EU within the World Trade Organization (WTO) and in the ambit of FTA negotiations. Michel Barnier, the then EU Commissioner for Regional Policy who was acting as the representative of the EU Commission in the Praesidium, proposed to add 'foreign direct investment' in the provision describing the CCP. This suggestion happened without further discussion (Article III-315), perhaps overshadowed by the need to address the US intervention in Iraq that divided opinion in Europe. The Praesidium endorsed the text of draft articles by the end of the day, and FDI thus entered the Constitutional Treaty—a Treaty that would ultimately never see light due to its rejection by French and Dutch voters in May and June 2005.

Following a period of reflection after the failure of the Constitutional Treaty ratification, the Member States eventually launched an IGC to amend the European Community (EC) Treaty. The IGC delivered a slimmed-down version of the Constitutional Treaty that preserved its major innovations, among which was the reworded provision on FDIs. The IGC did not want to discuss the boundaries of the CCP again and the addition of FDI stayed. Article 207 TFEU replicated the wording of Article III-315 and formally recognized the competences the Commission was long invoking.

> (1) The common commercial policy shall be based on uniform principles, particularly with regard to changes in tariff rates, the conclusion of tariff and trade agreements relating to trade in goods and services, and the commercial aspects of intellectual property, *Foreign Direct Investment*, the achievement of uniformity in measures of liberalization, export policy and measures to protect trade such as those to be taken in the event of dumping or subsidies. The common commercial policy shall be conducted in the context of the principles and objectives of the Union's external action.[5]

FDIs entered into the CCP and bestowed upon the EU exclusive competence over one of the most important areas of the global economy with no fanfare. As Meunier brilliantly put it, the competence shift

> was certainly not the result of intergovernmental bargaining since the outcome ran counter to the preferences of all Member States. Neither was it the result of pressures from business group, who were divided on the issue and not proactive in any way. The competence shift was more the result of

[5] Emphasis added.

a combination of serendipity, stealth, and prioritization than of straight Commission entrepreneurship.[6]

By adding FDI to the EU competences, Article 207 TFEU covers the conclusion of IIAs that aim to protect and/or liberalize foreign investments but only partially settles the controversy that surrounds it. One problem that emerged in the transitional phase derived from the choice of the term 'foreign direct investment' instead of the arguably less problematic 'international investments'. FDIs are nowhere defined: neither the Treaty nor those articles defining the remit of the CCP (Article 206 and Article 207 of the TFEU)[7] have shed light as to its meaning. As is often the case with EU law, a practical manifestation of this notion may instead be found indirectly in secondary law.[8] Other inputs could be derived from Court of Justice of the European Union (CJEU) case law, which has interpreted the concept of direct investment as 'investments of any kind undertaken by natural or legal persons and which serve to establish or maintain lasting and direct links between the persons providing the capital and the undertakings to which that capital is made available in order to carry out an economic activity'.[9]

Despite these statements, the absence of a clear notion of FDI has led to some doubts about the precise application of Article 207 TFEU and its implications on the international stage. The issue is clarified in the Comprehensive Economic and Trade Agreement between Canada and the European Union (CETA), the first EU investment agreement under the aegis of the new EU investment policy. According to CETA Article 8.1, both direct and portfolio investments concur to shape the definition of FDI covered by the agreement. This attests to the Commission's intention to focus its liberalizing agenda on market access for direct investment',[10] as confirmed by other EU investment agreements.

A second and more compelling problem reignited by Article 207 TFEU concerns the tension between the Union and its Member States over questions of competence, which remains an issue ontologically rooted in Community and

[6] Meunier (n 1), 10.

[7] Vidal Puig, Ramòn (2013), 'The Scope of the New Exclusive Competence of the European Union with Regard to "Foreign Direct Investment"', Legal Issues of Economic Integration.

[8] Council, Directive (EC) 88/361/EEC, OJ L 178, 8 July 1988: The Directive refers to 'direct investment' as 'investment of all kinds . . . which serve[s] to establish or maintain lasting and direct links between the person providing the capital and the entrepreneur to whom or the undertaking to which the capital is made available in order to carry on an economic activity'.

[9] Eeckhout, Piet, and Ortino, Federico (2012), 'Towards an EU Policy on Foreign Direct Investment.' In *EU Law after Lisbon*, edited by Andrea Biondi, Piet Eeckhout, and Stefanie Ripley.

[10] COM(2010)343 final.

EU law. In the name of efficiency and predictability, the EU's main intention was to exercise its competences on a broader range of aspects of investment promotion and protection. The Commission traditionally keeps fighting for larger areas of exclusive competence in external affairs, whereas the Council and especially the Member States generally strive to retain as many of their former sovereign prerogatives as possible. They often find consolation in the silences of the Treaty and in seizing the Court, as discussed in the following section.

C. The Commission, the Council, and the Court of Justice: Questions of competence and compatibility

Notwithstanding some discrepancies between the work done by the European institutions, the contours of the EU investment policy have begun to emerge more clearly. Unlike the treaties concluded by EU Member States, the 'EU model' covers investment at both the pre- and post-establishment phases and aims to maintain a high level of liberalization of market access commitments. More broadly, what the Commission intended to achieve within the policy for international investments was to secure a 'level playing field' among market participants by ensuring a predictable and transparent business environment without compromising the EU's essential interests.[11] The Commission succeeded at gradually replacing extra-EU BITs with agreements between the EU and third states,[12] and, more recently, has insisted on promoting sustainable development value chains and the green transition.[13]

Liberalization commitments are most often part of broad EU FTAs, such as those signed with Japan (2019), South Korea (2015), and the United Kingdom (2021) (see Table 2.1). The agreements with Canada (2017) and Mexico (negotiations concluded in January 2025) include investment chapters within broader FTAs, requiring conclusion and ratification by EU Member States following the completion of legal revisions. The EU has signed investment protection agreements (IPAs) to which the Parliament gave its consent and the Council its authorization to sign (as per Article 218 TFEU)—namely, the agreements with Singapore (2019) and Vietnam (2020)—both of which

[11] European Parliamentary Research Service (2022), *EU International Investment Policy: Looking Ahead.*

[12] Henquet, Thomas (2013), 'International Investment and the European Union: An Uneasy Relationship.' In *Investment Law within International Law*, edited by Freya Baetens.

[13] COM(2021)66 final.

Table 2.1 FTAs without investment provisions

Country	Type	Status
Japan	Economic partnership agreement (without investment chapter or separate agreement)	Entered into force on 1 February 2019.
South Korea	FTA (no investment provisions)	Provisionally applied since 1 July 2011, and was formally ratified on 13 December 2015.
United Kingdom	Trade and Cooperation Agreement (no investment provisions)	Entered into force on 1 May 2021.

Table 2.2 Mixed FTAs and IPAs

Country	Type	Status
Canada	FTA with investment chapter (Chapter 8)	Provisionally applied since 21 September 2017. Investment chapter requires Member States ratification, which is still ongoing.
Vietnam	FTA + IPA	FTA in force since 1 August 2020. IPA requires Member States ratification, which is still ongoing.
Singapore	FTA + IPA	FTA in force since 21 November 2019. IPA requires Member States ratification, which is still ongoing.

are still subject to Member States' ratification processes (see Table 2.2). The EU has also concluded an Interim Trade Agreement with Chile (entered into force on 1 February 2025), an FTA with New Zealand, and an Investment Facilitation Agreement with Angola (2024), while continuing discussions with Australia, India, and other countries (see Table 2.3). In 2013, it embarked on the negotiation with China of a comprehensive investment agreement, which was concluded in 2021, although the ratification process was effectively paused in result of the evolving dynamics of the wider EU–China relationship[14] (see Table 2.3). The Council has also outlined negotiation directives on investment with Euromed countries (Jordan, Morocco, Tunisia, and Egypt).[15]

EU negotiations of IIAs and their legal revision to verify internal consistency are largely conducted by the Commission, whereas the text of the

[14] In March 2021 the EU imposed sanctions on four Chinese officials for human rights abuses in Xinjiang, to which Beijing responded with its own sanctions on ten individuals and four entities in the EU, including Members of the European Parliament and of the Council's Political and Security Committee.

[15] However, current negotiations are not focused on investment protection yet.

Table 2.3 Other agreements

Country	Type	Status
Angola	Sustainable Investment Facilitation Agreement (no ISDS)	Entered into force on 1 September 2024.
Australia	FTA (inclusion of liberalizing provisions, no ISDS)	Negotiations started on 22 May 2018.
Chile	Advanced Framework Agreement (AFA). AFA comprises the Trade and Investment pillar (inclusive of investment protection provisions), and a separate Interim Trade Agreement (iTA) covering trade and investment liberalization.	The Interim Trade Agreement entered into force on 1 February 2025.
China	Comprehensive Agreement on Investment	Agreement in principle announced on 30 December 2020.
India	On 17 June 2022, the European Union relaunched negotiations with India for a FTA, and launched separate negotiations for an IPA and an Agreement on Geographical Indications (GIs).	Most recent EU proposal dated March 2022.
Indonesia	Negotiating since July 2016 for an FTA similar in coverage to what the EU achieved in its trade agreements with Singapore and Vietnam.	Most recent EU proposal dated December 2016.
Kenya	Economic Partnership Agreement (provisions on investment promotion).	Entered into force in July 2024.
Kyrgyzstan	Enhanced Partnership and Cooperation Agreement (provisions on trade in services and investment).	Signed on 25 June 2024.
Mercosur	FTA with no investment chapter.	Political agreement on an improved EU–Mercosur Partnership Agreement reached on 6 December 2024.
Mexico	FTA with a chapter on investment.	Negotiations on a modernised Global Agreement concluded on 17 January 2025.
New Zealand	FTA (inclusion of liberalizing provisions, no ISDS).	FTA entered into force on 1 May 2024.
Philippines	Trade and investment agreement.	Negotiations officially launched on 22 December 2015 and resumed in March 2024.

agreement is thereafter transmitted to the Council of the European Union and the Parliament for ratification (Article 218 TFEU). One of the most interesting novelties of the Lisbon Treaty is the broader power bestowed upon the Parliament. The Parliament shares full legislative powers with the Council in the CCP and it is involved in a co-decision procedure with the Council. It has addressed a wider range of issues, such as human rights, environmental protection, and social and economic development,[16] and has called for a clear definition of investor protection standards and parameters. As a result, whilst the Parliament has called for a common template—a sort of EU baseline—the Commission has rejected a one-size-fits-all model for investment agreements. Despite this differing perspective, the Commission broadly endorses the recent view of Parliament[17] that future EU international investment policy must ensure host states retain their right to regulate within their own territories, without potential violations of European investment protection guarantees.[18] The Parliament, in turn, welcomed the new approach envisaged by the new Investment Court System (ICS) mechanism replacing investor-state dispute settlement (ISDS), and the safeguard taken for public health, environmental protection, and public service.[19] It insisted, nonetheless, that investor protection should be accompanied by the exercise of due diligence and through the implementation of sustainable business practices.

Despite the existence of a common minimum denominator across the EU institutions, discrepancies stemming from the different roles played by each of them in international negotiations persist, especially in a field as sensitive as international investments. As a result, the Member States and the Commission already felt the urge to seize the CJEU twice, albeit none of the IPAs have entered into force.

The Court was thus called to trace once again the boundaries of the EU's exclusive competence with respect to trade matters. One first occasion for the Court to step in was offered in the context of the EU–Singapore FTA negotiations, where the Commission sought to solve a difference of opinion between the Commission and the Council on the interpretation of the Lisbon Treaty with respect to trade matters in the context of the FTA with Singapore.[20] More specifically, the uncertainty concerned the mixed or exclusive competence to sign and ratify trade agreements—with Member States sitting in the Council

[16] European Parliament, P7_TA(2011)0141 (6 April 2011), paras 6, 17.

[17] European Parliament, P8_TA(2015)0252 (8 July 2015), para 2.

[18] Calamita, Jansen (2012), 'The Making of Europe's International Investment Policy: Uncertain First Step', Legal Issues of Economic Integration, 311.

[19] European Parliament, P9_TA(2022)0268 (23 June 2022).

[20] Opinion 2/15, *EU–Singapore FTA*, EU:C:2017:376.

claiming competence to sign and ratify trade agreements alongside the EU (mixed competence), and the Commission insisting on the EU exclusive competence to do so. In its Opinion 2/15, the CJEU found that the EU FTA with Singapore 'falls within the exclusive competence of the European Union', except for portfolio investments and ISDS provisions, both of which belong to the competence shared between the EU and its Member States. Regarding the latter, the investor–state dispute settlement mechanism 'removes disputes from the jurisdiction of the courts of the Member States', and, as such, cannot be considered 'of a purely ancillary nature' and requires Member States' consent to be established.[21] It remains unclear which is the legal ground for establishing shared competence on ISDS matters. Regarding direct and portfolio investments, the difference lies in the control of assets. For example, establishing a company or acquiring one abroad are direct investments, whereas purchasing shares constitutes a portfolio investment. Unlike ISDS mechanisms, the Court proceeds more assertively in providing legal grounds for the shared competence underpinning portfolio investments:

> The conclusion of an international agreement—in the present instance with the Republic of Singapore—concerning non-direct foreign investment is, as EU law currently stands, likewise not 'provided for in a legislative act of the Union', within the meaning of Article 3(2) TFEU.[22]

As there is no legislation that bestows upon the Union competence to conclude agreements in the field of portfolio investments, Article 3(2) TFEU is not applicable. The Court went on in setting an even clearer boundary in this respect: international agreements concluded by the EU 'cannot "affect" rules of primary EU law or "alter their scope", within the meaning of Article 3(2) TFEU'.[23] This means that the ratification of broad FTAs involves Member States as long as they contain non-direct investments and investor–state arbitration clauses, which require shared competence.

Opinion 2/15 confirms a shift in competence conferred upon the EU by the Lisbon Treaty, albeit with clear limitations. As a result of this setback and rather than face the Court once again, the Commission chose to split investment chapters from the core trade provisions, introducing two independent agreements—the FTA and the IPA—thus shaping the dangers of mandatory

[21] Ibid, para 292.
[22] Ibid, para 236.
[23] Ibid, para 235.

mixed competences.[24] Further to Opinion 2/15, with respect to future trade negotiations, the Commission recommend presenting draft negotiating mandates for FTAs covering exclusive EU competence on the one hand, and separate mixed protection investment agreements on the other, with a view to strengthening the EU's position as a negotiating partner.[25] Trade and investment matters were thus split into two distinct treaties, to be ratified respectively by the EU only (the FTA) and by the EU and all its Member States (the IPA).

In reaction to this proposal and the considerable pressure it places on Member States, the Council reiterated that it is within its prerogative to decide on the launch of negotiations based on this proposal and 'to decide, on a case-by-case basis, on the splitting of trade agreements'.[26] The Commission has subsequently endorsed the Council's case-by-case approach. While the splitting approach has been applied to the agreements with Singapore and Vietnam—and is likely to influence those with the Philippines and Indonesia—the Council has clarified that agreements already concluded, such as those with Mexico and Mercosur, or currently under negotiation, such as with Chile, will remain mixed agreements.[27] In contrast, negotiations with India envisage an IPA alongside the main FTA. A different approach was pursued in the negotiations with Australia and New Zealand, in respect of which the Commission has not presented specific case recommendations for negotiating directives for investment agreements but has broadly aimed to a mutual liberalization of goods and services, leaving investment protection and resolution of investment disputes out of talks completely. To this group belongs the partnership agreement with Kenya as well. Lastly, in rethinking the best architecture for trade and investment protection agreements, a more extreme option on the EU table was the conclusion of a trade agreement with no investment agreement and thus avoiding the risk of being slowed down by national parliaments. At present, the FTA with Japan falls into this category as the willingness of the Council and the Commission to continue negotiations with Japan for a separate investment agreement has not reaped rewards.[28] The conclusion, in

[24] De Abreu Duarte, Francisco (2019), 'But the Last Word is Ours: The Monopoly of Jurisdiction of the Court of Justice of the European Union in Light of the Investment Court System', European Journal of International Law.

[25] COM(2017)492 final, para 6.

[26] Council of the European Union, 8622/18 (8 May 2018), para 3.

[27] Ibid.

[28] Although the Commission appeared committed in 2017 to continuing negotiations with Japan, this commitment has since faded:

> At the same time, negotiations continue on investment protection standards and investment protection dispute resolution. The firm commitment on both sides is to reach convergence in the investment protection negotiations as soon as possible, in light of their shared commitment to a stable and secure investment environment in Europe and Japan.

October 2023, of an agreement on cross-border data flows appears to confirm that an investment agreement is not a priority in the EU–Japan agenda.

Another challenge to the validity of the Commission's approach emerged in 2017, when the Belgian government asked the CJEU whether the CETA ICS—the

new dispute settlement mechanism renegotiated in line with the reformed approach to ISDS—was compatible with EU law. Based on Article 218 TFEU, the Belgian government's request was filed in September 2017 and was answered by the CJEU in May 2019 in its Opinion 1/17. In the meantime, the CJEU had found that investment treaties between Member States were potentially incompatible with EU law (the *Achmea* case) because the ISDS clause risks jeopardizing the autonomy of EU law.[29] Following the *Achmea* judgment, the Commission underlined that EU law already provides cross-border investors with judicial remedies,[30] and in May 2020 the Member States committed to the multilateral termination agreement for the termination of 'all bilateral investment treaties concluded between them by means of a plurilateral treaty or . . . bilaterally'.[31]

To the surprise of many, while intra-EU BITs were wound up, the CJEU reached opposite conclusions in considering the compatibility of the ICS provision of the EU–Canada Agreement with EU law. The heart of the Court's judgment is its reconciliation of the autonomy of EU law with the ICS system. There is an unusually strong acceptance by the Court of the EU legal system's coexistence with international law, rather than supremacy over it, but that acceptance is conditional upon the safeguards which the Court then sets out. These constraints, as Peers rightly points out, are not justified (as is usually the case) in terms of the Court's own institutional interests in the autonomy of EU

European Commission Press Release (8 December 2017), 'Joint Statement by the President of the European Commission Jean-Claude Juncker and the Prime Minister of Japan Shinzo Abe'.

[29] Case C-284/16, *Slovak Republic v Achmea* BV, EU:C:2018:158. While the issue of the compatibility of ISDS with EU law remained controversial, it was clarified in *Komstroy*, with respect to the Energy Charter Treaty:

> although the ECT may require Member States to comply with the arbitral mechanisms for which it provides in their relations with investors from third States who are also Contracting Parties to that treaty as regards investments made by the latter in those Member States, preservation of the autonomy and of the particular nature of EU law precludes the same obligations under the ECT from being imposed on Member States as between themselves.

Case C-741/19, *Republic of Moldova v Komstroy LLC*, EU:C:2021:655, para 61.

[30] COM(2018)547 final.

[31] Declaration of the Representatives of the Governments of the Member States on the Legal Consequences of the Judgment of the Court of Justice in Achmea and on Investment Protection in the European Union (2019).

law but in terms of the EU's political institutions' accountability to the democratic process.[32] From this standpoint, Opinion 1/17 constitutes an important stepping stone for the EU's desire to reform investment arbitration worldwide and signals a cautious opening in favour of international law, in respect of which the supremacy of EU law is not unfettered and cannot go as far as operating in the external relations of the EU.

While Opinion 1/17 can be saluted as a step forward in reinforcing the position of the EU as an international actor, suddenly moving away from the unrealistic and perilous idea of 'absolute supremacy' of EU law over international law in external relations does raise doubts as to its coherence.[33] Opinion 1/17, in fact, appears to validate the cutting-edge proposal (the ICS) of the Commission before a formal CJEU decision was taken. Despite the Court having increasingly developed a restricted view of the international freedoms allocated to Member States and other international institutions—as attested by a consistent jurisprudence of cases[34]—it appears that the Commission has taken innovative steps to draw the Court into its political orbit and shape the EU's external action accordingly.

D. The road for the future

No-one will gainsay that some peculiarities of EU law are quintessentially concerned with the preservation of its systemic structure, and, in particular, of the CJEU prerogatives. The journey taken by this book eschews compartmentalizing the EU legal system on the one hand and international rules on the other, especially as far as international investment matters are concerned. After half of a century in which the EU Member States had made little (if any) substantive changes to their investment treaties, the granting of an exclusive competence to the EU on FDIs marks the beginning of a new era, and not just for Europe. The new EU-led investment policy has the potential to engage the world investment community in exploring new paths towards far-reaching refinements and procedural reforms that align investment agreements with today's policy preferences. The establishment of new investment law and policy under

[32] Peers, Steven (2019), '"We *Aren't* the World": The CJEU Reconciles EU Law with International (Investment) Law' https://eulawanalysis.blogspot.com/2019/05/we-arent-world-cjeu-reconciles-eu-law.html. See also Part I, Chapter 3 and Chapter 4.

[33] De Abreu Duarte (n 24), 1212–19.

[34] A case in point is Opinion 2/13, *Accession to the ECHR*, ECLI:EU:C:2014:2454.

the auspices of the EU initiates a brand new season for the investment regime, with fresh opportunities to dig out further possibilities to address the systemic challenges of the investment arbitration regime.

The EU has worked intensively on developing a comprehensive approach to the protection of investors, both European investors abroad and foreign investors in the EU. Championing itself as a promoter of democracy and rule of law, the EU gradually readjusted the trajectory of its investment policy, especially by paying more attention to public policy objectives, although investment protection and promotion remain the sparks that ignited its policy aspirations. It seems that among other desired outcomes, the EU has proven its commitment to include obligations in the areas of protection of national security, the environment, public health, workers' and consumers' rights, industrial policy, and cultural diversity. Unlike Member States, whose BITs barely mentioned sustainable development, all the EU FTAs deal with sustainable development, environmental, and labour concerns. This has undeniably been inspired by the Canadian approach, which has helped shape the substance of EU negotiations under its new competence and test cohesion among the Member States, thus ensuring the pursuit of a common ground at the Council before the conclusion of future investment agreements.

These positive developments notwithstanding, granting a reliable and balanced investment environment is likely to be one of the main challenges for the EU, especially regarding demanding issues like climate change. In this regard, taking into account the interests of all involved stakeholders may unexpectedly lead towards undesired outcomes. States can profitably welcome a new approach that is more favourable to their right to regulate, but the impact of the resulting weakened investor expectations on Member States remains to be seen. In this regard, the path is fraught with even more uncertainty deriving from mandatory mixed competences, which, once again, leaves the Commission at a cross-roads as nothing can happen without the consent of the Council.[35]

As per Opinion 2/15, in the presence of agreements covering portfolio investments and containing ISDS clauses, mandatory mixed competences require the Member States' ratifications of the investment agreement, as it partly falls within the competences of the Union and partly within the competence of the Member States. As things stand, none of the concluded investment chapters

[35] Bungenberg, Marc, Reinisch, August, and Tietje, Christian (2013), *EU and Investment Agreements Open Questions and Remaining Challenges*, 165.

(CETA)[36] or investment protection agreements (Singapore,[37] Vietnam[38]) have entered into force. One preliminary problem that mixed competences unavoidably raises is the effect of a Member State unable or unwilling to ratify an agreement already negotiated between the EU, its Member States, and one or more third parties. This would be particularly problematic in bilateral settings because if one Member State does not ratify the agreement, its entry into force is prejudiced. While the EU is taking over international relations from its Member States, mixed agreements are here to stay[39] and might indeed be a signal of the Member States' strong resistance against the expansion of EU power, irrespective of the duty to cooperate,[40] which does not extend as to oblige it to ratify a mixed agreement.

Undeniably, the role of the EU in international relations has opened towards a more international law-friendly approach (Opinion 1/17). However, despite the EU's global ambitions, as reflected in Articles 3(5) and 21 TEU, the permanence of mixed competences is an indication that the advancement of the EU investment policy is likely to proceed one agreement at a time, and only if all the Member States agree.[41]

An interesting plot twist might be on the horizon. If the recent call by Parliament to amend the EU treaties is backed by the Council, mandatory mixed competences are likely to fade away.[42] In a historic resolution of November 2023, the Parliament has called for a 'strengthening of the Union's

[36] As of May 2025, seventeen Member States have completed the domestic ratification of CETA: Austria, Croatia, Czechia, Denmark, Estonia, Finland, Germany, Latvia, Lithuania, Luxembourg, Malta, the Netherlands, Portugal, Romania, Slovakia, Spain, and Sweden. The United Kingdom, which has left the EU, also ratified CETA while it was still a Member State. Member States that have not ratified CETA include the following: Belgium, Bulgaria, Cyprus, France, Greece, Hungary, Ireland, Italy, Poland, and Slovenia. https://www.consilium.europa.eu/en/documents-publications/treaties-agreements/agreement/?id=2016017.

[37] The EU–Singapore Investment Protection Agreement will enter into force after it has been ratified by all EU Member States according to their own national procedures. As of May 2025, the Member States that have not ratified the EU–Singapore IPA include the following: Austria, Belgium, Cyprus, France, Germany, Ireland, Netherlands, Poland, and Slovenia. https://www.consilium.europa.eu/en/documents-publications/treaties-agreements/agreement/?id=2018027&DocLanguage=en.

[38] The EU–Vietnam Investment Protection Agreement will enter into force when it is ratified by all EU Member States. As of May 2025, the Member States that have not ratified the EU–Vietnam IPA include the following: Austria, Belgium, Cyprus, France, Germany, Ireland, Netherlands, Poland, and Slovenia. https://www.consilium.europa.eu/en/documents-publications/treaties-agreements/agreement/?id=2019015&DocLanguage=en.

[39] Wessel, Ramsel, and Takács, Tamara (2017), 'Constitutional Aspects of the EU's Global Actorness: Increased Exclusivity in Trade and Investment and the Role of the European Parliament', European Business Law Review.

[40] Case C-28/12, *European Commission v Council of the European Union*, EU:C:2015:43.

[41] See Chapter 7 Section B.

[42] Proposals of the European Parliament for the amendment of the Treaties—European Parliament resolution of 22 November 2023 on proposals of the European Parliament for the amendment of the Treaties (2022/2051(INL)), OJ C, C/2024/4216 24 July 2024.

capacity to act by considerably increasing the number of areas where actions are decided by qualified majority voting and through the ordinary legislative procedure'.[43] Of particular interest for present purposes are the amendments to Articles 207 TFEU and 218 TFEU:

Art. 207 TFEU	Revised Art. 207 TFEU
1. The common commercial policy shall be based on uniform principles, particularly with regard to . . ., foreign **direct** investment, the achievement of uniformity in measures of liberalization, export policy and measures to protect trade such as those to be taken in the event of dumping or subsidies. The common commercial policy shall be conducted in the context of the principles and objectives of the Union's external action.	1. The common commercial policy shall be based on uniform principles, particularly with regard to . . . foreign investment, **including investment protection, economic security**, the achievement of uniformity in measures of liberalization, export policy and measures to protect trade such as those to be taken in the event of dumping or subsidies. The common commercial policy shall be conducted in the context of the principles and objectives of the Union's external action, **as well as its climate-neutrality objective.**
4(2). For the negotiation and conclusion of agreements in the fields of trade in services and the commercial aspects of intellectual property, as well as foreign direct investment, the Council shall act **unanimously** where such agreements include provisions for which unanimity is required for the adoption of internal rules.	4(2). For the negotiation and conclusion of agreements in the fields of trade in services and the commercial aspects of intellectual property, as well as foreign direct investment, the Council shall act **by a qualified majority.**
4(3). The Council shall also act **unanimously** for the negotiation and conclusion of agreement	4(3). the Council shall also act **by a qualified majority** for the negotiation and conclusion of agreements
	5. A permanent mechanism to monitor and examine foreign direct investment in the Union shall be established. This mechanism may be used to protect the European interest.

According to the proposal, one first step is to extend the CCP reach to investment protection and economic security (paragraphs 1 and 5), and bring the external action in line with climate-neutrality objectives. The main novelty, however, is to replace unanimity with a qualified majority for the conclusion of agreements in the field of FDI (paragraph 4(2)), and in the negotiation phases (paragraph 4(3)). These revisions are complemented with those advanced for

[43] Ibid, para 4.

Article 218 TFEU, which accord the Parliament a role almost as prominent as the Council:

Art. 218 TFEU	Revised Art. 218 TFEU
2. The Council shall authorise the opening of negotiations, adopt negotiating directives, authorise the signing of agreements and conclude them.	2. The Council shall, **after obtaining the consent of the European Parliament**, authorise the opening of negotiations, adopt negotiating directives, authorise the signing of agreements and conclude them.
	2a. **By way of derogation from paragraph 2, for agreements falling within the scope of Article 207, the opening of negotiations shall be conditional upon authorization by the European Parliament and the Council.**

If these amendments are approved, they would mark the end of mandatory mixity as we have known it. The amendments will strengthen the Union capacity to conclude IIAs overcoming the impediments raised by Member States within the Council. This move is expected to streamline the process and mitigate the risks of political deadlocks by taming the national interests with a new discipline. Member States, however, would still fight to keep their prerogatives, especially considering that throughout the entire EU history, each Member State was granted a position of power brokerage.[44] An unwarranted result of Member States facing binding norms, adopted wholly or partially against their will, could be a lowering of the standards to be adopted. If stripped of their shadow right of veto, Member States are likely to reach a general consensus on the 'narrowest' (or minimum) standard deemed to be beneficial for the Community as a whole. Despite the Commission's efforts to persuade the Member States that the measures are in the general interest and of sufficient importance to override the single interests, the removal of the veto power might generate distortive effects on the EU governance. These downgrading risks could be mitigated by the Parliament, which is enabled to give voice and power to fragmented interests whose 'membership' is more difficult to channel under qualified majority than unanimity. The challenge

[44] Weiler, Joseph (1999), *The Constitution of Europe: 'Do the New Clothes Have an Emperor?' and Other Essays on European Integration.*

here remains to control the uncontrolled reflexes of national interests in the international sphere.[45]

Perhaps it would not be too much to hope that enhanced unity in the EU relations over international investments will help overcome the uncertainties elsewhere, albeit it involves more complex demands and greater constraints on the actors, especially the Member States.

[45] Ibid, 251.

PART I
A PROMISE OF DEMOCRACY?

This Part introduces the readers to Chapters 3 and 4. It frames the principle of democracy as outlined, albeit nowhere defined, in the EU treaties, and explains how transparency and public participation have become the EU channels to spread democracy in the investment regime. Although many perspectives on the question of democracy in the EU seem plausible,[1] the manifestations of transparency and public participation are particularly revealing of the EU's pretensions towards a policy project *of* the people rather than just for the people even within the regime of international investments. Transparency and public participation constitute the preconditions to democracy. They foster better understanding, improve the quality of policy-making, and ensure systemic legitimacy and accountability. By extension, they enable the rule of law and serve as essential conditions for the realization of the Union, which will only truly be if its actions are made public and explained openly to European people.

Despite being often conflated and confused with each other, civil society participation and transparency are complementary manifestations of the principle of democracy and are equally important for the EU in reducing the gap between citizens, who feel increasingly alienated from economic relations and the complexities of today's multilevel system of governance. In this context, transparency operates as a vehicle through which governments inform the public about both how decisions are taken and the impacts their policies might generate. Participation materializes as a channel through which government and the public interact, enabling mutual understanding of the intentions of both. For the EU legal order, whose dual structure of legitimacy depends on the Member States and its citizens, 'participatory transparency' is instrumental

[1] This section does not aim to provide a definitive conclusion on the matter but rather focuses on how the EU's commitment to the value of democracy has been tentatively introduced and promoted within the investment system.

to the full realization of this order as it upholds the EU's fundamental pillars of democracy and protection of fundamental rights that underpin the aim to create 'an ever closer union among the peoples of Europe'. Participatory transparency ultimately confers upon citizens the opportunity to offer their input on investment policies: governments communicate their line of action, and the public is allowed to give feedback on this basis. It is in this sense that transparency has become a condition for participation since the public seeks to become involved in the debate after being put in the position of knowing what is happening.

Accordingly, each chapter tackles one issue: Chapter 3 deals with transparency and Chapter 4 with public participation.

***

Democracy was not part of the original vision of European integration, and it did not appear, in any form, in the European Economic Community (EEC) Treaty of 1957. Even the idealist pretension of the Rome Treaty towards an 'ever closer union among the peoples of Europe' was not a legal principle but has become a fundamental assumption for the Union, characterizing the entire EU story up until and beyond the Lisbon Treaty. It was assumed that the notion of representative democracy reflected the common tradition of Member States and could not be overridden by the EU.[2] However, unlike the imperfect habits of Member States' governments, the EU's self-celebrated mantra of governance without government[3] left citizens unable to throw out governments or to affect agents of EU governance. This somewhat paradoxical configuration of democracy in the EU is premised on Article 10 TEU: people are directly represented at the Union level in the European Parliament, and the Member States in the Council. This implies, however, that EU citizens are not in a position to vote out those in power since Member States representatives are not chosen in this manner.[4] As a consequence, an increasing indifference has epitomized a widespread sense of detachment from the EU governance since its very beginning, with some instances where this detachment turned into hostility towards the EU actions. Make no mistake: the problem of popular legitimacy (or rather the lack of it) in the EU decision-making process does not derive from the fact that the EU is not a state. The lines of the democratic deficit debate are well-known

[2] Williams, Andrew (2010), *The Ethos of Europe: Values, Law and Justice in the EU*, 165.
[3] Allott, Philip (2002), 'European Governance and the Re-branding of Democracy', European Law Review.
[4] Craig, Paul, and de Búrca, Gráinne (2020), *EU Law: Text, Cases, and Materials*, 188–91.

and have been extensively explored already.[5] What remains particularly problematic is that the EU exercises a huge amount of power over political, social, and economic issues—previously in the hands of Member States—without being entirely legitimated democratically.[6] Although the terms of the debate have shifted, mostly due to the Parliament's expanded legislative role, whenever the Union is incapable of adequately solving the problems with which it is confronted, the principles of accountability and representation come into question and appear even more compromised.

Democracy is hard to detect in the Union DNA, yet it is considered a structural principle of the EU,[7] one of the cornerstones of the EU edifice.[8] This apparent paradox can be partly explained through a teleological reading and the political messianism that have characterized the EU's narrative. Rather than embodying the ideal itself, the Union has been driven by the pursuit of an ideal—a vision of a better future and an ever-closer union among its peoples. This pursuit might explain why, for so long, the EU was able to operate without a veritable commitment to a principle it has consistently demanded of its aspiring members and professes to hold most dear.

As happens more often than not in the EU structure, what politics and its non-functioning political process were unable to do was corrected by the Court of Justice of the European Union (CJEU). If, on the one hand, the Court had little room to intervene in a decisional process that remains problematic, on the other, the Court slowly, and the Advocates Generals more speedily,

[5] Garcia, Soledad (1993), *European Identity and the Search for Legitimacy*; Bellamy, Richard, Bufacchi, Vittorio, and Castiglione, Dario (1995), *Democracy and Constitutional Culture in the Union of Europe*; Weiler, Joseph Haltern, Ulrich, and Mayer, Franz (1995), 'European Democracy and its Critique', West European Politics; Dehousse, Renaud (1997), 'Regulation by Networks in the European Community: The Role of European Agencies', Journal of European Public Policy; Majone, Giandomenico (1999), 'The Regulatory State and its Legitimacy Problems', West European Politics; Craig, Paul, and Harlow, Carol (1998), *Lawmaking in the European Union*; Weiler, Joseph (1999), *The Constitution of Europe 'Do the New Clothes Have an Emperor?' and Other Essays on European Integration*; Nicolaïdis, Kalypso, and Howse, Robert (2001), '"This is My Eutopia. . .": Narrative as Power', Journal of Common Market Studies; Aman, Alfred (2004), *The Democracy Deficit: Taming Globalization Through Law Reform*; Cardwell, Paul James (2011), 'Mapping Out Democracy Promotion in the EU's External Relations', European Foreign Affairs Review; Trew, Stuart (2013), 'Correcting the Democratic Deficit in the CETA Negotiations: Civil Society Engagement in the Provinces, Municipalities, and Europe', International Journal; Curtin, Deirdre (2014), 'Challenging Executive Dominance in European Democracy', The Modern Law Review; Habermas Jürgen (2015), 'Democracy in Europe: Why the Development of the EU into a Transnational Democracy is Necessary and How it is Possible', European Law Journal; Blockmans, Steven, and Russack, Sophia (2019), *Representative Democracy in the EU*; Craig, Paul (2021), 'Integration, Democracy, and Legitimacy.' In *The Evolution of EU Law*, edited by Paul Craig and Gráinne de Búrca.

[6] Weiler, Joseph (2011), 'The Political and Legal Culture of European Integration: An Exploratory Essay', International Journal of Constitutional Law.

[7] Case C101/08, *Audiolux v Groupe Bruxelles Lambert SA*, EU:C:2009:410, para 70.

[8] Case C353/99P, *Council v Hautala*, EU:C:2001:392, para 53.

stepped in to give effect to a broader discourse of political integration based on democracy. Democracy, recognized as a founding principle of the European Union,[9] has been progressively shaped by the Court through the twin notions of transparency and participation, framed as individual rights.[10] More specifically, the democratic development of the EU[11] hinges on participation in the exercise of power through a representative assembly[12] and the openness of decision-making processes. This, in turn, begs the question of how transparency and public participation have evolved to embody an expression of democracy within the EU legal order.

Transparency made its first appearance in the 1960s in the field of competition policy to limit the Commission's discretion to prohibit or permit the disclosure of documents but it was not conceived as an instrument to enhance democratic principles. Transparency as a democracy enhancer officially surfaced in EU law in the 1992 Declaration N.17 attached to the Maastricht Treaty. This was the first tangible act that acknowledged the importance of a general principle of a right to information[13] as part of a broader system of transparency in decision-making.[14] The Court, however, did not engage in vesting transparency of a particular legal status and insisted on a broader concept of 'openness' of the decision-making and of public authorities—a concept that is likely to have been inspired by a (Single) market-oriented justice. In *Netherlands v Council*, the Court recognized that the right to access documents and the principle of openness were essential requirements of democracy and could not be treated as an organizational matter purely internal to the institutions, but transparency remained unmentioned.[15] Article 255 of the Amsterdam Treaty[16] and its implementation through Regulation 1049/2001[17] crystallized a progressive

[9] Case T-135/96, *UEAPME v Council*, EU:T:1998:128, para 89; Case T-222/29, T-327/99, and T-329/99, *Martinez, De Gaulle* v *European Parliament*, EU:T:2001:242, para 200.

[10] Twining, William (2009), 'Diffusion of Law: A Global Perspective', The Journal of Legal Pluralism and Unofficial Law, 568.

[11] The issue is framed in this term for the first time in Case C-58/94, *Netherlands v Council of the European Union*, EU:C:1995:409.

[12] Case 139/79, *Maizena GmbH v Council of the European Communities*, EU:C:1980:250, para 34; Case 138/79, *SA Roquette Frères v Council of the European Communities*, EU:C:1980:249, para 33; Case C-300/89, *Commission v Council*, EU:C:1991:244, para 20.

[13] *Hautala* (n 8), para 47.

[14] Case C-064/05P *Sweden v Commission of the European Communities*, EU:C:2007:433.

[15] *Netherlands* (n 11), paras 18, 35.

[16] Treaty on European Union (Consolidated Version) Treaty of Maastricht, OJ C 325/5 24 December 2002, Article 255(1):

> Any citizen of the Union, and any natural or legal person residing or having its registered office in a Member State, shall have a right of access to European Parliament, Council and Commission documents....

[17] Regulation (EC) No. 1049/2001 of the European Parliament and of the Council of 30 May 2001 regarding public access to European Parliament, Council and Commission documents, OJ L 145/43, 31 May 2001.

affirmation of the right to access to documents of the institutions, notwithstanding the long-standing prudence of the CJEU towards the establishment of transparency as a general principle of Community law[18] and towards unreserved disclosures.[19]

Despite the Court's prudence, the Advocates General progressively construed transparency as a legal principle rooted in the democratic principle,[20] and originally derived from the most essential foundations of the Member States.[21] According to the Advocates General, the right of access to documents was inextricably related to the democratic nature of the EU institutions and was epitomized by the principle of transparency. Along with citizens' involvement in the decision-making process, they contended that transparency is necessary for a democratic society.[22] This appears even more compelling when looking at the overall legislative context of the EU and the objectives of the set of norms of which transparency forms a part (not only the Regulation 1049/2001 in question but, more broadly, the EU treaties). Advocate General Maduro framed the enhancement of transparency, particularly the right of access to documents,[23] in teleological terms, viewing it as an inexorable goal towards which the EU is gradually progressing. The implication is clear: the public's right of access to (institutional) documents constitutes a key element of the broader principle of transparency, which, in turn, is an integral part of the democratic principle. Transparency is a component of democracy because it strengthens the democratic nature of the institutions, legitimizes their actions, and makes them more accountable to the citizens, who, in turn, are in the position to carry out genuine and efficient monitoring of the exercise of the powers.[24]

Besides the fulfilment of an effective system of governance at the internal level, what is at stake, as Maduro rightly inferred,

> is the requirement of structural congruence, as the transfer of competence to the Community must not lead to diminished democratic control of power by the citizens of the Member States. . . . It would be unacceptable for certain powers, which were subject to democratic control mechanisms at national level, systematically to escape equivalent democratic control mechanisms

[18] *Sweden* (n 14), para 38.

[19] Case T-105/95, *WWF UK v Commission of the European Communities*, EU:T:1997:26; Joined Cases C-39-05/P and C-52-05-P, *Sweden, Turco v Council of the European Union*, EU:C:2008:374.

[20] Case C-41/00 P, *Interporc v Commission of the European Communities*, EU:C:2002:162, para 73.

[21] *Hautala* (n 8), paras 47–53.

[22] Case C-28/08P, *European Commission v Bavarian Lager*, EU:C:2009:624, para 212.

[23] *Sweden* (n 14), para 35–37.

[24] Case C-41/00 P *Interpor v Commission of the European Communities*, EU:C:2003:125, para 39.

> simply by being transferred to the Community, on the ground that they now form part of 'the States' foreign policy.[25]

Beyond the need to ensure consistency across Member States' approaches, what Maduro is inferring is the need for structural congruence between different areas of the EU actions, including the EU's external dimension. In the Lisbon Treaty, this inference finds its culmination: transparency is vested with legal status and, as such, has to be replicated externally as per Article 21 TEU. Transparency not only serves to legitimize the decision-making process and enhance the democratic nature of the EU internally but is also instrumental for the fulfilment of the broader objectives of the EU's external relations, as it ensures that the Union's actions on the international scene are shaped by the constitutional principle of, *inter alia*, democracy.

Enshrined in Article 15 of the Treaty on the Functioning of the European Union (TFEU),[26] the right of access to documents, institutional transparency, and the publication of documents produced throughout the legislative process are firmly established as Treaty provisions of general application, embodying a principle of good governance. Access to documents has been unequivocally elevated to the status of a fundamental right under Article 42 of the EU Charter of Fundamental Rights. It serves as a cornerstone for transparency and, consequently, for the exercise of democratic rights as it empowers citizens to scrutinize and engage with the legislative process.[27]

There is, however, a risk that transparency will not be used in the same manner by all citizens and that it will serve to promote privileged access to the political system for certain interest groups. It is in this regard that the second dimension of democracy—participation in the EU democratic life—comes into play. Participation is another way of imbuing decisions with greater legitimacy. Unlike the principle of transparency, the CJEU did not question the existence of such a procedural right but has consistently resisted claims to

[25] *Sweden* (n 14), para 53.

[26] Consolidated version of the Treaty on the Functioning of the European Union, OJ C 326, 26 October 2012 (TFEU), Article 15:

1. In order to promote good governance and ensure the participation of civil society, the Union institutions, bodies, offices and agencies shall conduct their work *as openly as possible*.
2. The European Parliament shall *meet in public*, as shall the Council when considering and voting on a draft legislative act.
3. Any citizen of the Union, and any natural or legal person residing or having its registered office in a Member State, shall have a *right of access to documents* of the Union institutions, bodies, offices and agencies, whatever their medium, subject to the principles and the conditions to be defined in accordance with this paragraph.

Emphasis added.

[27] Case C-57/16 P, *ClientEarth v Commission*, ECLI:EU:C:2018:660.

participation in the decision-making through the intermediary of a representative assembly.[28] In this sense, Williams is right in arguing that the realization of participation largely relies on highly controlled methods of interactions between the public and European institutions[29] or, at best, through litigation as part of individual effective judicial protection, as per long-established democratic traditions of the Member States.[30]

Somewhat similar to what it did for transparency, to strengthen democracy the Court referred to a broader concept of openness by allowing citizens to scrutinize considerations underpinning the legislative action.[31] Although it was quite assertive in acknowledging that Article 255 (Amsterdam Treaty) laid down the conditions to enable citizens to participate more closely in the decision-making process,[32] the Court has remained unwilling to accept that participation in the making of a legislative measure accord the applicants any enhanced prospects of being given standing to challenge it.[33] Advocate General Sharpston reiterates the point:

> Where a decision is reached by a legislative process, however, such public participation already exists. The legislature itself is composed of democratically-elected representatives of the public. When the decision-making process takes place within such a body, it benefits from indirect, but nevertheless representative, public participation.[34]

Without undermining the role the European Parliament plays in the EU decision-making process, it is a feature of modern democracies engaging with civil societies that a very significant part of the political discourse takes place outside the Parliament altogether.[35] This is noticeable in international affairs and particularly in the decision-making underpinning the negotiations of international agreements. Despite the new powers enjoyed by the Parliament,

[28] *Maizena* (n 12), para 34; *Sa Roquette Frères* (n 12), para 33.
[29] Williams (n 2).
[30] Case C-872/19 P, *Venezuela v Council of the European Union*, ECLI:EU:C:2021:37.
[31] *Sweden, Turco* (n 19).
[32] *Interporc* (n 20), para 39.
[33] Craig and de Búrca (n 4), 578–80; Case C-263/02 P, *Commission of the European Communities v Jego-Quéré*, EU:C:2004:210, paras 47–48.
[34] Joined Cases C 128/09, *Antoine Boxus and Willy Roua*; C 129/09, *Guido Durlet and Others*; C 130/09, *Paul Fastrez and Henriette Fastrez*; Case C-131/09, *Philippe Daras and Bernard Croiselet*; Case C-134/09, *Association des Riverains et Habitants des Communes Proches de l'Aéroport B.S.C.A. (Brussels South Charleroi Airport) ASBL – A.R.A.Ch and Bernard Page;* Case C-135/09, *Association des Riverains et Habitants des Communes Proches de l'Aéroport B.S.C.A. (Brussels South Charleroi Airport) ASBL - A.R.A.Ch, Léon L'Hoir and Nadine Dartois*, EU:C:2011:319, para 56.
[35] Joined Cases C-200/07, C-201/07, *Marra v De Gregorio and Clemente*, EU:C:2008:369, para 34.

the Commission remains the legislative initiator of trade and investment agreements (and of most legislation), and, therefore, the limited degree of engagement with the Parliament might not be sufficient to guarantee that citizens participate closely in such a process. Article 11 TEU introduced by the Lisbon Treaty remedies this shortcoming:

1. The institutions shall, by appropriate means, give citizens and representative associations the opportunity to make known and publicly exchange their views in all areas of Union action.
2. The institutions shall maintain an open, transparent and regular dialogue with representative associations and civil society.
3. The European Commission shall carry out broad consultations with parties concerned in order to ensure that the Union's actions are coherent and transparent.
4. Not less than one million citizens who are nationals of a significant number of Member States may take the initiative of inviting the European Commission, within the framework of its powers, to submit any appropriate proposal on matters where citizens consider that a legal act of the Union is required for the purpose of implementing the Treaties.

The provision implements a long-standing commitment on the part of the Commission to good governance, which finds its expression in the concepts of openness and participation laid down in the 2001 White Paper on European Governance. Article 11 TEU implements this path and materializes the EU's (mostly the Commission's) ambition to improve the involvement of citizens in policy shaping and nurture a culture of dialogue, consultations, and, more broadly, better communication. The provision is expressed in mandatory language ('the institutions, the Commission shall'). The European Citizens Initiative is one of the innovations introduced by the provision (paragraph 4) to promote the participation of citizens in the democratic life of the European Union, of which Regulation 211/2011 constitutes its legislative framework. For the first time, legislation has been enacted concerning the citizen's initiative, and, in addition to EU citizens, it is addressed to other three segments of the public: representative associations, civil society, and all stakeholders affected. The Court has, so far, oriented towards a cautiously open interpretation of this provision, thus sending a positive message about the nature of participatory democracy in the EU. Encouraging participation within existing democratic structures, however, does not imply bypassing or replacing these structures. Nor does it provide a miraculous solution to alleged and real shortcomings of the EU's democratic legitimacy. The added value of initiatives like ECI is in the opportunities they create and in the democratic debates citizens can trigger, regardless of whether the outcome is transformed into a formal proposal eventually.[36]

By fostering open debate on differing perspectives, EU policies are expected to achieve greater legitimacy,[37] enhance accountability to citizens, and bolster public confidence in EU institutions.[38] This extends not only to the perceived lawfulness of individual legislative measures but also to the legitimacy of the legislative process as a whole.[39] In this context, transparency and participation play a dual role: they inform the public about the Union's actions, ensuring its democratic legitimacy, and they cultivate a deeper understanding and engagement with the EU's initiatives. Perhaps even more significantly, transparency and participation are instrumental in fostering a sense of shared 'European spirit,' inspiring a new way of thinking and acting among the people of Europe. Despite its internal deficits in terms of democracy, what remains problematic internally might be vindicated externally (Article 21 TEU), especially in the presence of international agreements which manifestly seek to modify the legal order of the EU and clearly produce independent legal effects.[40] It is with this centripetal spirit that the EU surfaced the regime of international investments.

When the EU arrived in the international investment regime, a global process towards transparency was already developing, especially as regards the arbitration process. Historically speaking, investment arbitration took place under the strict condition of confidentiality, with little (if any) opportunity for public participation or knowledge about the existence of a dispute. Largely inspired by the commercial arbitration approach, for a long time confidentiality has prominently featured in investment agreements as well, with treaties being negotiated behind closed doors, no mechanism ensuring that the public will ever know about the claim brought, the positions taken by the parties, the decisions issued by the tribunals and the precise reasons for them.[41] Save for a few exceptions, such a policy of confidentiality remained the rule for quite a while, prudentially justified by the need to protect trade secret information, and to

[36] Case C-418/18 P, *Puppinck v Commission*, EU:C:2019:640, paras 71–84.
[37] Case C-157/21, *Poland v European Parliament*, EU:C:2022:98, para 52.
[38] *ClientEarth* (n 27), para 75.
[39] *Sweden, Turco* (n 19), para 59.
[40] *Puppinck* (n 36), paras 37–43.
[41] OECD (2005), *International Investment Law: A Changing Landscape: A Companion Volume to International Investment Perspectives*.

preserve the reputation of the actors involved (states and investors). The complexity of these agreements, coupled with the technical issues they address, has further contributed to the perception of the international investment regime as an obscure area of international law. Truth be told, this secretive approach worked relatively well for investors and to a lesser extent for states. Opacity allowed states to hide cases of corruption in the arbitral process but progressively exposed them to the uncomfortable need to justify their policy choices to their citizens. In particular, when the effects of foreign investments manifested in more practical terms, often at the expense of communities who lived in the area where the investment project took place, the lack of information made publicly available[42] and the limited public involvement in these policies quickly turned out to be a real problem.

International Investment Agreement (IIAs) are agreements rooted in a certain world view, which vindicate certain socio-economic interests.[43] This world view long remained shielded from public scrutiny, often even from parliamentary scrutiny thus deepening the gap between political choices, formal rules, and democratic governance. Democracy was usually listed under the preamble's commitments of investment treaties but no definitions were provided, possibly because the expectation that investment agreements had to ensure at least some adherence to democratic principles took time to emerge. The first signs of dissatisfaction date back to the 1990s when non-governmental organization (NGO) campaigns prompted, among other factors, the failure of the negotiations for a Multilateral Agreement on Investment. Pressure from organized citizens has grown considerably since then and materialized predominantly in direct actions like protests and occupations, or through court proceedings.[44] Direct actions targeted treaty-makers officials (especially through manifestations) and investors (especially through investment facilities' occupations), with subsequent investors' claims challenging state conduct's wrongfulness. Court proceedings epitomized public concerns about the relationship between the investment regime and national democratic spaces. While targeting investors, what civil society groups were seeking to obtain was some forms of engagement at the policy-making level—that is, obtain

[42] Gelos, R. Gaston, and Wei, Shang-Jin (2002), 'Transparency and International Investor Behavior', National Bureau of Economic Research Working Paper.

[43] Weiler, Joseph (2004), 'The Geology of International Law—Governance, Democracy and Legitimacy', ZaöRV.

[44] Cotula, Lorenzo (2017), 'Democracy and International Investment Law', Leiden Journal of International Law.

access to relevant information and, subsequently, influence the parameters of the investment regime.

Investment rules provided a particularly apt expression of the power of law to institutionalize distributive choices that impact the ability of citizens and states to respond to economic exigencies.[45] Unlike the EU, where democracy was an implied premise, in the investment regime democracy soon became an expectation necessary to overcome problems of systemic legitimacy and acceptance. The requests that emerged within the investment regime were twofold and interlinked with one another. First, there was a demand for greater transparency in investment arbitration, and, second, a demand for more accountability of the policy choices underpinning the negotiations of investment agreements. Different responses were advanced.

As for the first question, the problem was originally framed as a demand for third-party involvement in the context of environmental arbitrations. After the *Methanex* decision,[46] which was the first to grant third parties the possibility to submit briefs and recognize their useful contribution, public requests expanded in multiple directions. This expansion encompassed various aspects (e.g. the publication of documents produced within the arbitral process, the publication of the final award, and participation in the litigation process) but alternated with phases of prudential tightening since the litigating parties (claimant investors and respondent states) were reluctant to abandon confidentiality unreservedly. While states tended to remain more cautious towards the openness of the proceedings, arbitral tribunals gradually contributed to explicitly recognizing transparency as a normative principle and, albeit less consistently, admitting non-disputing parties' submissions. While formulations may vary across awards, arbitral tribunals agreed on the identification of the principle of transparency as one of the core components forming part of the fair and equitable treatment (FET) obligation that states have to grant to foreign investors. They have, however, been more cautious and proceeded on a case-by-case basis when called to decide about *amicus curiae* briefs. Despite the portrayal by its detractors, developments on the transparency front progressed slowly but consistently for over twenty years. As a consequence, the investment regime has been able to evolve towards the creation of new spaces for public engagement at the procedural level, finally overcoming the traditionally

[45] Schneiderman, David (2013), *Resisting Economic Globalization: Critical Theory and International Investment Law.*

[46] *Methanex Corporation v United States of America* (Partial Award, 7 August 2002).

deep-rooted predisposition towards secrecy and confidentiality, and now displays a marked orientation towards transparency in investment treaty arbitration.[47]

Different considerations pertain to the second question. While treaty-making presents greater scope for influencing and modifying the parameters of the investment regime, states have long remained reluctant to cede ground on this front. Unlike what happened for transparency in investment arbitration, arbitral tribunals had limited room to intervene on the accountability of the political choices underpinning investment policies, especially considering they were more part of the problem, or at least contributing to the problem to emerge, rather than in the position of delivering solutions. Since IIAs negotiations remained a prerogative of states, citizens began to question the accountability of governments to make decisions on their behalf, especially in light of the impact on the sovereignty of actors and forces produced beyond their nation's borders, and yet having real significance in people's lives.[48] Although these non-domestic forces—namely arbitral tribunals—lack the authority to create norms, their controversial role in reviewing (and sometimes sanctioning) significant public policy matters that extend beyond what investment rules would consider 'normal' has nonetheless allowed them to wield power in ways that distort political processes and undermine the very rationales of democracy.[49] For example, arbitral tribunals might sanction a legitimate legislative choice to not renew a permit to operate a hazardous waste facility situated in the proximity of an urban centre because of its alleged intoxicating effects on the soil, as it might violate the FET obligation or amount to indirect expropriation.[50] The distorting effect of these external forces prompted citizens to increasingly question how political choices underpinning investment policies were taken, often doubting in whose name these decisions were pursued, and what was the place (if any) for democratic governance in international investment law.

When the EU replaced the Member States in the domain of foreign investments (Article 207(1) TFEU),[51] the transparency narrative produced enough satisfactory progress within the arbitration process but was never articulated in democratic terms or linked to problems of accountability at the treaty-making level. If dealing with issues such as the publication of documents concerning

[47] *Biwater Gauff v Tanzania* (Procedural Order No. 3, 29 September 2006), para 114.
[48] Williams (n 2).
[49] Schneiderman (n 45).
[50] *Tecmed v Mexico* (Award, 29 May 2003).
[51] See Chapter 2.

the existence of an investment arbitration was becoming the new normal, the path to render 'accessible' the process by which investment treaties were concluded was fraught with uncertainties. This discrepancy was suddenly amplified by the online release of a leaked version of the Comprehensive Economic and Trade Agreement between Canada and the European Union (CETA) by a German media organization in August 2014. This move wrong-footed the EU and Canada and drew strong protests from the public and the media, both of whom urged the two sides to release the official texts of the negotiation. While for a long time the issue has not been a matter of particular concern, with the majority of states largely ignoring what transparency of negotiations could possibly imply, the public hostility towards secrecy in the negotiations rapidly became a matter of concern on both sides of the Atlantic.

Under its exclusive powers over foreign direct investment (FDI), the EU finds itself caught in a bind: should the response to the investment regime's lack of accountability be more Europe or less Europe?[52] The EU initially did not seize the chance to vindicate its values externally and opted for a less-Europe option, which was very much in line with preserving the investment system status quo. However, after a rather surprising U-turn (over the Canada trade deal), the EU settled for the more Europe option. The EU's initial cautious approach appears even more striking when contrasted with its proactive stance in the late 1990s, when the European Community became a leading advocate for incorporating a transparency dimension into trade policy. At the time, the Community recognized that greater transparency and engagement with representatives of civil society were essential for fostering understanding and acceptance of the multilateral trading system. In the trade context, transparency and dialogue with civil society were quickly acknowledged as key tools to enhance cooperation,[53] improve global economic governance, and reshape the World Trade Organization's (WTO) image. This rebranding aimed to present the WTO as a democratic organization that values cultural diversity, upholds environmental and labour standards, and acts in the interests of the broader global citizenry.[54]

Despite the initial reluctance, the EU quickly came to realize that international negotiations, and therefore the negotiations of investment treaties as

[52] Eckes, Christina (2019), *EU Powers Under External Pressure—How the EU's External Actions Alter its Internal Structures.*

[53] General Council, WT/GC/W/391 (12 November 1999); General Council, WT/GC/W/295 (5 August 1999).

[54] European Communities, Commission of the European Communities—Statement by Mr. Jacques Santer (Geneva WTO Ministerial 1998) https://bit.ly/3EzA7Sn.

well, were a political opportunity to extend the rules established in Brussels. Even if the domestic application of the democratic principle remained ambiguous within the EU, the investment regime presented a golden opportunity for the EU to correct the distortions brought about by investment rules in undermining democratic processes. The asymmetries that permeate the investment decision-making process gave the EU a chance to reduce the gaps between governments negotiating investment treaties, investment tribunals ruling upon these treaties, and societies/citizens practically bearing the effects of these treaties, and, more broadly, between the investment regime and national democratic spaces. Far from recognizing the existence of public participation as a normative principle, the pursuit of the value of democracy in its external relations steered the EU towards the creation of new channels to gather democratic inputs before, during, and after the negotiation process, ultimately with a view to including society in general.[55]

How this process of transparency and public participation has unfolded, and to what extent the value of democracy has been realized within the investment regime by the EU are questions explored in the following two chapters.

[55] Ortino, Federico (2012), 'Transparency of Investment Awards: External and Internal Dimensions.' In *Transparency in International Trade and Investment Dispute Settlement*, edited by Kunji Nakagawa.

3
Transparency as a democracy enhancer in investment arbitration

A. Overview

This chapter surveys the EU response to the global demand for greater transparency in investment arbitration. Despite the internal delay in recognizing transparency as part of the democratic principle, the EU aligned fairly quickly with international trends favouring greater transparency. At times the EU contributed to the consolidation of international instruments, and at times to their expansion by, for instance, providing non-disputing party access to all documents generated throughout the arbitral proceeding. These developments notwithstanding, the EU agenda on transparency remains ambiguous at best. It remains unclear, for instance, whether the EU would be inclined to compromise on transparency with countries traditionally sceptical about the inclusion of transparency obligations in investment agreements, like Japan. It is even less evident how the EU could persuade some of its Member States to endorse in full the transparency initiative without reservations, especially given that it took nearly a decade for the Commission's proposal to sign the Mauritius Convention to be ratified.

The chapter opens with a description of how transparency has become problematic in the investment system (Section B). It then briefly summarizes how transparency, or, rather, accessibility and availability of information, gradually evolved within the investment system and became part of a trend favouring transparency (Section C). Section D moves to analyse how the EU dealt with the investment regime's demand for greater transparency and, in conclusion, it highlights the ambiguities that still permeate the EU external action on the transparency front (Section E).

EU Values in Investment Law And Policy. Maria Laura Marceddu, Oxford University Press.
 DOI: 10.1093/9780191986208.003.0003

B. How the story began: A problem with investment arbitration's transparency

In November 2006, a group of three Tanzanian-based and two international environmental non-governmental organizations (NGOs) obtained *amicus curiae* status to submit a brief in the context of an investment claim between a UK water provider company, Biwater Gauff, and Tanzania.

Thanks to funding from the World Bank, the African Development Bank, and the European Investment Bank,[1] Tanzania embarked on a comprehensive programme of structural adjustments of the water and sewerage infrastructure to implement the existing infrastructure, which proved to be insufficient to provide adequate services to the majority of the population. After a five-year tendering process, Biwater Gauff, in partnership with the German-based firm HP Gauff Ingenieure, successfully secured a bid in 2003 to develop Tanzania's water and sewer infrastructure project. Together, they established a new company, City Water, to manage the project's operations. As part of a privatization initiative—one of the conditions tied to the project's funding—the tender process transferred responsibility for water production, transmission, distribution, and the operation and maintenance of the sewerage system from the Tanzanian public corporation DAWASA to City Water. Beyond operational functions, City Water's role was to build and collect revenue from the customers receiving these services. More specifically, it was required to make monthly rental payments, transfer a portion of the collected tariffs to DAWASA, and contribute to the first-time connection fund which would have subsidized water connections for poorer customers. As a result of City Water's mismanagement of the project, however, water rates rose immediately and customers began to complain. City Water failed to generate the expected income and quickly fell into financial difficulties. These difficulties were so severe that, just after eighteen months into what was supposed to be at least a ten-year arrangement, City Water had to renegotiate the terms of the underlying concession contract. Although the government had no obligation to renegotiate, it appointed an expert mediator to facilitate the process. The renegotiation process ended in failure. City Water's request to increase water rates as a result of a reduction in water available for distribution was considered without foundation and rejected.[2] Given City Water's inability to fulfil its contractual obligations, the Water Authority concluded that the project with City Water had to

[1] The funding amounted to USD 140 million. *Biwater v Tanzania* (Award, 24 July 2008), para 3.
[2] Ibid, para 477.

be terminated and the licence to be revoked. In May 2005, Edward Lowassa, Tanzanian Minister of Water and Livestock Development and a candidate for Prime Minister in the upcoming election, issued a press release stating that the termination of City Water's contract was due to persistent complaints from city residents about the company's incompetence.[3] In response, City Water contested the validity of the termination, asserting that it would continue providing services unless an arbitral tribunal 'decided otherwise'.[4] This stance was supported by Biwater, which had already initiated an arbitration proceeding under the lease contract.[5] City Water's senior management, however, was deported by Tanzanian officials, who entered City Water's offices, took control of the company's assets, and appointed new staff. A couple of months after these events, Biwater initiated an investment arbitration and claimed that politics had tainted their investment and that Tanzania violated the obligations contained under the 1996 UK–Tanzania Bilateral Investment Treaty (BIT) to (i) not unlawfully expropriate property, (ii) provide fair and equitable treatment to foreign investors, (iii) not impair the investment through unreasonable or discriminatory measures, (iv) ensure full protection and security, and (v) grant unrestricted transfer of funds.[6]

It comes as no surprise that the case attracted significant public interest. Not only because it involved the provision of a critical public service in a particular developing country but also because it raised larger (and often controversial) questions of international development policy[7] handled at the discretion of unknown and unelected people in secret.[8] Despite showing 'no compunction about making aggravating "disclosures" relating to the case',[9] Biwater requested the tribunal to maintain proceedings closed to the public until the release of the final award, and that the parties refrain from disclosing to a third party any of the pleadings and any correspondence between the parties and/or the tribunal exchanged during the proceedings.[10] These requests were prompted by Tanzania's decision to publish the Minutes of the First Meeting of the Tribunal, along with Procedural Order No. 2, online immediately after these documents had been transmitted to the parties by the tribunal. In light of these events,

[3] Schneiderman, David (2013), *Resisting Economic Globalization: Critical Theory and International Investment Law*, 65.

[4] *Biwater v Tanzania* (n 1), para 221.

[5] Ibid, para 211.

[6] Ibid, para 354.

[7] *Biwater Gauff v Tanzania* (PO No. 3, 29 September 2006), para 60.

[8] Mourre, Alexis (2006), 'Are Amici Curiae the Proper Response to the Public's Concerns on Transparency in Investment Arbitration?', The Law & Practice of International Courts and Tribunals.

[9] *Biwater Gauff v Tanzania* (n 7), para 41.

[10] Ibid, para 12.

Biwater argued that Tanzania's unilateral decision regarding the disclosure of the aforementioned documents was contrary to Article 47 of the International Centre for Settlement of Investment Disputes (ICSID) Convention[11] and Rule 39 of the ICSID Arbitration Rules,[12] and, on this basis, requested that the tribunal gather the parties to discuss the publication of materials related to the process on a case-by-case basis. Biwater clearly overlooked Tanzania's obligation to its citizens to ensure that accurate information about the dispute and its resolution is broadcast, and disregarded the fact that there was considerable public discussion and NGO activism about the case before the Tribunal was even selected, let alone before any of the documents in question was disseminated.[13]

When called to balance two competing interests—the need for transparency and the need to protect the integrity of the process—the tribunal recognized the public interest arising from the subject matter of the dispute and the potential harm of an unduly secretive approach (*a blanket refusal*). Despite acknowledging that the arbitral process could benefit from being perceived as more open or transparent, the tribunal eventually issued an order of confidentiality that accepted the Claimant's request for confidentiality, and underscored that media exposition risks aggravating the dispute and jeopardizing the integrity of the procedure.[14] Ironically, the order of confidentiality had the perverse effect of undermining participation in the dispute by third parties, and the five petitioners, albeit provided with standing, were not given access to any of the arguments either side made in the case. Despite the wider public interest in the matters at stake, public interest input was 'handcuffed' to avoid further aggravation of the dispute.

[11] ICSID Convention Article 47:

> Except as the parties otherwise agree, the Tribunal may, if it considers that the circumstances so require, recommend any provisional measures which should be taken to preserve the respective rights of either party.

ICSID Convention on the settlement of investment disputes between States and nationals of other States (1965), UNTS 8359.

[12] ICSID Arbitration Rules, rule 39:

> (1) If the Tribunal considers it necessary to visit any place connected with the dispute or to conduct an inquiry there, it shall make an order to this effect. The order shall define the scope of the visit or the subject of the inquiry, the time limit, the procedure to be followed and other particulars. The parties may participate in any visit or inquiry.
>
> (2) After consulting both parties, the Tribunal may allow a person or entity that is not a party to the dispute (in this Rule called the 'non-disputing party') to file a written submission with the Tribunal regarding a matter within the scope of the dispute....

ICSID Arbitration Rules (2003), ICSID/15/Rev. 1.

[13] *Biwater Gauff v Tanzania* (n 7), para 60.

[14] Ibid, paras 136, 146.

Different considerations flow from this arbitration. The most salient point is the space (if any) to accord to the disclosure of documents and non-party participation. Even more importantly, there is a foundational question of the premises upon which the space accorded to openness (disclosure) and accessibility (participation) is construed. Many have tended to combine and conflate these two spaces under the umbrella of transparency as the element most apt to respond to public interests that warrant opportunities for public engagement, especially as far as investor–state arbitration is concerned. They are not wrong per se: in arbitration proceedings, the level of public interest is fairly high given the fact that usually one of the parties is a state, the public is potentially affected by the outcome of these arbitrations, and the subject matter of these disputes often concerns governmental measures on the protection of public health, the environment, or local communities. In this context, transparency emerges as an essential prerequisite for the success of projects typically involving corporations from distant regions seeking to invest.[15] It undeniably serves as a critical factor underpinning the acceptability of arbitration. However, this suggest that transparency is but one piece of a broader narrative that is unfolding, albeit at times unconsciously, towards a different end: democracy.

Let us now examine how these democratic concerns about accountability, fairness, and legitimacy have surfaced within the investment arbitration system and explore the role the EU has played in shaping and addressing these issues.

1. How the story unfolded: In search for democracy in investment arbitration

For a long time, the issue of transparency itself has remained only tangentially present within the investment regime. Originally, the arbitration rules of most international institutions had not accorded much importance to openness, instead tending to adhere substantially to the confidentiality imperative. Despite a few exceptions found in the 1994 North America Free Trade Agreement (NAFTA)—such as Article 1127, which grants non-disputing parties the right to receive notice of any claim and copies of all pleadings, and Article 1128, which ensures non-disputing parties have access to all evidence submitted to the tribunal—there was little initial interest in creating a significant shift

[15] *Bear Creek v Peru* (Partial dissenting opinion of Professor Philippe Sands, 30 November 2017), para 7.

in state treaty practices regarding transparency.[16] Even less present was the issue of democracy, which was usually listed under the preamble's commitments of investment treaties but was nowhere defined. While a demand for greater transparency was progressively emerging and eroding the presumption in favour of confidentiality, the expectation that investment agreements had to ensure some kind of adherence to democratic principles took more time to materialize.

Transparency made its way into the investment system predominantly through third parties' requests to intervene in arbitral proceedings. It gradually began to be invoked with reference to the public availability of information about the activities related to investor–state arbitrations, the norms applied to determine disputes,[17] and the capacity for persons or entities to participate in the creation of such norms.

When confronted with the question of *amicus curiae* participation, a significant number of tribunals found that they have jurisdiction to receive submissions from third parties,[18] given the silence of most treaties in this regard and the absence of provisions explicitly denying this possibility. Albeit one might be tempted to read into this an indication towards openness, if not transparency, *amicus curiae* submissions were treated as a mere procedural issue. *Amici curiae* served as friends of the court and are allowed to provide the decision-maker with arguments and expertise the litigant parties may not provide,[19] insofar as they do not disrupt the process or unfairly prejudice either party.

The 2006 amendment process of the ICSID Rules is the first to formalize such a possibility by cautiously rendering the proceedings more *accessible* to third parties.[20] Arbitral tribunals, however, remained assertive in stressing that

[16] Calamita, Jansen (2014), 'Dispute Settlement Transparency in Europe's Evolving Investment Treaty Policy', The Journal of World Investment & Trade.

[17] Shirlow, Esmé (2016), 'Dawn of a New Era? The UNCITRAL Rules and UN Convention on Transparency in Treaty-Based Investor–State Arbitration', ICSID Review—Foreign Investment Law Journal.

[18] See among others: *UPS v Canada* (Decision of the Tribunal on Petitions for Intervention and Participation as Amici Curiae, 17 October 2001); *Suez Barcelona and Vivendi v Argentina* (Order in response to a Petition for Participation as Amicus Curiae, 19 May 2005); *Methanex v USA* (Award, 3 August 2005); *Electrabel v Hungary* (PO No. 4, 28 April 2009); *Glamis Gold. v USA* (Award, 8 June 2009); *Eli Lilly v Canada* (PO No. 4, 23 February 2016); *Grace v Mexico* (PO No. 2 on Amicus Curiae and Non-Disputing Party Participation, 5 April 2019).

[19] *Suez and Interagua v Argentina* (Order in response to a Petition for Participation as Amicus Curiae, 17 March 2006), para 13; *Eco Oro v Colombia* (PO No. 6, 18 February 2019), para 31.

[20] Three amended rules are particularly significant in this context. First, amended Rule 32 stipulates that, with the parties' consent, individuals other than the litigants may attend or observe all or part of the hearings. Second, the revised Rule 37 allows non-disputing parties to submit a brief on matters within the scope of the dispute, with the tribunal determining the specific submission procedure. Lastly, amended Rule 48 grants the parties the right to veto the publication of the award, although the Centre is still required to promptly include excerpts of the tribunal's legal reasoning in its publications. ICSID Arbitration Rules (2006), ICSID/15 April 2006.

non-disputing parties' submissions had not to be considered as a mechanism to obtain information from the disputing parties or affecting their rights, nor that the *amicus curiae* acceptance conferred petitioners the status of a party, the right to access the file of the case or to attend hearings.[21]

Despite this marked tendency towards confidentiality, the issues of openness and accessibility to the arbitral process gradually gained prominence in the investment arena. Insofar as accessibility and openness were equated with the idea of procedural assistance, arbitral tribunals appropriately circumscribed the role of non-disputing parties' intervention in the proceedings. The question became more complex when openness began to be associated with an expectation of knowledge and information *for the participants* involved in the investment regime—for example, about matters of compliance and effectiveness and the operation of the norms, rules, and procedures underlying the regime. A first problem lies in ascertaining who are the investment regime's participants. One could argue that international investment agreements primarily govern the (economic) relationship between foreign investors and the host state, which, notably, also become the litigating parties in the event of a dispute. From this perspective, states and investors constitute the 'identifiable people', while the level of openness and accessibility to the process is restricted to the extent that non-disputing parties (i.e. non-participants) can provide added value to the tribunal's deliberations. In this scenario, openness and accessibility to the proceedings are not aims that any tribunal has the power to impose in the absence of parties' agreement.[22] Transparency is acknowledged solely as a component of the broader obligation imposed on host states to treat foreign investors fairly,[23] enabling investors to plan their activities in alignment with their legitimate expectations.[24]

The problem with this conception concerns the extent to which international investment law can affect policy options, and ultimately the democratic space at the domestic level. Potentially, international investment agreements (IIAs) can have far-reaching implications across several policy areas—like energy policies, manufacturing, financial services, water and sewerage, telecommunication, etc. Beyond these substantive impacts, the inclusion of investor–state

[21] *Philip Morris v Uruguay* (PO No. 3, 17 February 2015); *Foresti v South Africa* (Letter Regarding Non-Disputing Parties, 5 October 2009).

[22] *Rand investment v Serbia* (Dissenting opinion of MG Kohen, 29 August 2019).

[23] Several tribunals have acknowledged transparency as part of the FET, e.g. *Metalclad v Mexico* (Award, 30 August 2000); *Waste Management v Mexico* (Final Award, 30 April 2004); *Mobil Exploration v Argentina* (Decision on jurisdiction and liability, 10 April 2013); *Infinito Gold v Costa Rica* (Award, 3 June 2021).

[24] *Watkins Holding v Spain* (Award, 21 January 2020).

dispute settlement clauses empowers tribunals to resolve disputes that carry significant economic, social, and political consequences, often without being fully democratically legitimated. While states formally retain their negotiating powers, the effects of foreign investments and the arbitral awards that follow are largely, if not exclusively, borne by citizens. These individuals, who may have a vested interest in the outcomes, are frequently excluded from the process. This dynamic underscores the existence of participants beyond the immediate litigant parties—states and investors—who bear the consequences of foreign investments yet lack the ability to deliberate or influence the policy decisions underpinning IIAs. Recognizing these broader stakeholder interests demands a paradigm shift towards fostering greater engagement at the international level. This shift would involve creating new spaces for participation and advancing systemic openness and accessibility, ensuring that all affected parties have a voice in shaping the rules and decisions that impact them.

Although states and investors formally remain the parties to a dispute, it is hard to ignore the presence of persons beyond those immediately involved as parties and potentially affected by the investment' and arbitrations' outcomes. As the *Biwater* case demonstrates, the consequences of an unsuccessful investment plan to supply water and sewerage were ultimately suffered by citizens, whose welfare had to allegedly be enhanced by the privatization operation.[25] The presence of a critical public service—like access to water—bears a reasonable relationship to the rational policy of keeping citizens apprised of matters that affect their lives. Some arbitral tribunals have linked this rationality of keeping citizens (and, more broadly, affected parties) informed about the presence of a public interest that arises from the subject matter of the dispute at stake.[26] It sounds rather obvious, at least in principle, that it is in the wider public interest to ensure that accurate information about the parties' dispute and its resolution is broadcast and that affected parties' stances are considered as long as they fall within the scope of the dispute. This, however, is not always easy to achieve in practice, especially if the arbitration is ongoing and the public exposure risks prejudicing the fairness of the process. As a result, the recognition of a public interest in investment arbitration needs to be mediated with the preservation of the integrity of the adjudicating process.

The consequences that flow from this are twofold: first, there is a problem with how informing the public and soliciting inputs at a negotiating level

[25] *Biwater* (n 1), paras 377–387.

[26] *Biwater v Tanzania* (PO No. 5, 2 February 2007), para 51 citing *Methanex v USA* (Decision of the Tribunal on Petitions from Third Persons to Intervene as Amicus Curiae, 15 January 2001), para 49.

before anything has been done—that is, accessibility to the treaty-making phase. Second, there is a problem of public scrutiny vis-à-vis arbitral tribunal decisions—that is, the openness of the tribunal's decision-making phase. Looking at these problems from a different angle, they could well be read as requests for different, and possibly broader forms of accessibility and involvement both at substantive (negotiation) and procedural (arbitral proceeding) levels. Interestingly, but perhaps unsurprisingly, this is the point where democracy comes into play. Accessibility and involvement are just other ways to refer to transparency and public participation, which, incidentally, constitute the twin foundation for the value of democracy as articulated within the EU system of justice. Albeit overlooked for a long time and, to a certain extent, still in the making, a more democratic orientation based on the twin notions of transparency and public participation was the answer the investment system had to look for. The demand for public participation was propelled by the EU in a rather original fashion, as will be discussed in Chapter 4. The demand for greater transparency was not met with a timely response and the EU somehow aligned with international trends, as argued in the remainder of this chapter.

C. How transparency became the new normal: International trends favouring greater transparency

Despite a perception of transparency as systemically beneficial (*Methanex*, 2001), a recognition of a trend towards transparency in the investor–state arbitration process (*Canfor Corporation*, 2005), and a widespread sense of confidence in the transparency of the ICSID system (*Azurix*, 2007), the path towards greater transparency within the investment system remains fraught with uncertainties.

Overall, a consensus emerged among tribunals recognizing transparency as an integral part of the obligation to treat foreign investors fairly and equitably. The publication of laws, regulations, administrative practices, and procedures related to or impacting investments has been regarded as a corollary to this obligation, with tribunals maintaining consistent approaches in this regard. Similarly, the publication of awards raised no particular doubts for arbitral tribunals; it was congenial to ensure systemic intelligibility and, therefore, legitimacy. The ICSID revised Rule 48 insisted on this direction and, even in case of disagreement between the parties, provided for a prompt publication of, at least, the excerpts of the tribunals' legal reasoning that led to the delivery of an arbitral award. The rationale for this consolidated trend, especially within the ICSID realm,[27] lay in the expectation that a manifest explanation of the reasons underpinning arbitral decisions—procedural transparency—renders investment arbitration intelligible, acceptable,[28] and, therefore, somewhat more legitimized.

This trend was further corroborated by the practices of some states, most likely influenced by the General Agreement on Tariffs and Trade (GATT) Article X:1, which mandates that trade-relevant information be published in a manner accessible to third parties, and GATT Article X:2, which stipulates that rules can only be enforced if they are published prior to their application. Cases in point are Canada and the US, which have shown a particular propensity to include provisions favouring procedural transparency.[29] The 2004 Canada model BIT expressly envisaged prompt publication of all laws, regulations, and procedures that might apply to the matters covered by the agreement,[30] and provided that even in cases where the parties disagree, any arbitral award should be made public, safe for the deletion of confidential information.[31] Interestingly, the model also contemplated the possibility for those interested to provide comments. Such a possibility was also granted, in an even more detailed manner, by the 2004 US model BIT, according to which any interested persons should be given the 'opportunity to comment on proposed measures'.[32] Likewise, both the 2004 and 2012 US models listed the documents to be made available to the public, excluding protected information.[33] Not all NAFTA countries displayed the same commitment towards transparency, with Mexico's approach lagging slightly behind. Albeit obligations of transparency of laws[34] or the publication of the awards were included in a few of its investment agreements,[35] other aspects, such as the openness of the hearings[36] or the possibility of accepting *amicus curiae* submissions, remained largely ignored.

[27] Most ICSID awards have been published one way or another. Non-ICSID awards are published sporadically and there is no central register to keep track of the number of unpublished proceedings. Dolzer, Rudolf and Schreuer, Christoph (2012), *Principles of International Investment Law*.

[28] *CECFT v Gabon* (Decision on Annulment, 11 May 2010); *Tenaris and Talta v Venezuela* (Decision on Annulment, 8 August 2018).

[29] Mollestad, Cristoffer (2013), 'See No Evil? Procedural Transparency in International Investment Law and Dispute Settlement', PluriCourts Research Paper; Calamita (n 16).

[30] 2004 Canada Model BIT, Article 19(1).

[31] Ibid, para 4.

[32] 2004 US Model BIT, Article 11(2).

[33] 2012 US Model BIT, Article 29(2) and (4).

[34] See, for instance, the Australia–Mexico BIT (terminated on 30 December 2018), Article 6.

[35] See, for example, the UK–Mexico BIT (entered into force 25 July 2007), Article XVI(4).

[36] The only exception is the Mexico–Panama FTA (entered into force 1 July 2015) Article 10.22(2).

As a matter of practice, the publications of laws related to investment and awards did not generally pose significant challenges. Even EU Member States referred to the publications of laws in their BITs, although the publication of awards was not compulsory. The situation becomes more complex, however, when greater transparency is sought before a decision is delivered, that is while the arbitration proceedings are still pending. As the *Methanex* and *Biwater* cases indicated, requests for increased transparency originally materialized through non-parties seeking to intervene as *amici curiae*. Ancillary to these requests, there emerged an implied expectation of access to the documents produced during the proceedings (including hearings), as such documents have the potential to directly or indirectly affect non-disputing parties.

In terms of transparency within the arbitral process, the North American experience once again led the way. The concept of a 'non-disputing party' was broadly applied within the Canadian framework, referring to anyone with a significant presence in the territory of a Party who wished to file a written submission with a Tribunal.[37] These submissions were allowed on the condition that they could effectively assist the tribunal, address a matter within the scope of the dispute, and provide a public interest perspective on the subject matter of the arbitration.[38] The 2004 and 2012 US model BITs also allowed non-disputing parties' submissions but limit them to questions of interpretation.[39] Largely echoing the 2003 Free Trade Commission statement, both Canada and the US model BITs left non-disputing parties' applications at the discretion of the arbitral tribunal, which remained in charge of ensuring that these submissions do not disrupt, unduly burden, or unfairly prejudice the process.[40]

Taking stock that states have traditionally accepted *amicus curiae* submissions from suitable third parties in cases featuring matters of public interest, arbitral tribunals have remained open to granting such possibility. Nonetheless, they have insisted on the need to identify a particular public interest that goes beyond a general interest[41] and the interests of the petitioners. In *Von Pezold v Zimbabwe*, for example, the tribunal rejected the petition made on behalf of four indigenous communities who claimed rights over the land object of Zimbabwe's forestry concessions because it did not believe the non-disputing parties to be independent or neutral.[42] Similarly, in *Eco Oro v Colombia*, the

[37] Ibid.
[38] 2004 Canada Model BIT (n 30), Article 39(4).
[39] 2012 US Model BIT (n 33), Article 28(2).
[40] 2004 Canada Model BIT (n 30), Article 39(1) and (5).
[41] *Eco Oro v Colombia* (n 19), para 34.
[42] *Von Pezold v Zimbabwe* (PO No. 2, 26 June 2012), para 62.

tribunal insisted on the need to demonstrate how the arbitration could have had a direct impact on the applicant's rights, and how the outcome could have affected a specific interest that goes beyond a generalized human rights issue, like the right to live in a healthy environment.[43]

A more problematic aspect related to the question of whether giving non-disputing/third parties access to proceedings' documents and/or hearings, especially if investment agreements were completely silent in this regard (such as EU Member States' BITs). More often than not, the question of access to documents has been answered negatively. Along the lines of *Biwater*'s position, more recent cases like *Pac Rim v El Salvador* denied third parties access to documents in the name of procedural integrity and deferred the issue at the parties' discretion. A notable exception in this landscape was *Foresti v South Africa*, which constitutes a rare example of a third party being allowed to see parties' filing despite objections from one party.[44] The *Foresti* tribunal took the view that access to documents ('those papers submitted to the Tribunal by the Parties') is necessary to enable the non-disputing parties to focus their submissions upon the issues arising in the case and to see what positions the Parties have taken on those issues. Non-disputing parties must also be given adequate opportunity to prepare and deliver their submissions in sufficient time before the hearing for the parties to be able to respond to those submissions.[45] *Foresti* was also the first tribunal that invited parties and non-disputing parties to provide feedback about the participation procedure, and that committed to discussing the comments of the parties and non-disputing parties in the award.[46]

When participation concerned attendance to hearings or the possibility of making oral submissions, even the *Foresti* tribunal took a more cautious approach. Despite the tribunal's commitment to the cause, the case was eventually discontinued before a final award. Hence, appreciating the impact the submissions ultimately had on the outcome remains a purely speculative exercise. Generally speaking, tribunals have been quite restrictive in granting non-disputing parties the possibility to attend hearings,[47] especially in the presence of manifest parties' objections.[48] The issue appears particularly problematic if

[43] *Eco Oro v Colombia* (n 19), para 34

[44] Unlike the *Border Timber* decision where the tribunal found it has no discretion to grant access over a party's objection. *Border Timbers v Zimbabwe* (Award, 28 July 2015), para 38.

[45] *Foresti v South Africa* (Award, 4 August 2010), para 28.

[46] Ibid, para 29.

[47] *Suez Barcelona and Vivendi v Argentina* (n 18); *Foresti v South Africa* (n 21); *Chevron v Ecuador* (PO No. 8, 18 April 2011); *Encavis v Italy* (Decision on the Non-Disputing Party's Application, 15 June 2022).

[48] *Suez Barcelona and Vivendi v Argentina* (n 18), paras 6–7; *Chevron v Ecuador* (n 47); *Border Timbers v Zimbabwe* (PO No. 2, 26 June 2012), para 63; *Infinito Gold v Costa Rica* (PO No. 2, 1 June 2016).

compared to the principle of public hearings in judicial proceedings as embodied in national laws. This has inevitably reinforced the image of investment arbitration as a privileged channel for foreign investors vis-à-vis domestic investors.[49] If arbitral tribunals remained extremely cautious in exercising discretion to allow non-disputing parties to attend hearings in the absence of parties' permission, some states continued to make concrete efforts towards a more transparent investment arbitration system.

Even on participatory fronts, the American and Canadian investment treaties advanced some rather impressive novelties in terms of openness. Article 38(3) of the 2004 Canada model, for example, provided that unless the parties object, hearings shall be open to the public and that the documents generated within the arbitral process shall be made publicly available, except for confidential information. On the whole, this devotion to transparency, regularly implemented over time, has been able to draw other states towards these good practices.[50] A good example of the effects generated by the NAFTA countries in favour of more transparency is the 2006 Central America Free Trade Agreement (CAFTA) agreement, signed and currently in force between the US, the Dominican Republic, Costa Rica, El Salvador, Guatemala, Nicaragua, and Honduras. Article 10 of its Chapter 10 (Investment) provided for the publication of materials from the very beginning of an arbitral proceeding, along with an obligation to publish documents generated in the course of the arbitration. Interestingly, CAFTA appeared to go even 'beyond the NAFTA by regulating the powers of tribunals to restrict access to information' and 'by requiring that proceedings take place in public'.[51]

Taken together, these are unequivocal indications of changes in favour of more transparency, especially if one considers that for a long time, the public has usually known almost nothing about international arbitration[52] and, save the disputing parties, no 'unauthorised persons were present' during the proceedings.[53] The debate around transparency remained complex to unpack and in the absence of an

[49] Marceddu, Maria Laura and Ortolani, Pietro (2020), 'What Is Wrong with Investment Arbitration? Evidence from a Set of Behavioural Experiments', European Journal of International Law, 424–6.

[50] See e.g. the agreements signed between Canada and some African states, which have embodied the transparent practices of the 'Canadian way', such as the Canada–Benin BIT (entered into force 12 May 2014); Canada–Côte d'Ivoire BIT (entered into force 14 December 2015). Similarly, see also the most recent experiences of some TTP countries, probably drawn towards transparency by the US in the context of the transpacific deal negotiations.

[51] Harrison, James (2011), 'Recent Developments to Promote Transparency and Public Participation in Investment Treaty Arbitration', University of Edinburgh School of Law Working Paper.

[52] Limbasan, Natalie and Malintoppi, Loretta (2015), 'Living in Glass Houses? The Debate on Transparency in International Investment Arbitration', BCDR International Arbitration Review, 31.

[53] Hobér, Kaj (2014), 'Arbitration Involving States.' In *Leading Arbitrators' Guide to International Arbitration*, edited by Lawrence W Newman and Richard D Hill.

agreement, the tribunals were left to decide transparency matters on a case-by-case basis.

During the first decade of the 2000s, the international community appeared more prepared to explore new approaches towards procedural transparency and recognize transparency as a desirable objective in a treaty-based investor–state arbitration system.[54] In 2009, the UNCITRAL Working Group II (WG) was ready to consider transparency as a matter of priority[55] and worked for more than four years on the elaboration of new standards favouring greater transparency in investment arbitration. Eventually, the process culminated with the adoption of the Rules on transparency in treaty-based investor–state arbitration in July 2013 (the Rules on Transparency).[56]

The Rules on Transparency consisted of a formulation of transparency standards that states are encouraged to use.[57] They comprise eight articles that reverse the presumption of confidentiality in investment treaty arbitration in favour of a presumption of openness[58] and can operate autonomously or as an integral component of the UNCITRAL Arbitration Rules.[59] As per Article 1, the Rules can be applied to any arbitration initiated under the UNCITRAL Arbitration Rules and based on investment treaties 'concluded on or after 1 April 2014'.[60] The Rules do not apply retroactively to those agreements signed off before the cut-off date, for which the contracting parties are expressly required to 'opt in' to their application'.[61] This constituted the most critical aspect of the Rules: they only apply to those arbitrations conducted under the UNCITRAL Arbitration Rules and which are based on an investment treaty concluded on or after 1 April 2014, unless the parties have opted out of the

[54] UNCITRAL, 'Report of the Working Group (Arbitration and Conciliation) on the Work of its Forty-Eighth Session (4–8 February 2008)', UN Doc. A/CN.9/646, para 68.

[55] UNICTRAL, 'Report of the Working Group II (Arbitration and Conciliation) on the Work of its Fiftieth Session (9–13 February 2009)', UN Doc. A/CCN.9/669.

[56] UNCITRAL, 'Report of the United Nations Commission on International Trade Law Forty-Sixth Session (8–26 July 2013)', UN GAOR Sixty-Eighth Session Supplement No. 17, UN Doc. A/68/17, para III.A.

[57] UNCITRAL, 'Report of Working Group II (Arbitration and Conciliation) on the Work of its Fifty-Third Session (4–8 October 2010)', UN Doc. A/CN.9/712.

[58] Schill, Stephan (2014), 'Editorial: Five Times Transparency in International Investment Law', The Journal of World Investment & Trade.

[59] Reith, Claudia (2015), 'The New UNCITRAL Rules on Transparency 2014: Significant Breakthrough or a Regime Full of Empty Formula?', Yearbook on International Arbitration.

[60] UNCITRAL Rules on Transparency in Treaty-based Investor–State Arbitration and Arbitration Rules (as revised in 2010, with new Article 1, paragraph 4, as adopted 16 December 2013), UN GAOR Sixty-Eighth Session Agenda item 79, UN Doc. A/68/462 (16 December 2013), Art. 1(2) (UNCITRAL Rules on Transparency).

[61] Ibid, Article 1(2)(a) and (b). See also UNCITRAL, 'Report of Working Group II (Arbitration and Conciliation) on the Work of its Fifty-Eighth Session (4–8 February 2013)', UN Doc. A/CN.9/765, para 17.

Rules. This implied that for the thousands of treaties concluded before April 2014, the Rules will not apply, unless the parties have expressly agreed to do so. To remedy this shortcoming in scope, the WG considered different options to ensure the wider applicability of the Rules and eventually came up with the United Nations Convention on Transparency in Treaty-based Investor–State Arbitration, also known as the Mauritius Convention.[62] The Convention provides a mechanism for states to consent to the application of the Rules to treaties concluded before April 2014. According to Article 2 of the Convention, the Rules on Transparency apply regardless of whether the arbitration is conducted under UNCITRAL rules, provided that both the respondent and the home state are parties to the Convention, or the respondent is a party and the claimant agrees to apply the Rules on transparency. The Convention was adopted by the UN General Assembly on 10 December 2014[63] and entered into force on 18 October 2017, having three instruments of ratification, acceptance, approval, or accession—coming respectively from Canada, Mauritius, and Switzerland.

The Rules on Transparency seek to render the arbitration process transparent from the very outset (i.e. before the constitution of the arbitral tribunal) so that the general public is informed of the commencement of the proceedings (Article 2)[64] and has access to relevant documents (Article 3, unless the exceptions of Article 7 come into play). The Rules provide for two schemes of participation: one for third persons (Article 4) and another for non-disputing parties (Article 5). Contributions from the former should be of effective assistance to the tribunal in the appreciation of the facts, whereas the latter is restricted to issues of law or interpretation, save those instances where parties might have information essential to the arbitration at stake. Hearings are public unless the tribunal, after consultation with the parties, excludes the public from certain parts of the hearings, especially if there is a need to protect confidential information or the integrity of the process.[65]

Taken together, the contributions of the Mauritius Convention and the Rules on Transparency break the dominant conceptualization of the arbitral procedure as a form of confidential and private justice.[66] As of 2025, the

[62] UNCITRAL, 'Report of the United Nations Commission on International Trade Law Forty-Seventh Session (7–18 July 2014)', UN GAOR Sixty-Ninth Session Supplement No. 17, UN Doc. A/69/17, para 106.

[63] UNGA Res 69/116 (18 December 2014) UN Doc. A/RES/69/116 (Mauritius Convention).

[64] UNCITRAL, 'Report of Working Group II (Arbitration and Conciliation) on the work of its Fifty-Fifth Session (3–7 October 2011)', UN Doc. A/CN.9/736, para 43.

[65] UNCITRAL Rules on Transparency (n 60), Article 6.

[66] Schill (n 58), 203.

Convention comprises twenty-five signatory states and nine ratifying states[67] signalling a quite small, but not completely insignificant tendency pointing towards transparency. More encouraging observations can be drawn from the Rules, which so far have been included in more than 100 IIAs[68] and model BITs.[69] These developments notwithstanding, the very question as to their effectiveness ultimately depends on their general acceptance. A significant number of states and regional economic integration organizations are opting for including the Rules in future treaties rather than ratifying the Convention, signalling a willingness to rebrand the system but not to dismantle completely its confidentiality roots. It seems necessary to verify whether these recent provisions might tip the scale towards the creation of a general principle of transparency (and third-party intervention), at the same time avoiding the negative consequences that too-expanded participation might have at the procedural level. It would be naïve to dismiss the issue of loss of privacy and confidentiality completely, especially in light of the potentially negative side effects on respondent states and investors alike.

Where the EU positions itself in this evolving scenario is discussed in the following section.

D. A delayed response from the EU investment policy

Unlike Canada and the US, the EU Member States did not embrace the transparency narrative extensively. Occasionally, they provided for the publication of awards but, broadly speaking, the issue remained either unaddressed or only partially regulated.

An empirical review of the BITS concluded by the Member States between 2006 (when the ICSID Rules amendment process took place) and 2024 displays a fragmented picture concerning the matter of transparency.[70] Even before the entry into force of the Lisbon Treaty (2009), several EU countries referred to transparency in their BITs. This batch accounts for roughly 40 per cent of the EU Member States but limits the transparency reach to the

[67] Full list available at: https://uncitral.un.org/en/texts/arbitration/conventions/transparency/status.

[68] Full list available at: https://uncitral.un.org/en/texts/arbitration/conventions/foreign_arbitral_awards/status.

[69] 2022 Italian Model BIT, Article 25(1); 2021 Canada Model BIT, Article 36; 2018 Dutch Model BIT, Article 20(13).

[70] The results are based on a personal research conducted on all Member States BITs from 2006 to 2024.

publication of laws related to the investment, or to the obligation of prompt response when the counterparty is soliciting information. Only one investment agreement—the Mexico–Spain BIT (2008)—provided for the publication of the arbitral awards. Unsurprisingly, the most developed transparency provisions were those included in the agreements signed by Canada with Eastern European or Baltic countries.

While for some states, like Croatia and Finland, it is not possible to draw comparison given the absence of BITs after 2009, the rest of the 'pioneering' group appears extremely cautious about improving its transparency performances during the EU-led investment policy despite the traction transparency was gaining globally. For example, Latvia did not include transparency provisions in its 2010 BIT with India. Similarly, Romania reduced the breadth of its pre-Lisbon commitment to openness of public participation by narrowing its transparency obligations. Austria and Slovenia still included transparency provisions in the investment agreements they negotiated after Lisbon, albeit without improvements worth reporting.

On the opposite side of the spectrum, there is a cluster of Member States that began to include transparency obligations predominantly after Lisbon. Along with Slovakia, France and Greece extensively embraced the transparency narrative, with a specific commitment in their BITs to apply the UNCITRAL Rules to *any* investor–state claim arising under the treaties in question. The refinements reached by these agreements indicate that exciting times may lie ahead. Portugal, Spain, and, perhaps surprising to some, Hungary soon followed this trend.[71] In a 2018 BIT with Turkey, Lithuania even introduced an obligation for investors to apply nationally and internationally accepted standards of corporate governance for transparency practices, thus recognizing transparency as part of a broader contribution to the sustainable development of the host state and local community.[72]

Outside these two major groups are the EU states that have demonstrated a certain degree of commitment to greater transparency, both before 2009—by making a significant number of their investment treaties, if not all, publicly available—and after the initiation of the investment policy under the EU's aegis, such as by signing the Mauritius Convention. Denmark, Germany, Italy, Luxembourg, and the Netherlands belong to this group. A significantly weaker

[71] Hungary's most recently signed BITs includes one with Bahrain (signed on 4 September 2024), which is not publicly available; one with Georgia (entered into force on 24 January 2025); one with San Marino (entered into force on 12 August 2023); and one with Oman (entered into force on 24 October 2022), all of which incorporate the UNCITRAL Rules on Transparency.

[72] Lithuania–Turkey BIT (signed on 28 August 2018, not yet entered into force), Article 16(3).

commitment to transparency is displayed by Poland. This sounds like a deliberate choice against transparency especially considering that only a handful of the several investment treaty arbitrations Poland is facing are visible.

The fragmented approach among Member States towards transparency in investment agreements is a reflection of the broader problem within EU law concerning the lack of meaning and purpose for the concept of openness. As illustrated in Part I, openness is a vaguely articulated characterization of the EU democratic principle. The prudent tightening of some EU Member States, which, at least before the Lisbon Treaty, remain particularly reluctant to abandon confidentiality seems to epitomize this vagueness, as furthermore attested by the Court's prudence and the EU institutions' unassertiveness in giving transparency any legal recognition. From an EU law standpoint, transparency was instrumental to the right to be informed and was a corollary of the effective exercise of the right to be heard but it long remained just a somewhat desirable feature, whose exact purpose has been difficult to pin down. Thanks to the impulses of the Advocates General, transparency gradually became one of the foundational ideas underpinning the EU value of democracy (the other one being participation) necessary for the full realization of the EU legal order's dual structure of legitimacy that builds on the Member States and the European citizens. Transparency, however, is just a stand-alone component of the broader principle of openness, which, in turn, leans closer to the EU value of democracy. In the EU, openness is instrumental to the full realization of 'an ever closer union among the peoples of Europe' where decisions are taken 'as *openly* as possible and as closely as possible to the citizen'. Although openness is deemed to be congenial to instil confidence in the decision-making procedure, bring public trust in institutional mechanisms, and reduce the concerns of civil society,[73] no strict parameters are identified for its unfolding. As frequently happens in law, this vagueness allows for the inclusion of less expressed ways to engage with democratic promotion both as standalone measures (e.g. transparency) and also as part of wider agreements,[74] regardless of the forms and shapes embodied by the EU democracy.

While this responds to the fulfilment of the EU's external action objectives, it begs the question of how EU values are attained and realized in relationships with third states. Economic instruments (like FTAs and international

[73] Lenaerts lists transparency among the 'trust-enhancing principles' underpinning the (then) Community legal order. Lenaerts, Koen (2004), '"In the Union We Trust": Trust-Enhancing Principles of Community Law', Common Market Law Review, 317.

[74] Cardwell, Paul James (2011), 'Mapping Out Democracy Promotion in the EU's External Relations', European Foreign Affairs Review.

investment agreements) have acquired the potential not only to contribute to the full realization of the EU's internal legal order but also to disseminate the EU's principles globally. Interestingly, these instruments can serve, and have already begun to serve, as channels for transmitting, *inter alia*, EU values to other countries, encouraging them to adopt and align with their principles. It is on this premise that it is possible to identify an EU path towards the promotion of democracy, which was off to a slow start but gained depth along the way, as discussed in the remainder of this section.

1. Institutional approaches

When the EU arrived on the international investment scene (2009), the demand for greater transparency in investment arbitrations was largely met by other players, like Canada and the US, and, in a relatively short time, transparency was accepted as the 'new normal', with official recognition even in international instruments, like the Mauritius Convention. Initially, the EU reaction was cautious and somehow aligned with international trends favouring greater transparency proceeding mostly by consolidating international instruments. Only at a secondary phase did the EU seek to contribute to their expansion more proactively.

Transparency did not emerge as a central theme in the 2009 Council negotiating directives for an agreement with Canada, nor was it a guiding principle in the development of an EU-led investment policy. It was primarily associated with trade aspects, and while there was some indication to include transparency obligations[75] regarding the administration, implementation, and application of regulations affecting international investment, transparency remained largely detached from the realm of investment arbitration. The Commission, at least initially, endorsed this line of action, despite an independent Sustainability Impact Assessment report having already raised doubts about the likeness of sustainable economic benefits or, for what it matters, any economic benefit at all from investment arbitration.[76] More bluntly put, as far as investment arbitration is concerned transparency was not treated as a matter of priority for the EU.

[75] COM(2016)470 final, para 42.

[76] A Trade SIA Relating to the Negotiation of A Comprehensive Economic and Trade Agreement (CETA) between the EU and Canada (2011), 360

The plea for openness, however, did not take long to emerge. Within the EU, the Parliament has been seminal in this sense, having called for more transparency in investment policy on several occasions. One of the first steps towards greater transparency was made in 2011. Seeking to establish an 'integrated and coherent investment policy', capable of ensuring positive contributions to economic progress and sustainable development,[77] the Parliament suggested introducing changes to the investment dispute settlement regime 'to *include greater transparency*' and the possibility to use *amicus curiae* briefs.[78] A few years later (2013), after the negotiations with the US for the Transatlantic Trade and Investment Partnership (TTIP) agreement had already begun, the Parliament insisted on the urgency of increasing the level of transparency through public access to documents.[79] On that occasion, the Parliament argued that transparency improves democracy and accountability within the EU, insofar as European citizens 'can fully participate in the democratic process and exercise public scrutiny'.[80] The focus was on informing citizens and enabling their participation in the Union's decision-making process, thereby enhancing public trust in the European institutions.[81] Clearly, this approach was more aimed at legitimizing the EU rather than making the investment system itself more democratic.

The most assertive contribution of the Parliament towards greater transparency is a 2015 Resolution in the context of the TTIP negotiations. Emphasizing the concerns already expressed by civil society on several occasions, the Parliament, in an even more demanding way, referred to 'transparency' twenty-one times and, unexpectedly, for the first time touched upon treaty-making (negotiation) aspects.[82] Specifically, the Parliament called for the replacement of investment arbitration with

> a new system for resolving disputes between investors and states which is subject to *democratic principles* and scrutiny, where potential cases are treated in a *transparent* manner by publicly appointed, independent professional judges in *public hearings* and which includes an appellate mechanism, where consistency of judicial decisions is ensured, the jurisdiction of courts of the

[77] European Parliament, P7_TA(2011)0141 (6 April 2011), para 2.
[78] Ibid, para 31. Emphasis added.
[79] Open access to information was introduced in the early 1990s with the Council Directive 90/313/EEC of 7 June 1990 on the freedom of access to information on the environment, OJ L 158, 23 June 1990, paras 56–58.
[80] European Parliament, P7_TA(2014)0203 (11 March 2014), para D.
[81] Ibid, para 3.
[82] See Chapter 4.

EU and of the Member States is respected, and where private interests cannot undermine public policy objectives.

The Parliament took stock of the malaise that has begun to characterize investment arbitration, especially in the context of the TTIP negotiations, and invoked the democratic principles as the conditions for the new envisaged system. Accessibility and transparency were invoked as conditions to ensure democratic scrutiny and corresponded to the openness of the tribunal's decision-making phase. This corroborates the point made in the first pages of this chapter: the Parliament was advocating for different, and possibly broader, forms of accessibility and involvement at the procedural (arbitration) level. At that point, the Commission followed suit. The 2015 'Trade for All' report recognized the importance of rendering policy-making transparent and evidence based. It took up the Parliament's suggestion to replace investment arbitration with a clear orientation to readdress the problems of arbitrators' lack of transparency with no hesitations: 'the question is not whether the system should be changed but how this should be done'.

The EU's attention to transparency was largely devoted to reversing the confidentiality of the arbitration process. It is only at a later stage that the EU's approach moved beyond the mere procedure and evolved to a point of explicit recognition of the need for further inclusion and participation of European citizens at the treaty-making level, as analysed in Chapter 4.

The EU's contribution to the transparency narrative in investment law took time to take off but eventually became a potentially transformative force. By solidifying the concept of a relatively high degree of procedural transparency at the global level—undeniably influenced by existing practices—the EU further legitimized the emergence of a new public dimension within investment law. This dimension is particularly dedicated to considering all interests involved and aligns more closely with the value of democracy, marking a shift towards a more inclusive and accountable approach.

The following section surveys how the EU transparency obligations operate in more practical terms in the investment arbitration process.

2. The EU FTAs and Investment Protections Agreements: The beginning of a new era

On the whole, all EU FTAs display a strong commitment towards transparency. Even in those FTAs that provide for investment liberalization (without investment arbitration clauses) transparency is articulated under two main general obligations. First, there is the well-known obligation to promptly publish any law, regulation, and judicial decision connected to the matters covered by the agreement,[83] if possible also via electronic means.[84] Second, there is an expectation that any measure of general application is accompanied by an explanation of the objective and the rationale underpinning it.[85] Another particularly salient and fairly widespread point is the identification of interested (natural or legal) persons that may be affected by a measure of general application.[86] Although these provisions primarily reference trade rather than investment matters, they nonetheless acknowledge the far-reaching impacts of FTAs beyond the contracting or litigant parties directly involved. Transparency, in this context, is essential for fostering a predictable legal and regulatory environment and promoting improved administrative practices, thereby extending their relevance to investment frameworks as well.

The issue of transparency is thus framed as a channel for *the ability to participate*— intended here as the capability to participate for interested persons— and is developed under similar premises also in some 'Trade and Sustainable Development' chapters of EU FTAs. In the EU agreements with India and the Mercosur countries, for example, there is an obligation to act transparently concerning trade and investment measures that may affect the protection of the environment or labour conditions and vice versa (environment or labour protective measures that might affect trade or investment).[87] In those instances, the rationale behind transparency is to ensure *awareness* around the measure in question and provide 'reasonable opportunities for interested persons and stakeholders to submit views'. Transparency is an instrument to raise awareness: governments inform their citizens of their line of action by releasing documents to the public domain (prompt publication). It is at this moment that the EU upgrades transparency to a new level: transparency could

[83] EU–Australia FTA (EU textual proposal of 2018), Chapter Transparency Article X.3; EU–Indonesia (EU textual proposal of 2018), Chapter Transparency Article X.3; Agreement between the EU and Japan for an economic partnership (entered into force, 1 February 2019), OJ L 330, 27 December 2018, Article 17.3; EU–Mercosur FTA (signed on 6 December 2024), Chapter Transparency Article 3, Chapter Trade and Sustainable Development Article 3; Free Trade Agreement between the European Union and New Zealand (entered into force 1 May 2024), OJ L 866, 25 March 2024, Article 23.3; Trade and Cooperation Agreement between the European Union and the United Kingdom of Great Britain and Northern Ireland (entered into force 1 May 2021), OJ L 149, 30 April 2021, Article 335.

[84] EU–Chile Interim Trade Agreement (entered into force 1 February 2025), OJ L 2953, 20 December 2024, Article 28.3.

[85] EU–Australia FTA (n 83), Chapter Transparency Article X.3(b).

[86] EU–Australia FTA (n 83), Chapter Transparency Article X.2; EU–Indonesia FTA (n 83), Chapter Transparency Article X.2; EU–Mercosur FTA (n 83), Chapter Transparency Article 1.

[87] EU–Mercosur FTA (n 83), TSD Chapter Article 3; EU–India FTA (EU textual proposal of 2022), TSD Chapter Article X.13.

also become a channel for the government and the public to interact, enabling mutual understanding of the intentions of both. Governments communicate their line of action (transparency, strictly speaking), and the public is allowed to give feedback on this basis (participatory transparency).[88]

This shift towards the dual paradigm of transparency and participation is replicated across investment chapters and, therefore, is extended to the decision-making of arbitral tribunals as well. The agreements with Canada, India, and Vietnam incorporate the UNCITRAL Rules on Transparency. Even those agreements where the Rules have not been included—the EU agreements with Singapore and Mexico—further elaborate on the issue of transparency. The default approach remains to make public all documents related to the initiation of an arbitration. This can be done either via strictly applying Article 3 of the UNCITRAL Rules or by expanding this list—as in CETA, and the EU–India agreement—or by way of exception, as in the EU–Vietnam agreement. Without referring to the UNCITRAL Rules, the EU–Singapore agreement reached the same outcomes and imposed an obligation to make public also the minutes or transcripts of tribunal hearings,[89] whereas in CETA the documents are available upon request.[90] This implies that any interested person has potential access to the entire proceedings' materials, without interfering with the litigation.

Hearings are open to the public, again either via the UNCITRAL Rules (CETA, EU–Vietnam FTA) or as a stand-alone provision (EU–Singapore and EU–Mexico agreements). In seeking to safeguard confidential or protected information, appropriate arrangements are taken to hold in private the parts of the hearing requiring specific protection.[91] The EU–India text proposal does not explicitly mention public attendance to hearings, although it is said that private hearings operate by way of exception to protect confidential information.

As regards non-disputing parties' participation, CETA limits their interventions exclusively to matters of interpretation[92] and allows *amicus curiae* submissions only via the UNCITRAL Rules. Likewise, the FTA with Vietnam clarifies that those submitting their briefs (*amicus curiae*) should be

[88] See Chapter 4.
[89] EU–Singapore Investment Protection Agreement (signed on 13 February 2019, pending Member States ratifications), Annex 8 Article 1(1)(f).
[90] Comprehensive Economic and Trade Agreement (CETA) between Canada, of the one part, and the European Union and its Member States, of the other part (entered into force provisionally on 21 September 2017), OJ L 11, 14 January 2017, Article 8.36(3).
[91] Ibid, para 5.
[92] CETA (n 90), Article 8.38.

independent of either Party's government, and their submissions should specify the nature of their interest. Beyond *amici curiae*, whose submissions operate again through the UNCITRAL Rules, the EU–India agreements broadly refer to third persons seeking to intervene—the intervener—by attending hearings and making oral statements.[93] The intervener is defined as 'any natural or legal person who can demonstrate a direct and present interest in the result of the dispute'.[94] Interventions from interveners are limited to support in whole or in part the award sought by one of the parties.[95] Similarly, the EU–Singapore FTA mentions *amicus curiae*[96] but more broadly identifies and relies on the category of 'third persons' as persons that are not a disputing party and not a non-disputing Party to the Agreement.[97] Annex 8 outlines a very detailed procedure for submissions on issues of fact or law the third person wishes to address. The terminology nuances are blurred in the EU–Mexico investment chapter, which refers to third persons and *amici curiae* interchangeably.

The EU approach towards transparency has been significantly inspired and, to a certain extent, modelled upon the transformative effects of the existing instruments on investment arbitration. The diffusion of the UNCITRAL Rules indeed indicates that when it comes to procedural transparency, the EU tended to align with existing trends, rather than leading change. Yet despite this slow kicking off, the EU sought to create new spaces for public engagement, going beyond the reach of the existing instruments. For example, the EU–Mexico text and the EU–Singapore FTA provide the parties with an opportunity to respond to third persons' submissions,[98] clearly following up on the *Foresti*'s approach. It is in this detail that lies the real novelty of the EU approach: transparency has become a condition for participation since the public seeks to become involved in the debate after being put in the position of knowing what is happening.[99] From this standpoint, transparency and participation are complementary sides of the broader principle of democracy that is, in the EU's eyes, the proper response to address the legitimacy issues affecting the investment regime. Overall, drawing inspiration from international trends

[93] EU–India Investment Protection Agreement (EU textual proposal of 2022), Article 3.23(3).

[94] This clearly echoes the language used in the tentative agreement with the US, TTIP (EU proposal as of 2016) Article 23(1).

[95] EU–India IPA (n 93), Article 23(1)–(3).

[96] EU–Singapore IPA (n 89), Rules 40–42.

[97] Ibid, Article 3.

[98] EU–Mexico Economic Partnership, Political Coordination and Cooperation Agreement (EU–Mexico Global Agreement) (signed 17 January 2025), Investment chapter Article 24; EU–Singapore IPA (n 89) Annex 8 Article 3(6).

[99] Marceddu, Maria Laura (2018), 'Implementing Transparency and Public Participation in FTA Negotiations: Are the Times a-Changin'?' Journal of International Economic Law.

and capitalizing on a global push for greater transparency, the EU's investment policy introduces a more democratic orientation to investment arbitration, rooted in the twin pillars of transparency and public participation.

Further confirmation of this intuition comes also from the investment agreement between China and the EU (CAI). While the whole agreement may not look as innovative as the EU portrays it to be, the transparency provisions present striking features. For example, Article 3*bis* of Section II (investment liberalization) grants the right to a party to request the other party to supply information about the operation of a 'covered entity' (the CAI term for state-owned enterprises). Information is intended in a broad sense and includes the percentage of share, the voting structure, the voting rights, the organizational structure, the annual revenues, etc. The request for information is incumbent upon governments, removes any fears of retaliation from EU firms, and offers a useful means to nudge China to police the behaviours of state-owned enterprises.[100] Other provisions to consider are Articles 1, 5, and 6 included in Section IV (investment and sustainable development). Article 1 places CAI very much in line with other EU agreements by providing for prompt publication of laws related to the investment and offers non-state stakeholders the possibility to submit their views. Articles 5 and 6 strengthen the steer towards transparency by creating unprecedented spaces for non-state actors to access the dispute settlement process, which is specific to this section and modelled after that of the World Trade Organization, albeit without official adoption and implementation process. Respectively, Article 5 is concerned with strict transparency: all the documents generated throughout the proceedings are publicly available and hearings are open; whereas Article 6 deals with participation. Any natural or legal person independent from either party government can submit their briefs on a matter that is directly relevant to a factual or a legal issue under consideration, in observance of the practicalities outlined in the provision. If implemented, this would put strong pressure on China on environmental and labour issues, especially from EU NGOs.

For the sake of completeness, separate, but ultimately rather unexpected, observations apply to the EU agreement with Japan, which has appeared to be quite sceptical about the inclusion of transparency obligations since Japanese BITs have been largely silent in this respect.[101] According to a leaked version

[100] Gao, Henry S (2022), 'The EU–China Comprehensive Agreement on Investment: Between Strategic Opportunity and Strategic Autonomy', Asian Yearbook of International Economic Law.

[101] Japan–Korea BIT (entered into force 17 May 2014).

released by Greenpeace Netherlands in June 2017,[102] the Commission's line of action concerning transparency looked consistent within the EU–Japan investment agreement given the incorporation of the UNCITRAL Rules, and a commitment towards access to documents and third-party interventions (as discussed during the fourteenth round of negotiations). However, an agreement on investment matters between the EU and Japan has not been reached[103] and does not seem likely to happen any time soon. Only time will tell if this approach will ultimately be embraced by Japan, albeit the current stalemate indicates that the EU line of action already displays contradictions, as elaborated in the section closing this chapter.

E. Shadows and contradictions of the EU agenda

Transparency has gradually acquired a key role as an *in statu nascendi* principle in international arbitration due to its close link to legitimacy and accountability, in respect of which transparency is often considered as the minimum standard. Despite this importance, the matter is still unsettled with tribunals conflicting on whether transparency constitutes a general principle under international law.[104] Regardless of its status under international law, Sands rightly argues that one way to enhance the legitimacy of arbitral tribunals' decision-making process remains the delivery of awards that consider the specific interests of local community raised through third-party submissions—even if the tribunal ultimately disagrees with the reasoning presented in those submissions.[105]

The very act of considering submissions from those affected by or holding an interest in an investment serves as a safeguard for the legitimacy of the regime. To maintain systemic legitimacy, investment arbitration must account

[102] The leaked texts are available on the Greenpeace website: <https://trade-leaks.org/jefta-leaks/>.

[103] EU–Japan, The Trade Agreement in Principle <https://policy.trade.ec.europa.eu/eu-trade-relationships-country-and-region/countries-and-regions/japan/eu-japan-agreement/agreement-explained_en>:

> At this point, we have finished negotiations on all parts of the Japan agreement with the exception of investment protection. On this we clearly need further discussion with Japan to achieve a satisfactory outcome, as the EU has made very clear that there is no possibility to return to an old-style Investor-to-State Dispute Settlement (ISDS) system.

[104] See, e.g., *Champion Trading v Egypt* (Award, 27 October 2006), para 164 asserting that the claimant has not proved that the State has violated 'the principle of transparency under international law'. See also *Rand Investment v Serbia* (n 22), para 4, where Kohen insists on the principle of freedom, by virtue of which tribunals do not have the power to impose on states something like transparency to which they have not consented.

[105] *Odyssey v Mexico* (PO No. 6—Decision on the Application for Leave to File a Non-Disputing Party Submission (Amicus Curiae), Dissenting Opinion of Philippe Sands, 20 December 2021), para 1.

for the interests of domestic regulatory regimes, which are typically anchored in democratic frameworks. Transparency operates as both an enhancer and an essential expectation for upholding such legitimacy. Initially arising as an expectation of access to knowledge and information for participants, transparency has evolved into a demand for involvement, with the potential to influence final outcomes, thereby establishing itself as a precondition for meaningful participation.

However sound in principle, in practice the EU agenda towards these expectations remains ambiguous at best. Albeit substantiated by international trends, it is undeniable that the EU has made remarkable progress in accelerating the diffusion of transparency and public participation as principles to be implemented throughout investment arbitrations. What purportedly distinguishes the EU is its pronounced commitment to democracy, reflected in the consistency between its internal and external actions (Article 21 Treaty on European Union (TEU)). This commitment is embedded in the EU's mission to promote its values globally (Article 3(5) TEU) and serves as a source of inspiration for the rest of the world. It would be shortsighted to overlook evidence of this commitment in the negotiations with Canada, Singapore, Vietnam, and Mexico, as well as in the text proposals for ongoing negotiations with other countries. While it might be relatively straightforward to implement transparency with countries like Canada that are long familiar with transparency practices, other players, like Japan, may pose new challenges. The issue cannot be dismissed because of the difficulties deriving from the Member States ratification processes of investment agreements containing investment arbitration clauses (as per Opinion 2/15) and is likely to shadow the EU leadership as a transparency leader—not only in its external relations. However sound and striking the EU commitment is on paper, especially with countries like China, it remains unclear whether the EU would be inclined to compromise on transparency with countries traditionally sceptical about the inclusion of transparency obligations in investment agreements. Beyond its external projections, it took nearly a decade for the EU to sign and ratify the Mauritius Convention.[106] While the European Parliament has consistently advocated for greater transparency in ISDS and criticized the delays in ratifying and implementing the Convention,[107] much discretion ultimately rests with Member State regarding the extent to which they fully endorse the transparency initiative without

[106] The EU officially signed the Mauritius Convention on 2 July 2024, following the Council's approval and the Parliament's consent, OJ L 2118, 31 July 2024 para 1.

[107] European Parliament P9_TA(2022)0268 (23 June 2022), para 49.

reservations. As it stands, the number of Member States that have ratified the Convention remains low, despite the widespread global adoption of the UNCITRAL Rules on Transparency.

All these considerations portray the EU as a receptive norm taker and enhancer. While it is fair to acknowledge the EU's attempts to implement democracy, especially if compared with Member States' poor individual records on transparency, the challenges posed by those countries particularly cautious in embracing a more democratic orientation for arbitral proceedings inevitably cast a shadow on the leading global role of the EU and its persuasiveness towards one of its foundational values.

4

Rethinking public participation in investment decision-making

A. Overview

This chapter examines how the EU efforts, despite their slow inception, have contributed to advancing public participation in investment law-making. Specifically, it explains how the EU has sought to correct some distortions brought about by the investment decision-making in undermining democratic processes.

The chapter opens by briefly describing the complexity that permeates the investment decision-making, insisting on the fact that those actually bearing the effects of foreign investments have rarely, if at all, been involved in the decision-making process (Part B). It then refines the public demands that have increasingly challenged such an exclusive approach (Part C) and examines the participatory mechanisms put forward by the EU to soothe popular anxieties about the legal and political processes underpinning investment rules that threaten the performance of democratic institutions (Part D). Apparently guided by the idealistic pursuit of a Union *of* people, the EU seizes the chance to capitalize strategically on (global) public opinion to generate consensus around the European Commission's agenda (Part E).

B. Investment decision-making in modern times

The Santurbán páramo is an ecosystem situated in the Andean region, close to the Venezuelan border. It is an ecological and cultural site in the Colombian high mountains that supplies water to millions of people and contains gold and other minerals. The site is particularly rich in terms of biodiversity as it provides refuge for endemic species, including the iconic spectacled bear.

EU Values in Investment Law And Policy. Maria Laura Marceddu, Oxford University Press.
 DOI: 10.1093/9780191986208.003.0004

Santurbán has rapidly become an 'evolution hot spot'[1] and has attracted significant commercial interest, especially because of its mineral resources.

In 1994, a Canadian mining company, Eco Oro (then known as Greystar) obtained a licence for exploration and exploitation[2] in the La Angostura village, within the Santander department, which is the department that hosts the páramo of Santurbán. The company started carrying out a programme of surface mapping, sampling, and diamond drilling, and between 1995 and 2001 expanded its activity by acquiring additional rights over the Angostura deposit. While Eco Oro slowly continued to expand its activities, the Colombian Constitutional Court issued decisions C-339/02 and T-666, establishing the state's obligation to protect páramos and clarifying that areas of ecological importance—including páramos—require higher levels of protection.[3]

As international business poured in and mining explorations surged, tensions escalated, with artisanal miners and activists seeking to preserve the ecosystem and the highland waters from pollution. In 2009 an investment from the International Finance Corporation in Greystar's La Angostura project prompted a reform of the 2001 Mining Code explicitly excluding mining activities in the páramos ecosystems, followed by a Constitutional Court ruling which reiterated that environmental authorities may declare certain ecosystems excluded from mining areas, even if those areas are not listed expressly in legislation or included in national regional parks or forest reserves.[4] In light of these developments, Eco Oro's application for an open-pit licence was thus ruled out by the environmental authorities because of its setting in the páramo zone,[5] and violent protests spread in several areas of the country.[6] Following these unfortunate events that impacted the company's market value, the company opted for an environmentally friendly rebranding of its corporate mission and name—from Greystar to Eco Oro—to assuage the concerns that had emerged thus far.[7] Right after the company rebranding, the Canada–Colombia FTA entered into force (August 2011).

[1] Cotula, Lorenzo (2020), '(Dis)integration in Global Resource Governance: Extractivism, Human Rights, and Investment Treaties', Journal of International Economic Law.

[2] *Eco Oro v Colombia* (Decision on Jurisdiction, Liability and Directions on Quantum, 9 September 2021), Contract of Assignment between Minas Los Diamantes Ltda and Greystar Resources Ltd—Permit No. 3452, para 98.

[3] Cotula, Lorenzo and Perrone, Nicolas (2024), 'Seeing Santurbán through ISDS: A Sociolegal Case Study of Eco Oro v. Colombia', Leiden Journal of International Law, 4; *Eco Oro* (n 2), Annex A.

[4] Ibid, Annex A.

[5] Ibid, para 113.

[6] Ibid, para 118.

[7] Ibid, para 131.

Eco Oro continued its operations until 2013, when they were suspended following additional delineations of the páramo area. A particularly contentious issue revolved around the exact boundaries of the páramo, which were ultimately defined and formalized in 2014 through Ministerial Resolution 2090. The Resolution divided the páramo into three zones—the preservation, the restoration, and the sustainable use zones. The document outlined certain exceptions to the prohibition on mining operations. Specifically, mining activities in the restoration zones of the páramo located within the municipalities of Vetas, California, and Suratá could proceed if authorized. Additionally, the Resolution granted a broader exception for projects that held a valid mining concession contract and an environmental control and management instrument, allowing them to continue operations even if situated within the páramo boundaries. This regulatory flexibility underscored the tension between environmental preservation and the continuation of pre-existing economic activities.

Over 50 per cent of Eco Oro concession lay within páramo but the project appears to fall under the exception upon the condition of being authorized to mine in the restoration zone.[8] In 2016, the government of Colombia approved a National Development Plan for 2014–2018 (Law 1753) that included new mining provisions. The approval was accompanied by further protests among those residing in the páramo area that culminated in citizens' legal actions before the Constitutional Court, which issued two decisions. In 2016, the Court struck down the mining exception,[9] and in 2017 called off the government's first delimitation of the páramo because of constitutional non-compliance with the requirements of consultation with the communities in and around the páramo and ordered the Government to provide a new delimitation within a year.[10]

Despite the mining authorities supporting the La Angostura project, after the first ruling, Eco Oro decided to initiate an arbitration process relying on the investment chapter included in the Colombia–Canada FTA, claiming that its legitimate expectations built upon pro-mining legislation were violated, that it was deprived of certain rights (lawful expropriation and minimum standard of treatment (MST)) and the value of its investment was destroyed. The decision on jurisdiction rendered by the arbitral tribunal in September 2021 rejected the expropriation claim but upheld the breach of the MST. The tribunal did

[8] Ibid, para 154.
[9] Constitutional Court of the Republic of Colombia, Judgement C-035 (8 February 2016).
[10] Constitutional Court of the Republic of Colombia, Judgement T-361 (30 May 2017).

not reach a unanimous position, and by majority ruled that while Colombia's measures were not discriminatory, its conduct was not flawless and it was legitimate for the investors to expect a predictable commercial framework for business planning and investment.[11] Arbitrator Sands disagreed with the finding on legitimate expectations and argued that a degree of inconsistency in state conduct is inevitable where multiple interests are at stake.

A key aspect of this decision, which complements the analysis in Chapter 3 and holds significant relevance for the current discussion, pertains to the participants within the investment regime. More specifically, the case underscores persistent challenges regarding the involvement—or lack thereof—of stakeholders beyond the traditional respondent states and claimant investors in arbitral proceedings and, more broadly, within the decision-making processes that shape investment agreements. This highlights the enduring exclusion of broader interests and actors from a system that directly impacts diverse public and private stakeholders. In the *Eco Oro* case, several organizations sought to obtain rights to submit an *amicus curiae* brief—namely Comité Santurbán, the Centre for International Environmental Law (CIEL), the Asociación Interamericana para la Defensa del Ambiente (AIDA), MiningWatch Canada, Institute for Policy Studies (IPS), Global Economy Project and the Centre for Research on Multinational Corporations (SOMO).[12] None of them was accorded such a right. Their submissions were dismissed as too general and lacking specific relevance to the legal scope of the dispute.[13] While the tribunal did not reject per se the legal grounds identified by these submissions, it considered that the petitioners have not shown 'how generalised issues of human rights, and particularly the right to live in a healthy environment, may be said to relate to the scope of the specificities of this dispute'.[14] Similarly, the tribunal rejected the request to obtain access to documents but granted the petitioners the right to attend hearings.[15]

The *Eco Oro*'s petitioners are illustrative of the presence of a plethora of actors with different visions and interests. For example, those living in the Santurbán páramo area were primarily concerned with preserving water from pollution ('water before gold' was their effective way of putting it),[16] whereas artisanal miners aimed to preserve a certain social identity and fibre they

[11] *Eco Oro* (n 2), para 804.
[12] *Eco Oro v Colombia* (PO No. 6, 18 February 2019), para 1.
[13] Ibid, para 29.
[14] Ibid, para 28.
[15] Ibid, para 41.
[16] Cotula (n 1).

have been providing for decades. Artisanal mining, however, has an environmental footprint and has been subject to regulations restricting mining activities. These internal divides are further exacerbated by the influx of foreign investors, even though the Eco Oro model was ostensibly designed to bridge local, national, and global interests.

On the whole, the case is particularly illustrative of the tensions that exist across different actors' perceptions and interests. These tensions reveal deep-rooted identity issues and are anchored on a certain value orientation that determines different visions with respect to the law, the dispute in question, and, more deeply, different representations of environmental protection, development, and natural resource exploitation. Yet reference to local actors in the dispute is found just on two occasions. First, they are mentioned as a term of reference to detect discrimination vis-à-vis foreign actors:

> the Tribunal does not find there was any evidence of an intention expressly to target Eco Oro, or that Eco Oro was inadvertently targeted. It is clear from the local demonstrations that many artisanal miners and local populations were equally concerned at the prospect of losing both their mining rights (to the extent they had such rights) and their livelihood, which had been dependent upon mining being undertaken in their localities.[17]

Second, they highlighted 'the State's inconsistent conduct regarding the Páramo both before and after the adoption of the measures, as well as the persistent uncertainty surrounding its delimitation, which continues to this day'.[18] In essence, this reflects an unresolved issue that has not been adequately addressed by state agencies,[19] further compounding the ambiguity surrounding the delimitation of Santurbán.

The interests at stake in this context are not merely political but also reflect significant tensions at economic, social, and legal levels, necessitating a deeper rethinking of the structural framework. Investment arbitration tends to oversimplify and flatten this societal complexity by framing solutions predominantly in binary terms—that is, determining whether host states are liable or not. Consequently, investment arbitration is ill-suited to address more intricate issues, such as the fragmented nature of the state and the multifaceted relationships between citizens, states, and investors. This largely underscores

[17] *Eco Oro* (n 2), para 640.
[18] *Eco Oro v Colombia* (Partial Dissenting Opinion of Horacio A. Grigera Naón, 9 September 2021), para 24.
[19] Cotula and Perrone (n 3), 14.

the need to reconsider the role and space accorded to participants in the investment regime. In this scenario, it becomes evident that traditional forms of civic participation—such as voting, demonstrating, contacting public officials, or boycotting—are inadequate, or at the very least ill-suited, to ensure meaningful participation for all stakeholders, whether nationals or non-nationals. A critical point to consider is that while investors (non-nationals) may not directly participate in the negotiation process, they often possess the means to influence the content of investment treaties.[20] Conversely, local actors who are most affected by investments are frequently relegated to a peripheral, if not entirely absent, role in overseeing and shaping decision-making processes. This imbalance underscores the need for a more inclusive and participatory approach to investment governance, particularly given that investment treaties are inherently political choices that reflect and vindicate specific socio-economic interests.[21]

It is not surprising that different governments and interest groups having different visions of justice and development legitimately advocate for diverse objectives to be pursued and raise questions on how political choices are made. This thus begs the question of how to reduce the gap between governments negotiating investment treaties and societies practically bearing their effects: Should public participation be a prerogative of certain categories of citizens (e.g. business groups) or does anyone potentially affected by foreign investments have a say? If the latter, to what extent should public participation complement what is expected to be delivered from representatives in governments? Should popular initiatives that have a substantially negative impact on investment interests be dismissed? At what stage, how, and to what extent should these inputs be collected and taken into consideration? What forms are the most suitable to ensure effective and meaningful participation?

Some input to these questions has been coming from the EU. Just tangentially touched by investment norms' democratic relapse, the EU was rather abruptly forced to deal with crowds of activists marching and protesting against the Comprehensive Economic and Trade Agreement between Canada and the European Union (CETA) and, shortly after, the Transatlantic Trade

[20] For example, in the United States, groups like the International Chamber of Commerce and the State Department's Advisory Committee on Transnational Enterprises have encouraged the initiation of a bilateral investment treaty programme since the 1970s. See Magraw, Kendra (2015), 'Investor–State Disputes and the rise of Recourse to State Party Pleading as Subsequent Agreements or Subsequent Practice under the Vienna Convention on the Law of Treaties', ICSID Review—Foreign Investment Law Journal, 142; Vandevelde, Kenneth T (1988), 'The Bilateral Investment Treaty Program of the United States', Cornell International Law Journal, 201.

[21] Weiler, Joseph (2004), 'The Geology of International Law—Governance, Democracy and Legitimacy', ZaöRV.

and Investment Partnership (TTIP) negotiations. The unfortunate circumstances encouraged the EU to adjust its trajectory and deliver original contributions to the participation cause. As a result, the EU (mostly the Commission, with input from the Parliament) devised sophisticated and experimental forms of governance to guarantee, at least in principle, wider inclusion of interested social groups in its decision-making process. In practice, however, these experimental forms have not resulted in institutional shifts of equivalent magnitude. This is in part due to investment rules' stiffness, and in part because the EU is also motivated by hegemonic aspirations of global law-making authority, which sit uncomfortably with democratic progress. The EU remains interested in promoting democracy through public participation, especially if and when it aligns with its agenda-setting objectives. This inward-looking approach does not necessarily undermine the intention to correct the political processes weakening perpetuated by investment rules but it is not shielded from strategic considerations.

Moving from these premises, in this chapter I inquire about the EU's rethinking of public participation to foster democratic progress in investment decision-making. For present purposes, the decision-making process begins at the negotiating phase of an investment agreement and ends when an award is rendered, should a dispute arise. Strictly speaking, arbitral tribunals, like *Eco Oro*, do not create norms. The issue of whether arbitral tribunals and, more broadly, international adjudicators make law instead of simply interpreting is controversial and will not be taken into account here, as it is already explored in the literature.[22] What remains relevant for present purposes is that by controversially reviewing (and sanctioning) high public policy matters in light of what investment operative rules consider 'normal', arbitral tribunals have the power to distort political processes in ways that undermine democracy's rationales[23] and affect a plurality of actors. The questions raised in *Eco Oro* reveal tensions that go beyond the terms of the dispute and concern a global tightening of environmental protection that is unfolding alongside neoliberalism advancement and offers a good starting point for a discussion on the space to accord to investment agreement participants. The demand for arrangements and spaces for local voices and representation in investment decision-making

[22] Zarbiyev, Fuad (2021), 'On the Judge Centredness of the International Legal Self', European Journal of International Law; Zarbiyev Fuad (2012), 'Judicial Activism in International Law—A Conceptual Framework for Analysis', Journal of International Dispute Settlement; see also Chapter 6.

[23] Schneiderman, David (2013), *Resisting Economic Globalization: Critical Theory and International Investment Law*, 113–35.

took time to emerge. Even the EU approach took time to adjust to this demand, as outlined in the following section.

C. A plea for public participation in investment decision-making

In a highly integrated world, it has become common wisdom to improve democratic processes in a way that takes into account the interests of those affected by decision-making. In principle, a large number of states agree with this line. In practice, however, arrangements to take into account local voices are often inadequate or incomplete, those outside the decision-making process are in no position to influence the process, and arbitral tribunals are unfit to rectify this gap. In principle, even Canada and the EU intended to consult civil society in the negotiations that would have led to the CETA agreement, but, in practice, uncertainties and deficits feature their commitment to public inclusion since the outset of the negotiations.

In the EU legal system, the responsibility for initiating investment and trade negotiations rests with the Commission, which takes the lead in the negotiation process. As a matter of procedure, the process starts with an impact assessment and a public consultation on the agreement's expected achievements, followed by an informal scoping exercise, which sets out what both parties wish to negotiate in more precise terms. In the context of the CETA negotiations the Commission played by the rules. A preliminary web-based consultation was held between February and March 2008, a sustainable impact assessment (SIA) was released in 2011, a joint report on the EU–Canada scoping exercise was published in March 2009, and paved the way for the beginning of CETA negotiations at the EU–Canada summit in May 2009 in Prague. Based on the information gathered during these preliminary steps, the Commission deemed enhanced economic cooperation between Canada and the EU to be desirable. It then recommended to the Council the formal initiation of negotiations. The Council holds the authority to either approve or reject the request, and if authorized, it sets the negotiating directives. Once the Council grants authorization, the Commission proceeds with the negotiations and, after each round or at other critical junctures, provides reports to both the Council and the Parliament.

On the whole, the CETA negotiations were largely conducted behind closed doors with European Commission officials, government representatives, some province officials on the Canadian side, specific Member States (France,

Germany, and the UK) on the EU side, and business lobby groups sitting at the discussion table[24] to help the Commission to identify potential trade barriers with Canada. The Canada–EU negotiations were not a high-profile case for Europeans, confidentiality was simply business as usual, and the presence of business lobbies did not pose particular concerns. Unsurprisingly, the draft texts compiled during the negotiations were not made public and the final texts would have become public only after the negotiations were closed.

For a long time, secrecy featured international negotiations of investment agreements, and more broadly of international agreements, without posing particular concerns. Traditionally, diplomatic or governmental representatives work behind closed doors to reach a mutually acceptable agreement, with few official documents subsequently being released to the public and limited (if any) public participation in political debate.[25] One partial explanation for confidentiality in international negotiations is that originally these interactions were mostly bilateral and between developed and developing countries, had less far-reaching implications (or so governments assumed),[26] and government representatives were expected to be accountable enough to decide in their constituencies' best interest.

Despite championing democracy as one of its funding values, even the EU has been no exception to this secretive and close approach to investment decision-making, or at least was when it entered the investment regime. During the CETA negotiations, business-oriented groups played a particularly prominent role. Among them, the three most influential were the European Round Table of Industrialists (ERT), BusinessEurope, and the European Services Forum. In contrast, civil society representatives did not receive comparable visibility or influence. This imbalance of inputs appears even more astounding considering that doubts on the net economic benefits of foreign investments were cast since the outset in the SIA report, with a particular reference to investment arbitration:

> There *may* be some positive social and environmental impacts from investment encouraged under CETA as a whole.... Regarding social issues, [i]t is important to stress that a *reduction in 'policy space'* as used in this assessment

[24] Hübner, Kurt, Balik, Tugce, and Deman, Anne-Sophie (2016), 'CETA: the Making of the Comprehensive Economic and Trade Agreement between Canada and the EU', Notes de L'Ifri.

[25] Hull, William Isaac (1908), *The Two Hague Conferences and Their Contributions to International Law.*

[26] This was particularly true for developing countries, with Pakistan's Attorney-General describing investment treaties as 'a piece of paper, something for the press, a good photo opportunity and that was the end of it'. Investment Treaty News (16 March 2009).

> *exclusively refers to the ability of governments to make policies that have clear social (as well as economic and environmental) benefits*. . . . This brings into question the efficacy of ISDS [Investor-State Dispute Settlement] in contributing to the objective of its advocates of preventing capital flight and enhancing investment with the end goal of contributing to the 'the well-being of society.' Likewise, it is *questionable that including ISDS in CETA would create a net/overall social sustainability benefit for the EU and/or Canada*. . . . The question then becomes what is the ideal structure for an investment enforcement mechanism in maximising what is referred to hereafter as 'sustainable economic benefits.'[27]

The SIA report also cautioned that the increase in foreign direct investments (FDIs) generated by CETA, particularly in Canada's oil sands and mining sectors, could lead to heightened environmental impacts due to the environmentally intensive nature of these industries.[28] Similarly, the report noted concerns among Canadian stakeholders about potential competitive disadvantages for Canada, the inclusion of an ISDS mechanism, and issues related to water delivery and management.[29] While these concerns posed challenges for some stakeholders, the report highlighted that CETA was likely to be more enthusiastically welcomed by others:

> The Investment Chapter in CETA . . . would also provide benefits to multinational companies and foster forms of intangible business relationships, which may have economic benefits; and stimulate the flows of capital and differentiated goods. Any benefits from an Investment Chapter may have a multiplier effect given that an important part of the EU–Canada economic relationship is based on investment and certain more intangible linkages.

In this light, CETA negotiations confirm a distorting trend in decision-making participation: non-business stakeholders remained in a disadvantageous position with marginal influence on the exercise of decisional power. On the contrary, the business lobby appeared well placed to influence the negotiators. Even admitting that the business lobby possesses more persuasive means to reach political channels, within the EU context the privileged position of business stakeholders remains somewhat congenial to advance the Commission's agenda on further integration. This explains the long history of collaboration

[27] EU–Canada SIA Final Report (June 2011), 19–20, 310–11, 328–30. Emphasis added.
[28] Ibid, 354.
[29] Ibid, 249, 277, 331, 343.

that powerful corporations have had with the Commission since the establishment of the Single Market. ERT, for example, lobbied strenuously for the completion of the Common Market and its proposition, as formulated in the 'Europe 1990: An Agenda for Action', was adopted, almost word for word, in the Commission's 'White Paper on Completing the Internal Market'.[30] It is not a coincidence that this lobbying occurred when the Commission was seeking to deepen the Common Market as a response to the economic crisis. The pressure from industrial leaders for the unification of European markets was precisely what the Commission was looking for. The rest of the story is well known: the ratification of the Single European Act, which entrenched the principle of mutual recognition in trade and capital mobility, instituted a qualified voting majority on issues on the realization of the Single Market[31] and ultimately set the objective to establish the Single Market before the end of 1992.

While for ERT, and other corporate lobbies, the Single Market looked like a profitable opportunity, one may be tempted to speculate that business stakeholders' inputs were not taken into account to ensure a pluralistic decision-making process but because their (predominantly profit-oriented) interests aligned with those of the Commission and could help develop a consensus on the European construct. From the Commission's standpoint, the Single Market in fact was a bold innovative step toward a higher degree of integration, a highly politicized choice of ethos, and a new political culture,[32] despite Member States' reluctance to cede more powers to the Commission. Albeit moved by different reasons, the direct political intervention of business stakeholders thus becomes pivotal in developing consensus on the Single Market plan, whose implementation needed corporate actors as much as corporate actors could benefit from a harmonized regulatory environment for frictionless trade across Member States.

From this standpoint, it is not hard to conceive CETA and, more broadly EU free trade agreements (FTAs), as further steps towards increased integration, insofar as they level the international playing field and ensure that international norms reflect and harmonize with the EU regulatory preferences. Fritz has described this bi-directional collaboration between the EU and business actors as 'reverse lobbying', that is, the 'public authority (the Commission) lobbying business to lobby itself'.[33] This reveals that the special place accorded

[30] Hermann, Christoph (2007), 'Neoliberalism in the European Union', Studies in Political Economy.
[31] Ibid.
[32] Weiler, Joseph (1999), *The Constitution of Europe 'Do the New Clothes Have an Emperor?' and Other Essays on European Integration*, 89–90.
[33] Fritz, Thomas (2015), *Public Services Under Attack—TTIP, CETA, and the Secretive Collusion Between Business Lobbyists and Trade Negotiators.*

to business input in the decision-making process is a by-product of the strong ideological commitment of the Commission to European integration, in respect of which a more general commitment to democratic decision-making occupies a marginal role.

An attentive observer would not miss the resemblance between the imbalances in EU decision-making and the distorting forces that have meanwhile gained prominence in investment decision-making. The more the number of investment arbitrations surged, the more investment matters became relevant to civil society. The more the power delegated to technocrats was augmented, the more citizens began to question the accountability of governments to make decisions on their behalf. This became especially evident in the investment regime due to the burdens placed on local actors in the presence of flawed foreign investments and adverse arbitration awards. These outcomes, shaped by external forces not produced domestically, began to have an increasingly significant impact on people's lives. The distorting effect of these forces was mostly generated by non-domestic (international) adjudicators ascertaining what could be considered 'a normal exercise' of sovereign decision-making and eventually sanctioning abnormal domestic regulatory controls, as happened with the *Eco Oro* case. Citizens increasingly questioned the decisions that sanctioned their governments, wondering in whose name these decisions were being made. Predictably, suspicion towards international intrusions in domestic policies and processes began to mount significantly.

What was particularly problematic was not the secrecy per se, or at least not exclusively. Every decision-maker would sensibly agree that a certain degree of secrecy is necessary for negotiations to accept compromise and change positions without 'constantly worrying about what the public and the press might say'.[34] The gist of the problem is rather in the deliberate exclusion from the decision-making process of certain voices that could not be taken into consideration at all. The problem is not merely in the secrecy underpinning the negotiations of an investment agreement and during arbitral proceedings.[35] The problem is in the non-inclusion since the outset—that is, before anything happens—of parties potentially concerned with and affected by the decision-making process in question, like the inhabitants of the páramo in *Eco Oro*. From this standpoint, it is not an exaggeration to posit that investment decision-making suffers from an original distortion that cannot be straightened out effortlessly or rectified by arbitral tribunals subsequently, and

[34] Gutmann, Amy and Thompson, Dennis F (1996), *Democracy and Disagreement*, 115.
[35] See Chapter 3.

that remains inadequate to take into account the plethora of local voices and interests.

These distortions, however, are not irresistible. As the negotiations of CETA were soon about to demonstrate, 'what matters in the EU is not how a discussion begins; what matters is how it ends'.[36] Let us now turn to understanding how the discussion unfolds.

1. The CETA negotiations

While the CETA talks progressed largely undisturbed in the EU, on the Canadian side they were exposed to further scrutiny. With North American Free Trade Agreement (NAFTA) in mind, civil society groups mobilized much faster than in Europe and one of the leading society groups (the Council of Canadians) raised concerns about the content of CETA as early as 2008. Equally concerned about the promises of free trade in times of economic uncertainty, the Trade Justice Network provided a venue to share information with a variety of non-governmental organizations (NGOs) and with those interested in knowing more about CETA in order ultimately to push the Canadian government towards more transparent and inclusive negotiations.

For Canadians, one of the most controversial points of CETA was the inclusion of a chapter on public procurement. According to some leaked versions of the agreement, it seemed that the EU was seeking full coverage of all subcentral government procurement entities in areas particularly important to its companies, that is, energy and hydro utilities. Even more alarmingly, the EU was interested in the liberalization of municipally delivered services, like school boards, publicly funded academic institutions, hospitals, and other health service entities.[37] In response to these concerns, the Canadian activists successfully assembled a municipal front sympathetic to the idea of excluding municipal procurement from CETA but did not gain traction among Europeans. Although the municipal campaign was tactically important in developing a political base that shared societal concerns, the Canadian civil society groups were not able to impact the CETA negotiations considerably,

[36] Weiler, Joseph (2020), 'Europe Must Learn Quickly to Speak the Language of Power: Part I', *EJIL:Talk!* <https://www.ejiltalk.org/europe-must-learn-quickly-to-speak-the-language-of-power-part-i/>.

[37] Trew, Stuart (2013), 'Correcting the Democratic Deficit in the CETA Negotiations: Civil Society Engagement in the Provinces, Municipalities, and Europe', International Journal.

possibly because they were fairly ineffective in lobbying the federal and provincial governments.

The CETA negotiations abruptly changed course after some documents were leaked and released online in August 2014 by a German media organization. Unlike their Canadian counterparts, European civil society groups formed a more robust front against globalization promises and were quite successful in igniting public opinion. They represented the largest cohesion amongst civil society in the EU's history, were able to collect over 3 million signatures against CETA,[38] and organized strong protests from the public and the media, both of whom urged the two sides to release the official texts of the negotiation. While the leak accelerated the process, other factors concurred to change the course of events. Alongside CETA, the Commission started the TTIP talks that gave extra visibility to trade negotiations and became increasingly interconnected with the negotiation of the EU–Canada agreement. The objective to be pursued in the long term thus became broader: beyond the opposition to CETA (and TTIP), an unprecedented united front was resisting globalization, its false promises of growth and jobs, and, by extension, its distortion of the democratic process. The scepticism knew no borders and succeeded in galvanizing protesters from both sides of the Atlantic. What was once a matter of one agreement has rapidly escalated into a matter of principle against free trade. One possible explanation for this aversion is that European citizens have greater expectations of the state and the social system, as opposed to markets, to generate fair and efficient outcomes. Another factor beyond the pressure of civil society organizations on both the DG trade and the Canadian government was the opposition of some EU Member States—Germany, Austria, and France—vocally claiming to reject an agreement including an ISDS clause.

The situation heated up rapidly as civil society organizations raised numerous issues, forcing CETA negotiators eventually to revise some critical parts of the original text. One of the most unexpected challenges was the investment arbitration mechanism, which emerged as a major point of contention. Despite some concerns raised by the Parliament as early as 2011 that investment arbitration could generate situations of conflict between the adoption of legitimate public regulations and the protection of investors,[39] investment arbitration was and remained relatively commonplace in investment agreements

[38] https://citizens-initiative.europa.eu/initiatives/details/2017/000008_en.

[39] European Parliament, P7_TA(2011)0141 (6 April 2011).

both within Canada and the EU. It is no surprise that EU institutions neglected to foresee ISDS as a threat, and overestimated, especially the Commission, its own power over Member States. More specifically, the Commission on its part failed to grasp the aversion and continued to applaud the 'robustness' of international arbitration as an established feature for investment protection, whose absence would discourage investors and make a host economy less attractive than others.[40]

Following the protests, certain traits began to emerge more clearly in the context of the CETA and TTIP negotiations, and continue to resurface in investment arbitrations, as demonstrated by the recent *Eco Oro* case. These traits primarily centred around requests for the acquisition of 'participatory rights' for those affected by investment decisions but without standing. Specifically, these requests can be summarized as (i) the possibility to participate in the decision-making process that concerns those seeking involvement (co-decision-making), and (ii) a broader expectation for access to information before its adoption. Two main implications arise from these requests. First, for accessibility to be effective, it must be accompanied by readability. Second, there is the question of which interests from 'those seeking to participate' are considered legally relevant for the matter at hand, and how the external input would ultimately be filtered by decision-makers, with the further concern of how it could influence the final outcome of a political decision.

Admittedly, participation is a hardly neutral political concept[41] and one particularly abused. In the remainder of this chapter, I argue that these requests presented the EU with an opportunity to put forward one solution for a two-fold problem. Participation is one of the twin pillars of democracy (the other being transparency) and it could work to mitigate the inherent distortions of investment decision-making and arbitration on the democratic process while improving the EU's internal problems of decision-making and preserving its authority over Member States. The EU sought to soothe popular anxieties about the EU decisional processes by enhancing public participation, the expectation being to safeguard the performance of democratic institutions in international agreement negotiations (external dimension) while keeping a united front among Member States (internal dimension), as discussed in the following section.

[40] COM(2010)343 final.
[41] Mendes, Joana (2011), *Participation in EU Rule-Making*, 19.

D. The EU rethinking of public participation in investment decision-making

The protests against the CETA negotiations (and later against TTIP) put the EU in an uncomfortable position that could not be ignored. Less than a month after the conclusion of CETA negotiations, Jean-Claude Juncker (the then newly elected president of the Commission) acknowledging the intense debates that emerged around investor–state dispute settlement reiterated that

> [A]s Commission President, I will also be very clear that *I will not sacrifice Europe's safety, health, social and data protection standards or our cultural diversity on the altar of free trade.* Notably, the safety of the food we eat and the protection of Europeans' personal data will be *non-negotiable* for me as Commission President. Nor will I accept that the jurisdiction of courts in the EU Member States is limited by special regimes for investor disputes. The rule of law and the principle of equality before the law must also apply in this context. . . . In the [TTIP] agreement that my Commission will eventually submit to this House for approval there will be nothing that limits for the parties the access to national courts or that will allow secret courts to have the final say in disputes between investors and States.[42]

While investment arbitration was recognized as problematic, the civil manifestations also revealed an acute sense of public disaffection with the European construct and profound mistrust in its decision-making process. The discontent was not due to the EU–Canada agreement itself, or at least not entirely. The discontent epitomized a deep-rooted condition of the Union itself. The pro-market view, whose significance for European prosperity is undisputed, played a central role in the EU's construction of the Single Market and the advancement of further integration. However, this development often occurred at the expense of the political process, where citizens were gradually replaced by consumers and increasingly detached from decision-making. In such a configuration, the pursuit of fundamental values remains ideally noble but is often overshadowed by market logic. This is not the place to rehearse the litany of European democratic deficits. But, if in the decision-making process the individual becomes lost, has no meaningful role in European governance, and

[42] European Commission, (22 October 2024), 'Setting Europe in Motion: President-elect Juncker's Main Messages from his Speech before the European Parliament', https://ec.europa.eu/commission/presscorner/detail/en/SPEECH_14_705. Emphasis added.

is exposed and subjected to external forces, protesting is the last resort option to raise awareness. The detachment appears even more pronounced in certain Member States, which insisted on the inclusion of an ISDS clause in the transatlantic agreement, as they had already directed the Commission through the politically 'binding' negotiating mandate conferred upon it.

The CETA negotiations confirmed a pro-market inclination that exposed the EU to the criticism of an alleged lack of legitimacy (and to some, of competence too) to negotiate in the best interests of its citizens. The negotiations exacerbated lingering doubts about the reasons for exposing citizens to the intrusion of non-domestically generated forces fronts like arbitral tribunals reviewing regulatory measures related to health, culture, and safety. In the wake of the protests, the Commission had to face an old truth: in a supranational system like the EU, public trust in decision-making cannot be assumed but has to be gained by means different from those that generally worked in the realm of states, especially in the presence of issues as sensitive as investment arbitration. To move the agreement forward, the Commission needed to restore faith in citizens increasingly alienated from global economic relations and, to a different extent, keep a united front among the Member States without relinquishing the exclusivity of its competence to sign and ratify trade agreements involving foreign investments.[43]

Admittedly, the lack of public trust in EU decision-making necessitated a comprehensive response. The Commission, and to a lesser extent, the Parliament, had to undertake a process of reconciliation with civil society to assuage its concerns. This process unfolded on two levels: at an explanatory level, by granting access to negotiating documents, ensuring that the public could track the development of the process at any given time; and at a practical level, by strengthening avenues for public participation. In the remainder of this section, I will delve into these aspects in greater detail. Taken together, these measures represented a significant shift from the Commission's initial stance on ISDS. By addressing the distortions that had arisen within investment matters, the EU aimed to reduce the democratic deficit within its own borders, although the outcomes still appear unattained.

[43] As explored in Chapter 2, in the context of the EU–Singapore FTA, *Opinion 2/15* clarified that except for non-direct investments and investor-state arbitration clauses, the ratification of a free trade agreement no longer involves Member States, and it is run at a supranational level by the Commission, the Parliament, and the Council. See also Chapter 7.

1. The right to access documents of the decision-making process

In a supranational system like the EU, access to negotiating documents is an issue that emerged long before the negotiations of CETA. As early as 1992, the deepening of European integration prompted the EU to reflect on the legitimacy and accountability of its decision-making. It was in Declaration No. 17 attached to the Final Act of the Maastricht Treaty that the question of improving public access to information officially surfaced in EU law as a mode to strengthen the democratic nature of the institutions and the public's confidence in the decision-making process.[44] Access to the document produced in the decision-making process, however, was far from being seen as a general principle of Community law, let alone one instrumental to the enhancement of democratic principles.[45] The Amsterdam Treaty pushed the boat out a little further, and although access to documents of the EU institutions did not operate unfettered,[46] Article 255 marked a radical change in the European approach to transparency. This shift moved away from a focus solely on access to documents as a matter of internal institutional organization. Instead, it broadened the scope to encompass the EU's external action, as subsequently elaborated by the Court of Justice of the European Union (CJEU).[47] This evolution signalled a commitment to greater openness in both internal and external governance, reinforcing accountability and public access to information.

The Lisbon Treaty corroborated and magnified this approach of openness as a condition to ensure good governance. In rather assertive terms, Article 15 TFEU imposed upon the EU institutions a duty to conduct their

[44] Treaty of Maastricht on European Union (1992), Declaration on the right of access to information, OJ C 191, 29 July 1992.

[45] Lenaerts, Koen (2004), 'In the Union We Trust': Trust-enhancing Principles of Community Law', Common Market Law Review, 319.

[46] Regulation 1049/2001 clarifies that the disclosure of documents may be denied if there are impacts on the protection of public interests (such as public security, military matters, international relations, and financial, monetary, or economic policy) or private interests (such as commercial interests of a natural or legal person, court proceedings and legal advice, investigations, and audits). Regulation (EC) No 1049/2001 of the European Parliament and of the Council of 30 May 2001 regarding public access to European Parliament, Council and Commission documents, OJ L 145/43, 31 May 2001, Art. 4(1)and (2). See also Case C-353/99, *Council v Hautala*, EU:C:2001:661.

[47] Cases C-39/05 P and C-52/05 P, *Sweden and Turco v Council*, EU:C:2008:374, para 59:

> As regards, first, the fear expressed by the Council that disclosure of an opinion of its legal service relating to a legislative proposal could lead to doubts as to the lawfulness of the legislative act concerned, it is precisely *openness in this regard that contributes to conferring greater legitimacy on the institutions in the eyes of European citizens and increasing their confidence in them by allowing divergences between various points of view to be openly debated.* It is in fact rather a lack of information and debate which is capable of giving rise to doubts in the minds of citizens, not only as regards the lawfulness of an isolated act, but also as regards the legitimacy of the decision-making process as a whole.

work as openly as possible, and conferred upon EU citizens the *right* of access to any documents. However, when the CETA negotiations began (May 2009), the Lisbon Treaty was not yet in force (December 2009) and the EU institutions were divided on whether to grant access to documents generated throughout international negotiations. The Parliament was persuaded by the potential benefits of openness, whereas the Commission and the Council were more prudent, and feared that the disclosure of negotiating documents would undermine the EU's negotiating position. The public discontent that burst out a few years later, however, led the Commission to reconsider its posture in the CETA and the TTIP negotiations quickly, as illustrated by its progressive detachment from the Council's fears of disrupting the negotiations and the introduction of measures that dramatically reversed its approach.

The Commission thus decided to make the treaty texts or, in the absence of an agreement, the EU negotiating proposals freely available online. Following the summer leak by a German media organization, in September 2014 the Commission published the text of CETA and has published regular updates on the status of the EU's ongoing trade-related negotiations since. More controversially, the Commission also pushed for the publication of the Council's mandates. The Council's mandates are the instructions that Member States sitting in the Council give to the Commission, which, on behalf of the Union, negotiates the EU investment agreements accordingly. Albeit not legally binding, these instructions are 'politically' recommended given that the Council has to give its approval to international agreements. This means that the Commission mostly does what the Council tells her to do, especially to prevent opposition at a later stage. Probably unknown to the protesters that blamed the Commission, the decision to keep ISDS mechanisms emanated instead from a Council 'to-do list', as clarified in the TTIP negotiating directives:

> the Agreement should aim to provide for an effective and state-of-the-art investor-to-state dispute settlement mechanism . . . . State-to-state dispute settlement should be included, but should not interfere with the *right of investors* to have recourse to the investor-to-state dispute settlement mechanisms. It should provide for investors as wide a range of arbitration fora as is currently available under the Member States' bilateral investment agreements.[48]

[48] Council of the European Union (9 October 2014), 'Directives for the negotiation on the Transatlantic Trade and Investment Partnership between the European Union and the United States of America', 11103/13 DCL 1. Emphasis added.

The Commission once again found itself at a crossroads: on one side, it had to face mounting public discontent with investment arbitration; on the other side, there were some Member States unenthusiastic about abandoning ISDS and embracing changes necessary to instil public confidence towards the EU economic governance. This division is evident in the temporal interplay between the dates of the Council's directives and their public release. For example, the CETA directives originated in April 2009 but became public in December 2015;[49] the Singapore and Vietnam negotiations were launched on the basis of the Association of South-East Asian Nations (ASEAN) negotiating directives adopted in 2007, but were partially declassified at the beginning of 2016, and entirely in 2020[50] the negotiating directives to enter in a deal with Japan started in November 2012 and were made public in September 2017,[51] following a solicitation from the Trade Commissioner. This interplay has become much narrower over time, signalling a commitment to broader accessibility—for example, it took about a month for the Council to release the negotiating mandates with Australia[52] and New Zealand.[53]

While the mode and place of governance remain intact, the huge potential of this increased accessibility to information depends on the understanding of more technical aspects disclosed by such information and ultimately on its use for all potentially involved actors to play a much more informed, critical and involved role in the EU decision-making.

Unsurprisingly, the most immediate beneficiaries of this accessibility have been NGOs, lobby groups, the media, and academics. Yet even 'ordinary citizens' often lacking resources and expertise are given a more direct channel to access the process of governance. It is not the 'Union *of* people' yet, but it is steering towards the Union involving and interacting *with* people. One problem of this configuration, however, is to place beneficiaries in a position to understand the technicalities that characterize these agreements. While access to information is vital for attributing responsibility and fostering transparency,

[49] Council of the European Union (15 December 2015), 'Recommendation from the Commission to the Council in order to authorize the Commission to open negotiations for an Economic Integration Agreement with Canada', 9036/09 EXT 2.

[50] Council Decision (EU) 2019/753 of 30 March 2020 on the conclusion of the Free Trade Agreement between the European Union and the Socialist Republic of Vietnam, OJ L 186, 12 June 2020; Council Decision (EU) 2019/1875 of 8 November 2019 on the conclusion of the Free Trade Agreement between the European Union and the Republic of Singapore, OJ L 294, 14 November 2019

[51] Council of the European Union (14 September 2017), 'Directives for the negotiation of a Free Trade Agreement with Japan', 15864/12.

[52] Council of the European Union (25 June 2018), 'Negotiating directives for a Free Trade Agreement with Australia', 7663/18 18.

[53] Council of the European Union (25 June 2018), 'Negotiating directives for a Free Trade Agreement with New Zealand', 7661/18.

the assumption that even educated and politically aware citizens inherently understand their own needs and desires is, at best, an oversimplification.[54] This assumption becomes especially tenuous in contexts where specialized knowledge is required to identify and articulate those needs accurately. Despite improved accessibility, the complexity of these agreements often created a knowledge gap, leaving citizens unable to engage meaningfully in decision-making processes or hold stakeholders accountable, further complicating efforts to ensure equitable outcomes.

2. The right to know how decisions are taken

Following the emphasis on accessibility, efforts also expanded toward improving the intelligibility of trade and investment decision-making. This materialized mostly in online resources (accessible and intelligible for a wider audience) but was accompanied by other channels. On its website, the Commission (specifically the DG Trade) explained how international agreements are negotiated so that even those who are not familiar with Article 218 TFEU or are not EU law experts may have an idea on how decisions are taken. The Commission then created a general homepage which identifies the scope and purpose of its trade policy.[55] A dedicated subpage provides an overview of up-to-date information on current trade talks, and trade agreements already in place.[56] For each agreement, the Commission published a timetable of key meetings and agendas, reports, and other documents to inform about the different steps of the negotiation and implementation processes. For each negotiation, the Commission included statistics on the FDI flows, as well as some brief sections explaining what drove the choice to enter into trade and investment negotiations with that particular country. Along with these data, the Commission also publish short documents, the 'factsheets' that seek to provide clear and simple explanations of complex issues.[57] Complementary to this, the Commission regularly holds public meetings (mostly in Brussels) with interested stakeholders. These meetings provide participants with an opportunity to intervene in the discussion and pose questions about the agreement

[54] Morlino, Leonardo (2010), 'The Two "Rules Of Law" Between Transition to and Quality Of Democracy.' In *Rule of Law and Democracy*, edited by Leonardo Morlino and Gianluigi Palombella, 58.
[55] https://ec.europa.eu/trade/.
[56] https://ec.europa.eu/trade/policy/countries-and-regions/negotiations-and-agreements/.
[57] An example of these factsheets can be found here: https://policy.trade.ec.europa.eu/eu-trade-relationships-country-and-region/countries-and-regions/canada/eu-canada-agreement/factsheets-and-guides_en.

at issue to those in charge of conducting the negotiations. While these sessions cannot, for obvious reasons, replace expertise in legal, economic, and political issues, or policy-makers' expertise in treaty-making, they nonetheless signal a genuine attempt to unpack the complexity of investment texts for non-specialists so that the latter can grasp, or at least have an idea about, the contents of the documents to which they are given access.

Accessibility and intelligibility concurred to restore faith in EU decision-making and became preconditions for a more structured articulation of the right to participate in decisional governance. The most strenuous Commission efforts in this respect materialized in the redesign of the investment arbitration mechanism in a way that conciliates the reluctance of those Member States unwilling to abandon ISDS while considering civil society's hostilities against the inclusion of an ISDS clause in the CETA agreement. The new mechanism—the Investment Court System (ICS)—served this double purpose and provided ground to enhance public participation in investment decision-making.

3. The right to participate in the decision-making process

Surprisingly, in a system as legally protective as the EU, the distortions induced by investment tribunals have gone unnoticed if not defended by some Member States for quite a long time, despite a few arbitrations already flagging up problematic issues.[58] It did not take long, however, for ISDS' most problematic traits to become apparent. Investment tribunals were vested with the power to controversially review and sanction public policy matters that would go beyond what investment operative rules consider 'normal'. This practice led to arbitral awards involving millions of euros (or dollars), which were increasingly difficult to justify to the public. Such outcomes not only infringed on domestic sensitivities but also disrupted legitimate democratic processes. Moreover, the tribunals' activity subtly or overtly raised concerns about the overall effectiveness and legitimacy of EU decision-making, as the consequences of these awards often clashed with the public interest and democratic accountability.

[58] The *Micula v Romania* case exemplifies the tension between international investment obligations and the policy adjustments required for EU membership. The case arose from Romania's decision to partially withdraw a series of investment incentives initially granted to promote economic development in disadvantaged regions. This withdrawal was a prerequisite for Romania's accession to the EU, reflecting the need to align its policies with EU state aid rules. However, the abrupt termination of these incentives was deemed a violation of the Romania–Sweden BIT, highlighting the complexities and conflicts that can emerge when balancing international investment commitments with EU integration requirements. *Micula v Romania* (Final award, 11 December 2013).

The growing malaise against this modus operandi presented the EU a chance to reshape decisional processes in ways that favour more inclusivity, and that help build 'a new stage in the process of creating an ever *closer union* among the *peoples* of Europe, in which decisions are taken as *openly* as possible and as *closely* as possible to the citizen' (Article 1 TEU). As discussed in Chapter 3, the EU progressively put together a plan to take decisions *openly*. What remains to be done is bringing the decisional process *closer* to citizens.

The Lisbon Treaty does not expressively speak of a legislative role for its citizens. It certainly enhances symbolically and tangibly the voice of citizens in a constructive dialogue with the EU institutions through broad consultations (Article 11 TEU), though without expressively clarifying what their legislative strength might be. The decisional process is brought closer to EU citizens but their legal standing remains nebulous and the ultimate say lies with the CJEU. Chances are that Article 11 TEU will be relied on by claimants in litigation and, in the end, the Court will be compelled to face interpretative issues as to the concrete implications of participatory democracy in the EU. However, such a judicial confrontation has not yet materialized, leaving the specific contours of Article 11's application in this context unexplored for now.

To mitigate discontent with investment arbitration and meet participatory demands more concretely, the Commission revamped certain instruments while also seeking to expand participation through new channels. Public consultation is the mode prescribed by Article 11(3) TEU and has occupied a special place in the EU commitment to bring decisions closer to citizens long before ISDS troubles.[59] While ex-post evaluation of existing legislation and impact assessments of new initiatives serve to achieve the EU's objective of better law-making, consultation is *the* most manifest form to achieve a democratic law-making. Consultation is a form of participation at large[60] that offers an opportunity to intervene in decisional procedure to those who are formally deprived of decisional power, and supplies useful information 'at the most appropriate time: before anything has been done'.[61] By anticipating interests that may be affected by the outcome of the procedure, the consultations have served more as a channel to build a public exchange between the EU institutions and its citizens rather than an instrument to vest civil society with legislative standing. Yet their impact cannot be dismissed altogether.

[59] COM(2002)704 final.
[60] Mendes (n 41), 28.
[61] Merrils, John (2005), *International Dispute Settlement*, 3.

Two consultations are particularly relevant for present purposes. The first one specifically responded to the strong public interest[62] over the inclusion of investor-state dispute settlement in the TTIP negotiations. The second one sought to gather public input on the EU's idea to reform the investment system through the establishment of a permanent multilateral investment court. Structurally similar, both consultations were freely accessible online in all official EU languages and lasted about 90 days.[63] The TTIP consultation was structured around 12 key investment issues, concerning both substantive investment protection and ISDS questions, along with an additional open question to submit general considerations. Each question consisted of an explanatory introduction, a background description of the approach adopted in most investment agreements, a description of the EU objectives for the TTIP, some reference texts, the specific question, and the possibility for contributors to add further comments. The Multilateral Investment Court (MIC) consultation consisted of about fifty questions, comprising both multiple-choice options and open questions. The questions were highly detailed and covered both the procedural and substantive issues that the establishment of a multilateral court might entail. Each question focused on a specific aspect of the investment regime that the multilateral court would attempt to address. All the questions began with a brief explanation of a potential problem as well as some background information on the way the EU investment treaties have already dealt with this problem, with reference being made to the CETA agreement. The questions were generally posed in the following terms: 'in your view how important is this?'; 'to what extent do you consider this important?'; 'do you believe there should be specific provisions dealing with this?' The respondent is then given the opportunity to rate his/her agreement or disagreement on a five-point Likert scale, with 0 signifying complete disagreement and 5 complete agreement. In addition, some questions allowed contributors to comment on a specific topic they deemed worthy of further consideration.[64] As of result, the TTIP consultation mobilized EU civil society to an unprecedented degree (about 150,000 responses were collected). A significant number of collective submissions (about 70,000) came from NGOs and were made up of different batches containing identical or very similar answers to all questions. Among

[62] Brown, Colin (2017), 'A Multilateral Mechanism for the Settlement of Investment Disputes: Some Preliminary Remarks', ICSID Review—Foreign Investment Law Journal, 673.

[63] The TTIP consultation was organized between 27 March and 13 July 2014; the MIC consultation began on 21 December 2016 and ended on 15 March 2017.

[64] Marceddu, Maria Laura (2018), 'Implementing Transparency and Public Participation in FTA Negotiations: Are the Times a-Changin'?', Journal of International Economic Law, 681.

other submissions, the Commission received 3,144 individual replies from EU citizens, reflecting the interests of academics, trade union organizations, governmental organizations, consumer protection groups, business associations, and others. The MIC consultation submissions were fewer in number but more heterogeneous in nature.

In principle, instruments like the Consultations could implement a more democratic decisional process, and enhance the accountability of negotiators of supranational bodies like the EU. In practice, however, public consultations say both too much and too little. They say too much because opening the floor to all interested stakeholders might give more exposure to those players holding a louder voice and able to be more vocal in advancing their own views, like NGOs. They say too little because the final act adopted does not necessarily reflect the interests voiced in the procedure. Consultations tend to assuage policy concerns, like the legitimacy of the decision-making process, rather than altering the process by, for example, endowing participants with formal decision powers and institutional structures. Admittedly, a participated configuration of the decision procedure may enhance the level of its legitimacy but does not necessarily imply that democratic involvement improves.

When the TTIP consultation results were released online at the beginning of 2015, no significant changes were introduced to the CETA text concerning ISDS, the fate of which remained uncertain also in the transatlantic agreement. The stalemate was overcome thanks to the Parliament, which was pivotal in giving meaning to public involvement in EU decision-making and in steering the EU towards a new direction. By recognizing that the EU negotiating style 'has led to deficiencies in terms of democratic control of the negotiation process',[65] the Parliament recommended that the negotiations should be concluded more inclusively 'taking into account the concerns voiced by European citizens'. The Parliament added a step forward and called for an EU decisional process that incorporates public concerns, and recommends

> to *replace* the ISDS system *with a new system* for resolving disputes between investors and states *which is subject to democratic principles and scrutiny*, where potential cases are treated in a transparent manner by publicly appointed, independent professional judges in public hearings and which includes an appellate mechanism, where consistency of judicial decisions is ensured, the jurisdiction of courts of the EU and of the Member States

[65] European Parliament, P8_TA-PROV(2015)0252 (8 July 2015), para M.

> is respected, and where private interests cannot undermine public policy objectives.[66]

The Parliament gave the final push against ISDS, and, in September 2015, the DG Trade Commissioner Malmström announced the introduction of a new investor-state mechanism that would replace ISDS in all EU forthcoming negotiations: the ICS.

Briefly, ICS is a two-stage dispute settlement procedure that comprises a first-instance tribunal and an appellate tribunal. The standing tribunal is composed of tenured judges, a third of which are nationals of the EU, another third of the counterpart in question (e.g. of Canada in CETA), and the last third of other countries. A similar structure is replicated at the appeal level.[67] In November 2015, ICS featured the Commission's negotiating proposal with the United States, and, after the legal scrubbing, replaced the ISDS mechanism in CETA as well. While the negotiations with the United States ended without a conclusion at the end of 2016,[68] CETA became the first agreement containing the new investment court system, soon followed by the agreements with Vietnam and Singapore.

The proposal for an investment court system marked a significant departure in the EU's stance on investment governance. It signalled a shift from a primarily reactive strategy—focused on addressing public dissatisfaction and demands for greater involvement in decision-making—towards a more proactive and ambitious role in reshaping the investment regime's participation:

> What has clearly come out of the debate is that the old, traditional form of dispute resolution suffers from a fundamental lack of trust. However, EU investors are the most frequent users of the existing model, which individual EU countries have developed over time. This means that Europe *must* take the responsibility to reform and modernise it. We must take the global lead on the path to reform. . . . We want to establish a new system built around the elements that make citizens trust domestic or international courts.[69]

[66] Ibid, (xv). Emphasis added.

[67] See Chapter 6.

[68] The TTIP negotiations were launched in 2013, ended without conclusion at the end of 2016, and were declared obsolete in 2019. Council of the European Union (15 April 2019), Decision authorising the opening of negotiations with the United States of America for an agreement on the elimination of tariffs for industrial goods, 6052/19.

[69] European Commission (2015), 'Commission proposes new Investment Court System for TTIP and other EU trade and investment negotiations', https://ec.europa.eu/commission/presscorner/detail/en/IP_15_5651. Emphasis added.

Although the new procedure set for solving disputes still resembles arbitration in substance, what makes ICS important from an output perspective is how it epitomizes the changes embraced by the EU vis-à-vis its decisional process. One may be tempted to see this redesign as a meaningful incorporation of publicly gathered inputs. The most enthusiastic may even be tempted to speak of an important recognition of some sort of participatory rights that bestowed upon citizens at least some legal influence over the legislative process underpinning the replacement of ISDS. A closer look, however, reveals that the direct influence of citizens on policy choices is rather limited and that instruments like public consultations are not entirely apt to fulfil this function.

A particularly noteworthy innovation in terms of participation in EU FTAs is the establishment of various instruments and bodies designed to ensure broader inclusion and consultation. These include the Regulators Forum, Domestic Advisory Groups,[70] Supporting Units and Contact Points,[71] Specialized Committees,[72] Bilateral Dialogues,[73] and Civil Society Forums.[74] Together, these elements form a comprehensive network that gathers private and public inputs, and, in the long term, has the potential to enhance the institutional framework within which each agreement operates. The concept of advisory facilities as mechanisms to address gaps in the application of the law is not entirely new; it has been proposed on various occasions, albeit not extensively.[75]

The primary contribution of these autonomous advisory bodies lies in their ability to present the perspectives of diverse stakeholders, equitably

[70] Domestic Advisory Groups consult with stakeholders, contributing to the smooth implementation of agreements.

[71] Supporting Units facilitate dialogue and governance coordination, with Contact Points overseeing tasks like supervising institutional bodies, preparing for meetings, and responding to requests. Supporting Units help coordinate governance and dialogue, while Contact Points manage tasks like overseeing institutional bodies, preparing for meetings, and responding to inquiries. Comprehensive Economic and Trade Agreement (CETA) between Canada, of the one part, and the European Union and its Member States, of the other part (entered into force provisionally on 21 September 2017), OJ L 11, 14 January 2017, Article 26.5(2).

[72] Specialized Committees focus on specific trade-related areas such as services, investment, and intellectual property, providing expertise and facilitating effective communication between the parties involved. See e.g. CETA (n 71), Article 26.

[73] The Bilateral Dialogue helps maintain regular communication between the parties, supporting the Joint Committee and preventing potential issues from escalating.

[74] The Civil Society Forum, which convenes annually, further enhances transparency and participatory governance by allowing civil society representatives to discuss the functioning of the agreement, fostering broad public involvement in the process. Agreement between the EU and Japan for an economic partnership (entered into force, 1 February 2019) OJ L 330, 27 December 2018, Article 16.15 and Article 16.16; Free Trade Agreement between the European Union and New Zealand (entered into force 1 May 2024), OJ L 2024/866, 25 March 2024, Article 24.6 and Article 24.7.

[75] Bjorklund, Andrea (2011), 'Improving the International Investment Law and Policy System: Report of the Rapporteur.' In *The Evolving International Investment Regime: Expectations, Realities, Options*, edited by Jose E Alvarez and Others.

representing various interests on matters related to the agreement. These bodies assist the parties by voicing issues and raising awareness of contentious points. Their structure forms a complex network that ensures internal checks and balances. Through the Joint Committees, the parties are continually informed about potential issues, which can then be resolved at the sub-group level and incorporated into the agreement. The mediation of participation through the Joint Committee, to which each body reports its activities, mitigates the risk of compromising the procedural integrity of agreement implementation. This mechanism prevents any single party or interest group from becoming overly dominant, as power is distributed among counterbalanced, reciprocally operating mechanisms.

However, while the institutionalization of these new entities reflects the belief that broader participation enhances the acceptability and legitimacy of outcomes, it does not equate to full participation. This multilayered governance framework confirms the presence of non-state actors even in the international investment arena, formally acknowledging their socially and environmentally responsible role. Yet despite this progressive development, their influence remains constrained. These actors are largely limited to addressing issues that arise post-agreement, with minimal capacity to shape the negotiation process or influence the terms of the agreement itself. As a result, their participation, though valuable, falls short of meaningfully altering the underlying dynamics of decision-making during the negotiation stage, ultimately limiting their potential to bring about more inclusive and impactful changes in the overall structure of international investment agreements.

E. Great idealism or greater self-interests?

Concealed under the ideal of 'an ever *closer union* among the *peoples* of Europe', the structural choices made by the EU partly soothe popular anxieties about the distortions brought about by investment decision-making processes that threaten the performance of democratic institutions—that is, the inclusion of ISDS clauses in investment agreements.

A closer look reveals that the EU was also driven by a good measure of self-interest. Despite the enthusiasm for this 'let's fix it' programme and the pedagogical mission it felt invested in, the Commission's approach often appeared more focused on supporting or selling a predetermined outcome, rather than genuinely building a Union *of* people. While it is undeniable that the Commission corrected its trajectory because of the resistance of civil society campaigns, and that the Commission's approach set 'a virtually unprecedented departure from the treaty-making practice of the EU Member States',[76] the reasons underpinning this retuning appear to be less idealistic than one might wish.

Even in the domain of foreign investment, the EU's decision-making process does not fully align with the democratic values that the Union espouses and aims to promote (as per Article 3(5) TEU). While the EU's contributions are original and legally robust concerning the right to access documents, its approach to the issue of participation seems less compelling. Participation is often perceived as a complementary source of democracy as it brings citizens closer to decision-making, but it is not always clear how close citizens should be brought and therefore, to what extent participation could factor in the democratic nature of decision-making. Although the use of participatory rights has become more explicit within the EU investment policy, this has only marginally changed the legal influence of those affected by investment decision-making distortions.

Even with regard to the experiences of public consultations, it remains unclear what inputs were truly considered or to what extent, for instance, ICS was shaped by the feedback gathered from these consultations. There is a lingering question as to whether ICS was primarily introduced to satisfy the Council, rather than addressing the concerns of civil society as a whole. Even trying to be optimistic, the latter framing seems more accurate, particularly given that, despite some refinements, ICS closely resembles traditional investment arbitration, with foreign investors retaining legal standing before international tribunals, while third parties have none. From this standpoint, the TTIP consultation was a red herring, meant to draw attention to the expansion of public participation, when in fact it could have served to support an outcome more acceptable to the negotiating governments.[77] Make no mistake: on the surface, Member States coalesce on the idea that public participation enhances the legitimacy of the decision-making process. In practice, however, enhancing integration through public deliberation regarding public matters in the Union sphere may not be suitable for each Member State, especially if it implies conceding more (exclusive) power to the Commission or gets in the way of exposing contradictions and compromises that have traditionally been written under hundreds of bilateral investment agreements. Adopting a maximalist

[76] Calamita, Jansen (2014), 'Dispute Settlement Transparency in Europe's Evolving Investment Treaty Policy', The Journal of World Investment & Trade, 645.

[77] Ross, Alison (2016), 'Schwebel Criticises EU Act of "Appeasement"', Global Arbitration Review.

approach towards greater participation may be welcomed in countries like Norway[78] or the Netherlands, which have held public consultations on their investment model agreements, but not in every other Member State.

From a less apocalyptic perspective, ICS could be also treated as evidence that the public consultations exercised effect on political changes in the discussion of investor–state dispute settlement, and have ultimately impeded the inclusion of investment arbitration as we have known it. The main shortcoming of this approach lies in the ambiguity underpinning the legal status of initiatives like public participation, as it remains unclear whether participatory rights could be enforceable against the Commission. As early as 2002, the Commission, backed by the Court,[79] clarified that there was no room for a legal configuration of these public participation mechanisms, which remain non-legally binding. The consultations belong to the Commission's initiative (before the adoption of a proposal) and provide guidance and assistance to Commission officials in charge of running the consultation processes but do not 'command and control' them. Nor could expose the Commission to be challenged in Court on the grounds of alleged lack of consultation of interested parties.[80] Consultations, however, form part of the formalized and compulsory decision-making process envisaged in the Lisbon Treaty. There might be a case where claimants rely on Article 11 TEU, and the Court will be compelled to face the interpretative issues as to the concrete implications drawn from these principles. If opting for a narrow approach, the Court would undermine a provision that was meant to convey a positive message about the EU's inclusiveness and willingness to publicly engage and would render decision-making less accessible to those affected.

As things stand in the investment regime, demands for participatory rights are growing considerably. Public opposition is continuing to question investors' conducts and has begun to inquire about States' conducts as well.[81] In *Rockhopper v Italy*, for example, civil society protests played a pivotal role in preventing the Italian government from passing legislation that would have exempted the investor from a ban on oil and gas exploration within 12 miles

[78] Royal Norwegian Ministry of Trade, Industry and Fisheries, 'Model Investment Agreement—Public Consultations', 15/1625(2015). https://www.regjeringen.no/contentassets/e47326b61f424d4c9c3d470896492623/consultation-letter.pdf.

[79] The Court has been unwilling to accept that participation in the making of legislative measure accords the applicant any enhanced prospects of being given standing to challenge it. Case C-321/95 P, *Stichting Greenpeace Council (Greenpeace International) and Others v Commission of the European Communities*, ECLI:EU:C:1998:153.

[80] COM (n 59).

[81] Supreme Court of Spain, *Greenpeace v Spain* (20 June 2023), https://climatecasechart.com/wp-content/uploads/non-us-case-documents/2023/20230620_12221_judgment.pdf.

of the Italian coastline. These protests ultimately led the Italian Parliament to reinstate the previously revoked ban. As a result, the investor filed a claim for compensation, alleging violations of the protections granted under the Energy Charter Treaty, arguing that it would have obtained a production concession before the ban's introduction. The tribunal ultimately awarded the investor €190 million in compensation.[82] Despite clear differences in substance and language, it seems unlikely that if similar disputes are litigated before an ICS tribunal the outcome would be radically different. *Amicus curiae* submissions and consultations remain laudable attempts at rendering the different stages of the decision-making process more open, but their impact remains circumstantial and problematic to assess.

One factor that could alter this perspective would be to consider participation as a right. Participatory rights are already recognized in international instruments. Principle 10 of the Rio Declaration, for example, acknowledges that participation 'of all concerned citizens' is fundamental to best handling environmental issues and, when supported by good transparency practices, contributes to raising consciousness on policy-making. Participation is recognized also at a national level. A case in point is the Constitutional Court of Colombia that struck down the government's first delimitation of the páramo precisely because of the lack of participation of the communities in and around the páramo. The EU treaties recognize participation in some forms but do not stretch this recognition to the rights threshold. The EU approach responds more to what Habermas describes as 'cosmopolitan consciousness', which is congenial to countervail global institutions but not necessarily expand participation rights. The EU cosmopolitan consciousness has the potential to counterbalance the dynamics of the investment regime and the interests of its Member States. This is rooted in the notion of a global law-making authority like the EU (though Habermas originally referred to the United States), capable of fostering consensus on critical public policy issues of global significance. For instance, investor–state dispute settlement remains a highly contentious mechanism and its inclusion in future agreements is increasingly being called into question globally. Consensus, however, does not equate to rights. Even participation through *amici curiae*, which is vested with a right status, is ultimately deferred to the discretion of a tribunal that might well ignore the reasoning of these submissions, despite allowing them.

From a purely legal standpoint, the right to participation has yet to achieve the status of a principle in international relations, and the EU has rectified this

[82] *Rockhopper v Italy* (Final award, 23 August 2022).

framing only in part within the investment regime. Several factors concur to explain the EU's position. First, participation might give more exposure to certain actors than to others. NGOs are best placed to advance their message because they possess resources that less organized groups lack but are not world democratizers. A related risk concerns the Member States tempted towards popular law-making behind what is prescribed by the Treaties. Another plausible explanation lies in the fact that a too-expanded right to participate could overshadow the potential 'European added value' of any proposed Union action, as well as the 'cost of non-Europe' in the absence of action at the Union level.[83] From this perspective, participation might generate standards that would conflict with the values pursued by the Union—for example, liberalization versus the right to live in a healthy environment. This, in turn, would contradict and threaten the EU's aspiration of a supranational law authority that is superior and not reversible by any nation's legislature.[84] This inward-looking approach does not inherently contradict the aim of addressing the weakening of political processes perpetuated by investment rules; however, it remains influenced by strategic considerations, which may temper its corrective potential. The EU remains particularly interested in promoting democracy through public participation, especially when it aligns with its agenda-setting objectives, but less so when it contradicts its broader strategies.

Seen through these lenses, the EU's changes to investment agreements appear bold compared to the traditional state-led negotiation models. However, the expanded space for public participation is unlikely to significantly alter investment decision-making beyond what aligns with the EU's strategic goals. While participation makes strides on the political front, its impact on the legal framework remains limited. This may reflect the EU's broader tendency to separate politics from the law—a characteristic of its integration story, which often emphasizes governance 'through law'.

Despite its idealistic connotation, democracy for the EU was designed in the wake of the horrors of nationalism and democracy brought about by the Second World War. As such, it somehow operates by way of checking on power exercises through international experts (bureaucrats, technocrats, diplomates, judges) and remains at a remove from popular politics and will.[85] In this setting, there is room for transparency—as instrumental to check and

[83] Interinstitutional Agreement between the European Parliament, the Council of the European Union and the European Commission on Better Law-Making, OJ L 123, 12 May 2016, para 5.

[84] Rubenfeld, Jed (2004), 'Unilateralism and Constitutionalism', New York University Law Review, 2011.

[85] Ibid, 2020.

restraint power—but the space for public participation is much more limited and subjected to the EU's global making authority. Times have changed and the digital revolution has exponentially increased expectations of transparency and public participation, with civil society becoming particularly vocal in vindicating a role in world policies. Yet, and perhaps unsurprisingly, integration rather than participation remains the EU's preferred means to increase economic efficiency and bring the hyperpower to heel. This is reproduced in the investment decisional process and explains why incidental enablers and enforcers can only play within the boundaries assigned to them without altering the decision-making process significantly.

PART II

A PROMISE OF RULE OF LAW?

Part II of this book is articulated in Chapters 5 and 6, each of which addresses a pivotal aspect of the rule of law's development within the EU's investment law and policy framework. Intuitively, the rule of law constitutes 'the only reliable bulwark against the arbitrary exercise of power and means, in essence, that any legal dispute must be resolved in accordance with– and only in accordance with—the applicable norms provided for by law'.[1] However, providing a precise definition proves challenging because the concept of the 'rule of law' remains inherently nebulous. It can, at best, be tentatively described as a shared framework of assumptions and inclinations regarding the role of law in society, the hierarchy and interaction of legal sources, and the actual authority wielded by various actors and institutions. Another plausible approach is to consider the rule of law as a credible limitation on arbitrariness.[2] This Part, borrowing from Raz's observations, advocates for a conception that has substantive rather than moral content, and maintains that rule of law acts as a protection against a society of chaos and abuse.

Despite being enshrined as one of the founding principles of the EU (Article 6(1) of the Treaty on European Union (TEU)), the rule of law has remained somewhat amorphous and has taken time to acquire some substance in the context of international affairs, including the regime of international investments. Notwithstanding the relatively superficial and fluctuating nature of definitions and understandings, the EU institutions have tended to promote a comprehensive approach that includes substantive components (e.g. non-discrimination and equality before the law, respect of human rights) along with formal procedural elements (e.g. legal certainty, independence and impartiality of the judiciary, prohibition of arbitrariness). The latter is particularly

[1] Lanaert, Koen (2019), 'Upholding the Rule of Law through Judicial Dialogue', Yearbook of European Law.

[2] Morlino, Leonardo (2010), 'The Two "Rules of Law" Between Transition to and Quality of Democracy' in *Rule of Law and Democracy*, edited by Leonardo Morlino and Gianluigi Palombella, 40.

significant in the EU's external promotion and dissemination of 'its' interpretation of the rule of law, as well as in the gradual formation of an international consensus on investment law.

The procedural elements—such as legal certainty and judicial independence—stand out as particularly fitting examples of how EU values have sought to "*Europeanize*" the investment regime, achieving greater progress in these areas compared to others, such as human rights considerations. Hence, the analysis revolves around two complementary but distinct levels of inquiry. At a micro level, Chapter 5 concentrates on the 'rule of law' principles imposed on host states, that is, how host states behave according to certain rule of law parameters and what role the EU played in shaping those parameters, for example legal certainty obligations imposed on host states and the resulting legitimate expectations entertained in investors. At a macrolevel, Chapter 6 expands to judicialization, a legalizing approach particularly dear to the EU for imparting the direction according to which the investment regime *should* operate.

* * *

The rule of law has been heralded as one of the foundations of EU law to the extent that its institutions and bodies are submitted to legal norms, that judicial review by the EU Court ensures respect for these norms,[3] and that respect for the rule of law is essential for the respect of all other values.[4] The concept of rule of law forms one of the primary values on which the EU is founded, as is clear from Articles 2 and 21 TEU, the preambles of the EU Treaty and the Charter, and the preamble of the Convention for the Protection of Human Rights and Fundamental Freedoms. The rule of law is considered a foundational principle[5] inspired by the practice of the Member States,[6] and one that ensures that the evolution in the powers of the Community institutions does not undermine the rule of law and the institutional balance.[7]

The rule of law is a foundational value that guides also the EU's international action. However, despite the rule of law constituting an accession benchmark, a condition for the enjoyment of all Treaties' rights, and a guide to the EU's external action, it is not altogether clear what the EU is seeking to promote

[3] Case 294/83, *Les Verts v Parliament and Council*, EU:C:1986:166.
[4] Case C-156/21, *Hungary v Parliament and Council*, EU:C:2022:97.
[5] Case 92/78, *Simmenthal v Commission*, EU:C:1979:53, para 785.
[6] Case 16/65, *Bosch v Van Rijn*, EU:C:1962:3, para 61.
[7] Case C-50/00 P, *UPA v Council*, EU:C:2002:197.

exactly.[8] It appears that the rule of law is more easily invoked than understood and that 'everyone is in for it, but have contrasting convictions about what it is',[9] as reflected in the rather disorganized institutional approaches and initiatives advanced over the years—for example the Commission's Justice Scoreboard (2013) followed by the 2014 Framework;[10] the Council's Annual Rule of Law Dialogue (2014); infringement proceedings (Article 258 TFEU); and the Rule of Law Cycle (2019), a joint idea supported by the Parliament and implemented by the Commission. Central to these initiatives is Article 7 TEU, which establishes a procedure to address breaches that undermine the values enshrined in Article 2 TEU. The procedure is subject to the Council's unanimity, the absence of which renders its effectiveness as a mechanism for scrutinizing the activities of Member States questionable, if not unsatisfactory.[11] The effects deriving from the absence of a conceptually sound framework are noticeable in the lack of full adherence to the EU values after accession, as epitomized evidently, for example, by the cases concerning Hungary's restrictions of rights of opposition and the media, and Poland's judicial reform. From this standpoint, the rule of law is likely to suffer the same biases and inconsistent fate that beset the principle of democracy, thus inhibiting the EU's ability to draw other countries into its orbit of values.

From a less orthodox perspective, the lack of definitions and precise obligations around the concept of rule of law in the Treaties left a margin of discretion for its pursuit. In the EU's frequent practice, the concept of the rule of law evolved into a series of manifestations articulated by the Court, which gradually solidified into established principles. When applied to foreign policy, these principles became a cornerstone of European integration.[12] Despite the lack of a definition, the Court exercised a constitutional gap-filling role thanks to which the European Community (EC) was recognized as a 'Community based on the rule of law', and that paved the way for the emergence of further

[8] Pech, Laurent (2016), 'The EU as a Global Rule of Law Promoter: The Consistency and Effectiveness Challenges', Asia Europe Journal, 7.

[9] Bingham, Thomas (2011), *The Rule of Law*.

[10] An example of the chaotic approach is the challenge raised by the Council, which argued a lack of competence in the framework's creation. Specifically, the Council contended that neither the Treaties provided a legal basis nor did the Commission possess the authority to establish new supervision mechanisms related to the respect for the rule of law. The conflict was ultimately resolved through clarification that triggering the preventive mechanism—and determining a clear risk of a serious breach—required implied powers, which the Council could either exercise directly or invoke with the assistance of the Commission. Craig, Paul and De Búrca, Gráinne (2020), *EU Law: Text, Cases, and Materials*, 51.

[11] Williams, Andrew T (2009), 'Taking Values Seriously: Towards a Philosophy of EU Law', Oxford Journal of Legal Studies, 568–9.

[12] De Baere, Geert (2012), 'European Integration and the Rule of Law in Foreign Policy' In *Philosophical Foundations of European Union Law*, edited by Julie Dickson and Pavlos Eleftheriadis, 354.

benchmarks that would have gradually made sense of what the EU sought to promote when invoking the rule of law. The first time the concept was invoked by the Court was in *Les Verts*: the rule of law provided foundations for the EU (then Community), and posited that neither the Member States nor the EU institutions could be above the law, or could 'avoid a review of the question of whether the measures adopted by them conform with the basic constitutional charter, the treaty'—the judicial review process.[13] Before *Les Verts* the Court's jurisdiction was limited to determine an action for annulment to actions brought against a measure adopted by the Council and the Commission. The French association (*Parti écologiste Les Verts*) argued that this constituted a denial of justice. However, the Court interpreted the provision (formerly Article 173 EEC) as not explicitly excluding actions brought against the Parliament, even when such actions had legal effects on third parties.[14] It is thanks to this 'generous and dynamic interpretation of the Treaty'[15] that since *Les Verts*, it has become unquestionable that neither the EU institutions nor the Member States are above the law.

After *Les Verts*, the Court gradually put more flesh on the bones and through its caselaw elucidated what could have fallen within (or outside) the concept of rule of law. The right to be heard,[16] legal certainty,[17] legitimate expectations,[18] non-discrimination, and proportionality[19] were among the earliest manifestations detected and acknowledged by the Court in the time span of the Maastricht and Amsterdam Treaties. In line with the spirit of the time, after the fall of the Berlin Wall references to the rule of law became conspicuous, albeit largely symbolic at first. It is in the Amsterdam Treaty that the rule of law gained formal enshrinement in EU primary law as one of the EU's foundational principles, common to all Member States. In the following years (Nice Treaty), while consolidating the original manifestations of the rule of law, more emphasis was placed on the need to ensure access to justice and conformity of institutional measures with the Treaty.

Meanwhile, with the EU having established a comprehensive system of legal remedies and procedures, the Court emphasized its role as both guardian and

[13] *Les Verts* (n 3).

[14] Pech, Laurent (2010), 'A Union Founded on the Rule of Law: Meaning and Reality of the Rule of Law as a Constitutional Principle of EU Law', European Constitutional Law Review, 312.

[15] *UPA v Council* (n 7), para 71.

[16] Case 52/69, *Geigy v Commission*, EU:C:1972:73, para 806.

[17] Joined Cases 178, 179, 180/73, *Belgium and Luxembourg v Mertens*, EU:C:1974:36; Case 88–76, *Exportation des sucres*, EU:C:1977:61, para 719.

[18] Case 74/74, *CNTA v Commission*, EU:C:1975:59, 16; Case 152/88, *Sofrimport v Commission*, EU:C:1990:259, para 26; Case T-489/93, *Unifruit Hellas v Commission*, EU:T:1994:297, para 39.

[19] Case 29-69 *Stauder v City of Ulm* EU:C:1969:57; Case 118/75, *Watson and Belman*, EU:C:1976:79, 1209.

reviewer of the legality of measures adopted by the institutions, within the bounds of their discretion.[20] In the Community, the rule of law has thus begun to be articulated primarily along two dimensions: the first is legislative, which ensures that the measures of the institutions and Member States are in compliance with the Treaty. The second one is judicial and provides judicial protection against unlawful Community measures.[21] As Advocate General Maduro explains, the Court aimed to ensure structural congruity by giving form to a systemic judicial review of the lawfulness of the single measures (judicial dimension) but also of the system as a whole (legislative dimension). From this configuration, any transfer of state powers had to go hand in hand with a conferral of powers of review and rights of action without creating powers beyond the reach of the law and the courts.[22] A corollary implication that followed from this duality was the prohibition of arbitrariness of the executive power. The point is reiterated by the Court that reaffirmed the limits that the law imposes on certain political decisions. Regardless of what may be politically expedient at a particular moment,[23] the interference of executive authorities with individuals' rights is not permissible unless there are other compelling interests which are subject to judicial control anyway.

Since rights are effective only if they are justiciable, electing to place such a reliance on the law and its legal institution sounds like a prudentially wise choice for the achievement of the political and economic Community project. These choices made by the Court rendered virtues associated with the rule of law, the separation of powers, and the right to judicial review inherently cardinal in the EU legal system. Some gaps left in the jurisdiction, however, soon indicated that rule of law claims are highly contestable and that the rule of law was initially conceived as a process of ordering by the Court rather than as the expression of a value.[24]

This is ultimately revised and rectified by the Lisbon Treaty, which no longer describes the Union as being founded on certain principles but rather as being founded on certain key values. The shift from principles to values was unexpected, nonetheless congenial to reflect the 'untouchable core of the EU legal order and the core constitutional identity of the EU as a legal-political

[20] Case T 198/95, *Comafrica and Dole Fresh Fruit Europe v Commission*, EU:T:2001:184, paras 123, 134; Case T 373/100, *Philip Morris International and Others v Commission*, EU:T:2003:6, para 121; Case C-249/02, *Portugal v Commission*, EU:C:2004:483, para 40.

[21] Case C-273/04, *Poland v Council*, EU:C:2007:361, para 29.

[22] Ibid, para 32.

[23] Case C-402/05 P, *Kadi v Council*, EU:C:2008:11, para 45.

[24] Williams (n 11).

system'.[25] Albeit more refined, the list of the rule of law components articulated by the Court following the entry into force of the Lisbon Treaty remains not exhaustive.[26] It aligns with principles later formalized in the checklist adopted by the Venice Commission (2016), and posits that

> the concept of rule of law requires a system of certain and foreseeable law, where everyone has to be treated with dignity, equality, and rationality, and in accordance with the laws and to have the opportunity to challenge decisions before independent and impartial courts through fair procedures.[27]

This articulation was further clarified by the Commission in 2019:

> What is the rule of law?
>
> The rule of law is enshrined in Article 2 of the Treaty on European Union as one of the founding values of the Union. Under the rule of law, all public powers always act within the constraints set out by law, in accordance with the values of democracy and fundamental rights, and under the control of independent and impartial courts. The rule of law includes, among others, principles such as legality, implying a transparent, accountable, democratic and pluralistic process for enacting laws; legal certainty; prohibiting the arbitrary exercise of executive power; effective judicial protection by independent and impartial courts, effective judicial review including respect for fundamental rights; separation of powers; and equality before the law. [28]

The rule of law thus morphed into the well-known principles of legality (*a system of law, within the constraints set out by law*), legal certainty (*certain and foreseeable law, implying a transparent, accountable, democratic, and pluralistic process*), prohibition of arbitrariness of the executive power (*treated with rationality, prohibiting the arbitrary exercise of executive power*); effective judicial protection (*everyone has the opportunity to challenge decisions, under the control of independent and impartial courts*),[29] access to independent and impartial courts, separation of powers, and equality before the law.[30] All these constraints set out by the law for the exercise of public powers are effectively

[25] Pech, 'A Union Founded on the Rule of Law' (n 14), 316.

[26] Case T-245/15, *Klymenko v Council*, EU:T:2017:792, para 74.

[27] *Hungary v Parliament and Council* (n 4), para 19.

[28] COM(2019)163 final, para I.

[29] Case C-64/16 *Juizes Portugueses v Tribunal de Contas*, EU:C:2018:117, para 31; Joined Cases C-478/11 P to C-482/11 P *Gbagbo and others v Council*, EU:C:2012:831, para 52.

[30] *Hungary v Parliament and Council* (n 4) para 231; Craig and de Búrca (n 10).

summed up in the expression 'established by law', where the organization of the judicial system does not depend on the discretion of the executive but is regulated by the law emanating from the legislative.[31] The rule of law operates by insisting on a particular mode of exercising power, whose abuses are corrected by the law.[32]

In the Lisbon era, there is a strong emphasis on governance through law, particularly on the necessity of ensuring the independence and impartiality of the judiciary. This should not come as a surprise given the EU's external mission to promote and advance the rule of law in the world, but also in light of safeguarding the EU's autonomy. In a Community founded on the rule of law, the Court's review of legality serves as a constitutional safeguard for the autonomy of the EU legal order. This autonomy cannot be compromised or overridden by constraints imposed by an international agreement, even one stemming from a UN Security Council resolution, as highlighted in *Kadi*.[33]

The point is reiterated in Opinion 1/17: 'international agreements entered into by the Union must be entirely compatible with the Treaties and with the constitutional principles stemming therefrom'.[34] This does not impede a co-existence of some sort with international obligations insofar as they are in conformity with the constitutional safeguards and preserve the EU's order autonomy. What is particularly interesting in the realm of the investment regime is the emergence of another facet of the EU rule of law interactions with international law: the conditions of conformity are not justified as is usually the case in terms of the Court's own institutional interests in the autonomy of EU law but in terms of the EU's political institutions' accountability to the democratic process.[35] This accountability ensures that arbitral tribunals cannot challenge the level of public interest protection established by the Union through a democratic process. This is a step forward if compared to *Kadi*, but a leap in the dark if compared to Opinion 2/13 (concerning the EU access to the European Convention on Human Rights), which strenuously insisted on preserving the EU's autonomy against any interferences from any judicial body. In Opinion 1/17, it appears that the rule of law's condition of compatibility with EU

[31] Case C-508/19 *Prokurator*, EU:C:2021:290, para 50; Case C-132/20, *Getin Noble Bank*, EU:C:2021:557, para 71.

[32] De Baere (n 12) 357–8.

[33] The review of the lawfulness of an international obligation does not concern the agreement as such but its application to EU law, which has to conform with the Treaties. Case C-402/05, *Kadi*, EU:C:2008:461, paras 281–288, 316.

[34] Opinion 1/17, EU:C:2019:341, para 165.

[35] Peers, Steve (2019), 'We *aren't* the World': The CJEU Reconciles EU law with International (Investment) Law'; Opinion 1/17 (n 34), paras 151, 160.

treaties is a given (as per *Kadi*), and what needs to be preserved is the level of protection of public interest established by the EU measures, regardless of the adjudicating authority. It looks as if preserving the autonomy of the EU legal order has to pass through the protection of public interests, the degree of which is determined by the EU anyway. The autonomy of the Union's legal order is safeguarded when measures deemed necessary by the EU to protect public interests align with EU law and are not subject to review by any arbitral tribunal.[36]

What could look suspicious to the purists of the autonomy principle could be seen as an indication of the EU's response to the questions raised within the investment regime, and more broadly of the EU's mission to diffuse its values abroad. One may even be tempted to read into this an attempt at extraterritoriality towards judicial bodies external to the EU, yet bound to follow and protect its measures. Unlike what happened with democracy, the demands for the rule of law manifested more vividly in the investment regime and provided a great opportunity for the EU to advance the Union's comprehensive understanding of the rule of law as a value worth pursuing without divesting the EU's authority. On its part, the investment regime presented a particularly attractive chance for the EU to reshape some faulty parameters, most of which pertain to the conduct of states hosting foreign investments (Chapter 5), as well as to impart a systemic orientation modelled upon effective judicial protection and more in line with its autonomy (Chapter 6).

The EU's entry into the investment regime coincides with a moment of particular disquiet for the latter marked by the emergence of an increasing number of issues, somewhat related to one another. A key preliminary issue concerned the balancing of private and public interests.[37] The expansion of the rights granted in international investment agreements (IIAs) to private persons (investors) vis-à-vis the regulatory capacity of governments has raised questions about how to define the boundaries of protection afforded to private parties. It also highlights the conditions under which governments can legitimately regulate without incurring liability for breaching the substantial protections provided to investors.

One might expect (especially EU law scholars) that the problem of balancing competing interests can be solved through interpretation whenever changes in

[36] Ibid.

[37] More generally, some scholars have argued that 'international adjudication demands democratic legitimacy': von Bogdandy, Armin and Venzke, Ingo (2014), 'In Whose Name? An Investigation of International Courts' Public Authority and Its Democratic Justification', European Journal of International Law.

law or alterations of policies give rise to legitimate doubts concerning their implications. Despite the guidance from the Vienna Convention on the Law of Treaties, interpreting investment treaties has proven to be particularly complicated because of the legal uncertainty that features these agreements from the outset. IIAs, and bilateral investment treaties (BITs) in particular, do not clearly define what the obligations imposed upon host states are. They simply indicate the (investors' protection) principles to be taken into account, which, for their part, have consisted of rather vaguely worded provisions for a long time. A good example of this vagueness is the fair and equitable treatment obligation accorded to foreign investors by host states and that usually reads as follows: 'each Party shall accord to covered investments fair and equitable treatment and full protection and security'. Although the sense of terms like 'fair' and 'equitable' is rather intuitive, their open-textured nature comprises subtle nuances in meaning that each interpreter might more or less lean on, and their meaning might vary depending on the circumstances of a given case.

The open-textured nature of key terms as those characterizing host states obligations vis-à-vis investors has given the adjudicator (i.e. the arbitral tribunal) the power to choose among several plausible alternatives, each of which is lawful per se. It has thus become increasingly common for tribunals to assign different meanings to the same terms or clauses, often delivering interpretations that are unexpected, at least in the eyes of the disputing parties. This has led to broadly inconsistent and sometimes conflicting outcomes. Consequently, the system—particularly arbitrators—has faced significant criticism for impartiality, as their appointment often depends on prospective claimants.[38] While it would be particularly hazardous to demonstrate that arbitrators tend to favour investors or interfere with the legislative powers of the contracting parties, the data provided by the International Centre for Settlement of Investment Disputes (ICSID) (for 2022) nonetheless appear to corroborate this suspicion: 56 per cent of awards upheld the investors' claims in part or in full.[39] However, the United Nations Conference on Trade and Development (UNCTAD) statistics (for 2020) reduce the distrust to about 29 per cent of concluded cases decided in favour of the investor, and about 37 per cent decided in favour of the state.[40] One inference that might not readily transpire from these numbers is the legitimacy of the reasons behind states' actions

[38] Van Harten, Gus (2013), *Sovereign Choices and Sovereign Constraints*, 163.

[39] ICSID Releases 2022 Caseload Statistics (2023), available at: https://icsid.worldbank.org/news-and-events/communiques/icsid-releases-2022-caseload-statistics.

[40] UNCTAD Investor–State Dispute Settlement Cases: Facts And Figures 2020 (2021), available at https://unctad.org/system/files/official-document/diaepcbinf2021d7_en.pdf

that amounted to violations of investment law—for example the reasons underpinning a licence's revocation or a contract's non-renewal. This aspect is particularly problematic to justify to the public, especially when significant monetary compensation is due for restoration of the harm caused by the violation in question.[41]

Balancing investment protection with states' regulatory autonomy remains a challenging task, raising questions about the legitimacy of the adjudication process that reviews regulatory actions—a challenge compounded by the birth deficit of vaguely drafted treaty provisions, which has created several dilemmas for the investment regime. Since investment law is not sufficiently precise to allow for reasonable foresight of the consequences of actions, interpretations of the open-textured provisions in investment agreements have led to uncertain outcomes. The uncertainty of the consequences a given action entails, in turn, has resulted in further implications on both the public and private sides. On the private (investor) side, the lack of legal certainty has impeded the fulfilment of expectations legitimately conferred by investment treaties' rights. On the public (state) side, the lack of legal certainty risks have disturbed the government's power to alter the policy for the future up to a point where even the prospect itself of being hit with investment claims had the effect of deterring governments from changing their domestic regulatory framework—the so-called regulatory chill effect.

From this perspective, it is hard to imagine any attempt to balance private and public interests without legal certainty. It is legal certainty that ensures that laws are clear, precise, and predictable as regards their effects and the legitimate expectations they generate. It is the certainty of the laws that by conferring rights and imposing obligations creates boundaries between competing interests and ensures the fulfilment of legitimate expectations and regulatory stability. The EU is a system construed on the premise that law enhances certainty, predictability, and security, thereby benefits market economies by protecting contracts and property.[42] The problem in the investment regime, however, is that legal certainty alone might not be sufficient to ensure balance because the purpose of investment agreements fluctuates between the attraction of foreign capital and contribution to the development of the host state. As long as the balancing line between these two options remains a moving target in investment law, the dilemma of balancing is unlikely to be solved.

[41] Blackaby, Nigel (2004), 'Public Interest and Investment Treaty Arbitration', Transnational Dispute Management.

[42] De Baere (n 12), 364–5.

The recent global steer in favour of greater state regulatory autonomy in the investment regime seems to point towards a systemic reconfiguration where public interests must be safeguarded. Treaty language clarifications, the inclusion of stand-alone 'right to regulate' provisions, and exceptions (both of a general and a public security nature) all push in that direction and are likely to improve predictability. Expanding the state's regulatory autonomy reach, however, does not necessarily translate into balancing or certainty. Whether, and under which conditions, investors' rights cannot override public interests remains undefined and the investment-protection obligations a state voluntarily undertook when entering into an international investment agreement must be honoured.[43] The preservation of public interests through language clarifications is likely to generate more certain, or at least reasonable, expectations of certain outcomes. Yet it might not yield satisfactory results in terms of systemic balance, given that investment agreements fetter the state's exercise of its regulatory powers, ultimately leaving the contentious matter to the circumstantial scrutiny of international dispute settlement mechanisms.

It is against this conundrum that the EU might have had a solution to advance. In the EU legal system, legal certainty and balance stand together due to the existence of an 'overriding public interest' concept and to prominence of the judiciary. Legal certainty, as discussed above, is one of the earliest manifestations of the rule of law and constitutes one of the general principles recognized by EU law. In view of ensuring no distortions of market competition, legal certainty rests on the subcomponent of legitimate expectations. Legal certainty calls for clarity and accuracy in framing the laws and possesses a distinctively objective nature, while legitimate expectations are the result of precise and specific assurances that create foreseeable rights and refer to specific situations lawfully created.[44] Legitimate expectations relate primarily to changes in legal situations and are based on a balance between individual interests and general public interests.[45] Taken together, legal certainty and legitimate expectations are parts of the principle of legality and the Union's legal order. They ensure an equilibrium between the interests founded on legitimate expectations and the principle that the authorities act in accordance with the law.[46] This balancing exercise is especially pertinent in investment matters, where legitimate

[43] *Occidental v Ecuador* (Award, 5 October 2012), paras 529–530.

[44] Case C-346/03 and C-529/03, *Atzeni and others v Regione Autonoma della Sardegna*, EU:C:2005:256, para 142.

[45] Case C-184/16, *Petrea v Ypourgou Esoterikon kai Dioikitikis Anasygrotisis*, ECLI:EU:C:2017:324, para 65.

[46] Case T-51/89 *Tetra Pak v Commission*, EU:T:1990:15, paras 83–84; Case C-63/93 *Duff and others v Minister for Agriculture and Food and Attorney General*, EU:C:1995:170, paras 23–25.

expectations may be overridden by an overriding public interest. Indeed, under EU law, the presence of such an overriding public interest can justify infringing a right and dismissing an expectation. As per the Court's case law, examples of overriding reasons relating to the public interest are public health, social services, public education, safety, the environment, public morals, consumer protection, privacy and data protection, the promotion and protection of cultural diversity, animal health, and the protection of the urban environment.

The presence of an overriding public interest, however, does not operate unfettered as is reasonable to expect in a common market organization. Alterations at the policy level have to be expected, especially where there is no longer economic justification for a measure, but they should be accompanied by a reasonable warning and appropriate transitional measures so that those affected get acquired with them.[47] The point is well summed up in the *Sofrimport* case:

> The effect of that provision [Article 3(3) Regulation 2707/72] is to enable an importer whose goods are in transit to rely on a legitimate expectation that in the absence of an overriding public interest no suspensory measures will be applied against him.[48] [T]he provision in question is intended essentially to protect the legitimate expectations of traders. . . . However, that guarantee . . . protects traders *only if*, before shipping the goods, they have not been given a sufficiently clear indication that any suspension measures might affect goods in transit as well. Where such a warning has been given to traders, they are aware of the fact that goods which have been shipped, without the prior issue of a licence, are not immune from restrictive measures; there is no reason therefore to protect their legitimate expectations.[49]

However sound on paper, the matter is complex, even under EU law. It is unclear, for example, how to determine what period of time to be accorded for the applicant to adjust to the altered measure and possibly prepare to challenge them. Also, it remains unsettled whether the determination of a balance between the interests of those affected and policy change considerations corresponds to a proportionality test.[50] Leaving these issues aside, the EU approach remains potentially apt to provide a gateway also for the contentious matter of

[47] *CNTA* (n 18); Case T-472/93 *Campo Ebro and others v Council*, EU:T:1995:35, paras 50–52.
[48] *Sofrimport* (n 18), para 16.
[49] Ibid, 26. Emphasis added.
[50] Schønberg, Søren J (2000), *Legitimate Expectations in Administrative Law*.

balancing investors' expectations and states regulatory autonomy, especially in light of the absence of the overriding public interest prong and its corollaries within the investment regime.[51] I argue that the EU could provide a solution to determine whether investors' expectations are legitimate and the extent to which it would be legitimate for them to be frustrated. The responses so far, have been promising, yet the EU has not entirely seized its potential and the outcomes are not as audacious as they could have been, as argued in Chapter 5.

For the public interest prong to be functional it requires a context of impartial and independent justice to operate. Independence and impartiality are essential standards for the respect of the rule of law and constitute the conditions for the EU to advance 'its' value of rule of law internationally,[52] in a manner more articulated than as an afterthought.[53] According to a well-established line of case law, the concept of judicial independence has two aspects to it: external and internal. The external aspect, independence *strictu sensu*, requires the adjudicating body to be protected against external constraints liable to jeopardize the independent judgment. The internal aspect is linked to impartiality and requires objectivity and the absence of any interest in the outcome. This is essential to ensure a level playing field for all parties involved in the proceedings and their respective interests concerning the subject matter[54] as it guarantees equal access to justice, free from undue pressures, and ensures the enforcement of decisions. The adjudicators are expected to possess a 'psychological attitude of initial indifference' toward the dispute, demonstrating and appearing to remain equidistant from the litigant parties.[55]

The requirements of impartiality and independence are particularly fitting to respond to some systemic dysfunctionalities and balancing needs of the investment regime. Just as with democracy, the rule of law is an implicit foundation of the EU project and has the potential to serve as a promise for addressing issues of legal certainty (Chapter 5) and balance (Chapter 6) in other systems. On one hand, independence (external dimension) would respond to the need to mitigate the imbalances, whether real or perceived, of arbitrators' conflict of interests and their prospective appointments. On the other hand, impartiality

[51] Ortino, Federico (2024) 'The Public Interest as Part of Legitimate Expectations in Investment Arbitration: Missing in Action?' In *By Peaceful Means: International Adjudication and Arbitration: Essays in Honour of David D. Caron*, edited by Charles N Brower and Others.

[52] Case T-288/15, *Ezz and other v Councils*, EU:T:2018:619, paras 59–61.

[53] Williams (n 11).

[54] Case C-685/15 *Online Games and others v Landespolizeidirektion Oberösterreich*, EU:C:2017:452, paras 60–61; Joined Cases C-748/19, C-754/19 *Prokuratura Rejonowa* EU:C:2021:403, paras 172–174.

[55] Case C-17/00, *De Coster v Collège des Bourgmestre et Échevins de Watermael-Boitsfort*, EU:C:2001:366, para 93 citing Calamandrei fn 117.

(internal dimension) would respond to the need to deliver more certain and balanced outcomes by avoiding particularly restrictive interpretations that have at times imposed constraints on the policy space and regulatory functions of contracting parties in ways not intended or desired.

Open-textured provisions enshrined in investment agreements provide a gateway for tipping the balance towards a judiciary that would weigh incommensurable values that lack a common scale or metric—that is, liberalization and sustainability. While the pursuit of one does not have to exclude the other, if the indeterminacy of concepts like the fair and equitable treatment is resolved through interpretation, the balancing becomes a powerful tool in the hands of the judiciary, which, incidentally, is very much in line with the EU aspirations of judicialization. Bestowing upon the judiciary such a power, however, does not come without liabilities. A court that admits it is balancing admits it is out of its assigned territory in a democracy[56] and risks infusing potentially destructive political implications with the law, as Chapter 6 demonstrates.

[56] Shapiro, Martin (2020), 'Judicial Power and Democracy.' In *Judicial Power—How Constitutional Courts Affect Political Transformations*, edited by Christine Landfried, 21–35.

5

Balance and legal certainty

A. Overview

This chapter focuses on the role of the EU in reshaping certain parameters of conduct imposed on host states by international investment agreements (IIAs). This reconfiguration addresses the need for balance that has arisen, particularly in the interpretation and application of the fair and equitable treatment (FET) standard[1] and indirect expropriation,[2] in relation to regulatory stability. The EU's approach is guided by and modelled on its understanding of the rule of law, with the external promotion of this concept forming an integral part of its framework.

The demand for balance in the investment regime arises from the inherent uncertainty regarding the primary purpose of investment agreements, which oscillates between attracting foreign capital and ensuring the host state's development. While these objectives need not be mutually exclusive, very clear treaty standards that do not take away anything from investor's guarantee of regulatory stability have been quite rare and conflicting views have followed. One narrative has purported that if the attraction of foreign capital prevails, alterations in the domestic regulatory framework may be perceived as violations of the investment protections accorded by the relevant investment treaty, rendering the state liable for such breaches. Conversely, if the focus is on the host state's development, changes in government policy might reduce the extent of investors protection, requiring investors to bear the negative consequences of regulatory changes and/or change their conduct accordingly. However, reality is more nuanced than black and white choice, and often allows for middle-ground compromises that balance the maximum attraction of FDI with the host states' regulatory discretion.

Interpretation involves determining the linguistic meaning of a legal text, while application entails translating that meaning into legal rules for a specific case. However, without clear boundaries ensuring legal certainty, it becomes

[1] See e.g. *Bilcon v Canada* (Award, 17 March 2015).
[2] See e.g. *Bear Creek v Peru* (Award, 30 November 2017).

EU Values in Investment Law And Policy. Maria Laura Marceddu, Oxford University Press.
 DOI: 10.1093/9780191986208.003.0005

difficult to predict the consequences of a given action (problem n.1). This lack of predictability further complicates efforts to define the legality of conduct by the parties involved (problem n.2). In the investment regime, a persistent challenge is the lack of clarity in the law regarding its intended objectives. For example, the obligation to treat investors 'fairly' and 'equitably' might appear intuitive or even self-evident. However, each term carries subtle nuances that can shift in meaning depending on the specific circumstances of a case. This variability allows for different—though not inherently incorrect—interpretations. The open-textured nature of such provisions, combined with the resulting lack of legal certainty, poses significant challenges to the precise realization of the rights conferred upon investors under investment treaties. Moreover, even slight variations in how these provisions are interpreted can hinder a government's ability to adjust its policies in the future.

In addition to this, the inability to hold investors liable unavoidably exposes the system to the criticism of being imbalanced and inattentive to alternative social values, thus questioning the effectiveness of the promised material prosperity.[3] This is furthermore exacerbated by the fact that investment agreements give full rights of standing to foreign investors (claimants) and governments (respondents) but leave out third parties, despite the effects an investment may have on them. Examples of third parties could be Indigenous communities in whose land 'a corporation from a faraway place [arrives] to pursue an investment',[4] or domestic investors in competition with foreign competitors, or, perhaps less striking, citizens and consumers. None of those who fall under the 'third party' category is formally entitled to full standing in the investment adjudication, even though their rights or interests could be affected by the investment and are likely to be even more affected by a decision of an arbitral tribunal.[5]

This imbalanced allocation of rights and responsibilities appears to be particularly problematic if one considers that the negative economic consequences are potentially borne by third parties like citizens and consumers twice. First, because of the unexpected negative impact an investment may have locally; second, investment claims argued upon failed economic operations risk penalizing states that have allegedly deviated from the standard rational model prescribed by investment agreements. Indeed, failed investments are understood as investments that have not delivered the expected outcomes or have had

[3] Lang, Andrew (2011), *World Trade Law after Neoliberalism: Reimagining the Global Economic Order*, 1–7.

[4] *Bear Creek v Peru* (Dissenting opinion of Professor Philippe Sands, 30 November 2017), para 7.

[5] Albeit full standing rights are precluded, they may be granted access to hearing and/or the possibility to submit *amicus curiae* briefs.

negative effects on the delivery of the investments, yet are somehow explained and reviewed as alterations introduced at the regulatory level. This perspective reflects the historically unilateral approach to fairness in investment agreements, which predominantly sanctioned the host state's misconduct without questioning the conduct of foreign investors.[6]

As I will argue in this chapter, what emerged more prominently within the investment regime as a demand for balance conceals, in practice, a demand for legal certainty. Although tribunals have scarcely mentioned the latter as a rationale or a condition for the former, the EU possesses interesting tools to deploy for answering both. The EU principle of legal certainty does supply a convincing, albeit partial, response to the investment law demands of a proper allocation of rights and obligations. For the EU response to be fully effective, however, it should insist more on the concept of 'overriding public interest' as the condition for balance. Only in the acknowledgement of an overriding public interest does the possibility to permit a potential infringement of a right reside, and, consequently, the justification for trumping an expectation whenever in the presence of an overriding public interest. I consider the EU's efforts to implement legal certainty in investment agreements commendable, albeit it could have been more audacious in emphasizing an overriding public interest approach to deliver more effective results in terms of balance.

The chapter proceeds as follows. It introduces the problem of legal certainty within the investment regime and then offers a brief overview of the approach adopted within the EU (Section B). It then identifies the points where the EU approach could meet the demands for balance, and implicitly legal certainty, as they emerged within the investment regime (Section C). The EU modus operandi to address both issues of legal certainty and balance in its investment policy is then discussed in greater detail in Section D. Some concluding observations wrap up the chapter (Section E).

B. Legal certainty in the EU and investment legal regimes

1. The regime of international investments

This section surveys the recent renewable energy arbitrations that predominantly challenged Spain to frame the problem of legal certainty within the investment regime.

[6] Sornarajah, Muthucumaraswamy (2015), *Resistance and Change in the International Law on Foreign Investment*, 421.

Recent years have seen increasing pressure to embrace renewable energy. This acceleration is due to factors like climate change and the race to net zero, and global events such as the COVID-19 pandemic and the war in Ukraine's impact on energy supplies. Foreign investments have been pivotal in increasing the amount of electricity generated from renewable resources, principally wind and solar, and government incentive programmes certainly facilitated the energy away from certain types of fossil fuels.

Investments in the renewable sector are rather peculiar in nature. They tend to involve long-term agreements and display a significant level of potential state interference, given their lengthy exposure to political risk and uncertainty about the imbalance between risk and return. As such, any unexpected change in the support scheme risks altering the lengthy return on infrastructure development projects and, more broadly, the profitability of the entire investment. As a result, besides adequate instruments in support of these investments, states must ensure regulatory stability, predictability, and protection.[7] In Europe, following a series of EU proposals to reduce greenhouse gas emissions and facilitate the transition towards decarbonization, many Member States put in place incentive schemes to attract capital for renewables. Starting in the mid-2000s, most of these incentive programmes focused on subsidizing the tariffs paid to energy producers. Among them, the programme introduced by Spain proved particularly successful in attracting foreign investments.[8]

In the context of a profound financial crisis in 2008, the uncertainty that permeates changing market dynamics and the huge costs of renewables projects soon put these programmes to the test. Many European countries were unable to maintain their renewable energy support policies and their incentive schemes rapidly became economically unsustainable. What happened is that higher construction costs, for example for the construction of a solar plant, required financial support that renders the investment heavily reliant on supporting schemes and, therefore, more vulnerable to regulatory changes than other investments receiving less financial support, like those in natural gas and nuclear power. Exacerbated by the financial crisis, the incentive schemes quickly became unsustainable, burdening governments with significant debts;

[7] COM(2010)639 final. The relationship between legal certainty and renewable energy policies has long been established in the literature. See among others: Dolzer, Rudolf and Schreuer, Christoph (2012), *Principles of International Investment Law*, 145–9; Gatzert, Nadine and Kosub, Thomas (2015), 'Determinants of Policy Risks of Renewable Energy Investments', Friedrich-Alexander University Erlangen-Nürnberg Working Paper.

[8] Spanish Promotion Plan for Renewable Energy, originally promulgated in 2000 and revised in 2005: Plan de Fomento de las Energías Renovables en España 2000–2010 (30 December 1999); Plan de Energías Renovables en España (PER) 2005–2010 (26 August 2005).

for example, Spain's tariff deficit exceeded €29 billion, amounting to 3 per cent of its GDP.[9] To respond to this unforeseen situation, states wound back the incentive schemes to prevent the tariff deficit from growing further.[10] Once the price of renewable energy definitively proved to be unable to compete with electricity generated from coal or natural sources, states began to amend and derogate from the legislation underpinning the subsidy schemes until their eventual termination. These interventions affected the profitability of the investments and sparked dozens of claims[11] from investors, particularly against Spain. The influx of cases against Spain amounted to more than fifty claims (as of May 2025) filed at the International Centre for Settlement of Investment Disputes (ICSID), the Stockholm Chamber of Commerce (SCC), or before UNCITRAL tribunals. A similar fate, albeit with less intensity, was suffered by other EU countries, including Italy, Romania, and the Czech Republic, which introduced measures that progressively retract the financial incentives of the original subsidies scheme, up to a complete overhaul of the scheme. As a consequence of this change, investors could no longer benefit from the subsidies scheme and decided to initiate multiple investment arbitrations challenging host states' changes to the incentive regimes.

These arbitrations primarily rely upon the FET obligation (Article 10(1)), enshrined in the Energy Charter Treaty (ECT), which reads in the relevant part as follows:

> Each Contracting Party shall, in accordance with the provisions of this Treaty, encourage and create stable, equitable, favourable and transparent conditions for Investors of other Contracting Parties to make Investments in its Area. Such conditions shall include a commitment to accord at all times to Investments of Investors of other Contracting Parties *fair and equitable treatment.*

Investors contended that Spain violated the FET obligation by frustrating their legitimate expectations. They argued that many of the investments were made in reliance on the subsidies scheme and that they reasonably relied on Spain's representations that the regulatory regime would remain stable. In response,

[9] Mehranvar, Ladan and Sasma, Sunayana (2022), *The Role of Investment Treaties and Investor–State Dispute Settlement (ISDS) in Renewable Energy Investments.*

[10] Michalena, Evanthie and Hills, Jeremy Maxwell (2013), *Renewable Energy Governance: Complexities and Challenges.*

[11] Vadi, Valentina (2015), 'Beyond Known Worlds: Climate Change Governance by Arbitral Tribunals?', Vanderbilt Law Review, 1285.

Spain maintained that the subsidy scheme only entitled investors to a 'reasonable' rate of return. Specifically, Spain argued that in the absence of specific promises from the host state, it would have been unreasonable for the investors to expect an excessive limitation on the Spain government's power to regulate the economy in accordance with the public interest.

In ascertaining the merits of these claims, the birth deficit of vaguely written treaty provisions like the FET manifested evidently. The arbitral tribunals varied in how they resolved the disputes and used different analyses when reviewing the reasonableness of Spain's policy changes due to the vague language of Article 10(1) ECT. As the remainder of this section will show, each tribunal assigned a different weight often to the same factors, including the justifications underpinning the remodelling of the regulations, the extent of investor's expectations, and the allocation of costs and risks.

When applying the FET provision to the specific facts, nearly all tribunals recognize the protection of legitimate expectation as an important, if not the dominant, component of FET. These expectations pertain to the reasonable assumption a foreign investor can hold regarding the treatment of their investment. Such expectations typically arise from the legal and regulatory environment, specific commitments or promises made by the host state, and the host states' overall conduct towards the investor.

A primary point of interpretative divergence among tribunals concerns the nature of state commitments—in other words, whether they involve individualized undertakings or general provisions applicable to a broad group of entities. Some tribunals have dismissed investors' expectations of regulatory stability primarily because the claimants did not receive any specific promises or commitments from the respondents in that context.[12] In their view, a commitment to a group of investors did not amount to a commitment to any individual investors, and to find otherwise would amount to an excessive limitation on the power of the state to regulate its economic policy. Certain tribunals corroborate this view by positing that legitimate expectations at the regulatory level originate from specific *individualized* representations made to induce investors to invest in renewables.[13] In the absence of such a specific commitment, investors cannot form a legitimate expectation that the regulatory framework would not be altered.[14] According to other tribunals, there does not have to be

[12] *Stadtwerke München and others v Spain* (Award, 2 December 2019), paras 198, 308.

[13] *Philip Morris v Uruguay* (Award, 8 July 2016), para 426; *Horthel v Poland* (Award, 16 February 2017), para 238; *Isolux v Spain* (Dissenting Opinion of Prof. Dr. Guido Santiago Tawil, 6 July 2016), para 4.

[14] *RREEF v Spain* (Decision on Responsibility and on the Principles of Quantum, 30 November 2018), para 245.

a specific representation for a legitimate expectation to arise: a state's act or conduct, and acts of general legislation (to be read together with the general market condition at the time the investment was made), create a legitimate expectation of *relative stability*.[15] From this perspective, the FET standard carries with it an implicit expectation of protection of investors' basic and fair expectations, like stability.[16] Put differently, the FET enshrined in Article 10(1) ECT accords investors a legitimate expectation of relative stability of the regulatory regime. Although no state could reasonably be expected to freeze its laws,[17] the investor is protected from radical or fundamental changes.[18]

Beyond the form the manifestations may take,[19] an even more controversial point where tribunals diverge again is what determines a breach of the standard—the factual circumstances that might (or might not) determine such a breach. This determination depends on several factors, for each of which tribunals have assigned different weights. Unsurprisingly, this has led to varying outcomes, despite the factual and legal similarities across the claims under investigation. It is worth emphasizing that all these claims were based on Article 10(1) of the ECT and stemmed from changes to regulatory regimes originally designed to attract investments in renewables, which became economically unsustainable over time. The two most dividing points for tribunals in determining a breach of the FET standard revolve around (i) the gravity of the change, and (ii) the reasonableness of the measures pursued by the host state. As regards the former, tribunals have relied on factors to assess the severity of the change such as its abrupt, sudden, or radical nature. As regards the latter, the key factors brought into the assessment have been suitability, necessity, and fairness. Proportionality is where (i) and (ii) meet: if the change is not random, unnecessary, and does not deprive the regulatory framework of its essential features unexpectedly, then the gravity of the change could be balanced against the objective sought. A change is potentially proportionate only if the alteration(s) introduced in the regulatory framework maintains all interests at stake balanced against each other. In practice, however, what falls within the

[15] *Novenergia II v Spain* (Final Award, 15 February 2018), para 651; *Cube Infrastructure v Spain* (Decision on Jurisdiction, Liability, and Partial Decision on Quantum, 19 February 2019), para 245; *Micula v Romania* (Award, 5 March 2020), para 362; *SunReserve v Italy* (Award, 25 March 2020), para 817; *Renergy v Spain* (Award, 6 May 2022), paras 639–642.

[16] According to Tecmed, the FET obligation entails a protection of investor's basic and fair expectations. *Tecmed v Mexico* (Award, 29 May 2003), para 154.

[17] *Renergy* (n 15), para 639.

[18] *Eiser Infrastructure v Spain* (Award, 4 May 2017), para 363; *Novenergia II* (n 15), para 654; *SolEs Badajoz v Spain* (Award, 31 July 2019), para 308; *OperaFund and Schwab v Spain* (Award, 6 September 2019), para 508.

[19] *Renergy* (n 15), para 639.

boundaries of reasonableness is a delicate exercise and 'the line that separates legitimate modifications of the regulatory regime from changes that constitute improper breaches of the commitment to stability is not easily defined'.[20]

The tribunals that found a breach of the FET standard considered that Article 10(1) ECT entitled investors to expect that Spain (or any host state) would not drastically and totally change the regulatory regime on which the investment depends when pursuing a legitimate policy objective. For the tribunals embracing this vision, the measures adopted by Spain were not a '*normal* exercise of [its] regulatory powers'. While investors could not expect absolute regulatory stability, according to these tribunals the legislative changes introduced by Spain were so drastic and fundamental that severely violated the legitimate expectations of investors to obtain stable returns on their investments. In their view, the radical, fundamental, and unforeseeable dismantling of the regulatory regime fell 'outside the acceptable range of legislative and regulatory behaviour' as it exceeds in 'suddenness and severity what a prudent investor would reasonably have expected'[21] within the economic relationship with the host state. The implication is that Article 10 ECT protects investors against these changes[22] because the legal framework is not expected to change arbitrarily and without notice. Changes to the regulatory scheme are admissible only if modifications are necessary, suitable to the legislative intent they sought to achieve, and possibly accompanied by transitional periods.[23] While the requirement of suitability is relatively undemanding, the necessity criterion involves a more detailed analysis to determine whether less restrictive measures were reasonably available,[24] particularly in the context of a global crisis.[25]

In the reasoning of those tribunals that found a breach of the FET standard, the existence of an expectation of stability[26] has somehow become an obligation. The breadth of the rule stated in some awards like the *OperaFund* is staggering:

[20] *Kruck and others v Spain* (Decision on Jurisdiction, Liability and Principles of Quantum, 14 September 2022), para 200.

[21] *SolEs Badajoz* (n 18), para 462.

[22] *Cavalum* SGPS *v Spain* (Decision on Jurisdiction, Liability and Directions on Quantum, 31 August 2020), para 538; *Eiser* (n 18), para 363; *Novernergia II* (n 15), para 654; *InfraRed v Spain* (Award 2 August 2019), para 368; *OperaFund* (n 18), para 509.

[23] *Renergy* (n 15), para 910

[24] *RWE Innogy v Spain* (Decision on Jurisdiction, Liability, and Certain Issues of Quantum, 30 December 2019), paras 462, 554.

[25] Ibid, para 912.

[26] *Hydro Energy* 1 S.à r.l. *and Hydroxana v Spain* (Decision on Jurisdiction, 9 March 2020), para 673.

> The Tribunal agrees with both Parties and the tribunals in *Antin*, *Masdar*, *Novenergia*, and *Eiser* that Article 10(1) of the ECT includes an *obligation* to provide fundamental stability of the economic and legal regime in place, and that the FET protects against changes in the *essential characteristics of the regulatory regime relied upon by investors.*[27]

Fundamental stability is a legitimate expectation of protection ('against changes in the essential characteristics of the regulatory regime') that reaches the degree of an obligation under FET ('includes an obligation'). Stability becomes the threshold for investor protection,[28] in the absence of which the investment would not have been made in the first place. From this standpoint, the line between the point from where the obligation of stability begins and the point up to where the expectation of stability ends, or rather extends, remains blurred. Sornarajah is not wrong in arguing that it looks as if a stabilization clause is read into every contract, although the parties did not make the treaty to provide for contractual protection.[29]

On the other side of the spectrum, some tribunals have rejected the allegation of a breach of the FET standard. Those tribunals have been more lenient in reviewing the balancing exercise carried out by Spain when attempting to protect consumers[30] from a tariff increase without incurring violations of Article 10(1) ECT. In their view, the reduction of public expenditure that avoids excessive burdens on the consumers of electricity has been balanced against the need to encourage environmental protection and renewables, while protecting the legal rights of existing investors.[31] The *Stadtwerke* tribunal is seminal on the point:

> Spain's contested measures were proportionate in that that they did not have a significant *negative* effect on the Claimants' investment. . . . In the present case, the aim sought to be realized by Spain in adopting the contested measures was to protect the solvency and stability of the public electricity system. It is undeniable that such State aim was *vitally* important to the public welfare of Spain. In order to achieve that aim, Spain adopted an approach of '*shared sacrifice*,' that is, that those benefiting from the system should contribute to its continued operation and financial stability. With respect to the present

[27] *OperaFund* (n 18), para 508. Second and third emphases added.
[28] *Renergy* (n 15); *Eiser* (n 18), para 363; *Novernegia II* (n 15), para 654; *OperaFund* (n 18), para 508.
[29] Sornarajah (n 6), 420.
[30] *Isolux v Spain* (Award, 12 July 2016), para 823.
[31] *Renergy v Spain* (Dissenting Opinion of Professor Philippe Sands KC, 6 May 2022).

> case, the Claimants were required to forego a *modest* amount of revenue for the sake of preserving the electricity system. Thus, the aim, the method and the effect of the State measures were *reasonable*. From a relative perspective, one may therefore conclude that the burden on the Claimants was reasonably proportionate to the aim and purpose of the measures contested by them. The Claimants' argument that Spain's measures were not 'proportionate' is therefore rejected.[32]

From this standpoint, stability remains within the boundaries of an expectation (and not of an obligation) whose legitimacy is derived from its reasonableness. Stability is a matter that concerns the entire regime ('to protect the stability of the public electricity system') and, therefore, all interests involved—of both investors and consumers alike. Interestingly, the tribunal described the approach adopted by Spain as a 'shared sacrifice' by which both the public (Spain) and private (investors) sides are expected to sacrifice a reasonable measure of their freedom and power which they would otherwise enjoy to continue benefitting from the system ('those benefiting from the system should contribute to its continued operation and financial stability'). The tribunal refers to a system in which all actors involved should be proportionally bound by and entitled to the benefits of the law to which they are subjected,[33] implicitly characterizing it as a system based on the rule of law. According to this view, stability is the threshold for proportionality, a parameter that ensures a reasonable relationship between the burden placed on investors and the aim sought to be attained by the host state.

To sum up, despite the factual and legal similarities, a first set of tribunals interpreted the FET to encompass an obligation of regulatory stability. A second batch of tribunals interpreted stability as an expectation of systemic proportionality. Two considerations flow from this. First, uncertain premises generate different outcomes, despite factual and legal similarities. Second, uncertain outcomes produce imbalances. If it is unclear what is legitimate to expect in a given situation, how would it be possible to reach a balance of any sort?[34] It is the certainty of the laws that confers rights and imposes obligations that create boundaries between competing interests and ensures the fulfilment of legitimate expectations and regulatory stability. If the law, however, does not

[32] *Stadtwerke* (n 12), para 354. Emphasis added.

[33] Bingham, Tom (2006), *The Sixth Sir David Williams Lecture—The Rule Of Law* <https://www.cpl.law.cam.ac.uk/sir-david-williams-lectures/rt-hon-lord-bingham-cornhill-kg-rule-law>.

[34] *Electrabel v Hungary* (Decision on Jurisdiction, Applicable Law and Liability, 30 November 2012), para 113.

elucidate the criteria to meet the expectations, or whether investors' rights should (or should not) override public interests, it remains subject to circumstantial judgments. For the delivery of conclusive judgments, the law has to be certain, sufficiently clear, and predictable. This is the point at which the need to balance the competing interests of investors and states becomes apparent, prompting an implicit call for greater legal certainty. The EU has a potentially suitable approach to answer both, as outlined in the following sections.

2. The EU legal regime

The principle of legal certainty is one of several general principles recognized by Community law. I will survey the *Sofrimport* case to illustrate how legal certainty interacts with regulatory stability in the EU law context.

Sofrimport is a company incorporated under French law that shipped a cargo of cartons of Chilean dessert apples from Chile for import into the European Community (March 1988). In the same year, the Commission took some protective measures concerning imports into the Community of dessert apples originating in non-member countries. Initially, to monitor and surveil the imports of dessert apples from third countries the Commission introduced some measures[35] among which is the presentation of an import licence for free circulation of dessert apples within the Community (for the period until 1 September 1988). The Commission then considered that the continuation of such imports could lead to serious disturbance of the market given that the applications for these import licences exceeded the traditional quantity of imports of Chilean dessert apples. Therefore, it decided to suspend import licences for dessert apples originating in Chile,[36] to alter the original period of suspension[37] for reasons of management, and to enable an in-depth review of the overall situation of the market in dessert apples.[38]

Before the cargo arrived at the port of Marseilles (20 April 1988), Sofrimport had applied for an import licence for these goods (on 12 April 1988) with the French intervention agency, ONIFLHOR, which denied Sofrimport's application while its goods were still in transit because Regulations No. 962/88

[35] Commission Regulation (EEC) No 346/88 of 3 February 1988 introducing special surveillance of imports of dessert apples from third countries, OJ L 34, 6 February 1988.

[36] Commission Regulation (EEC) No 962/88 of 12 April 1988 suspending the issue of import licences for dessert apples originating in Chile, OJ L 95, 13 April 1988.

[37] Initially it was from 15 to 22 April 1988, and then to 18 to 29 April 1988.

[38] Commission Regulation (EEC) No 984/88 of 14 April 1988 amending Regulation (EEC) No 962/88 suspending the issue of import licences for dessert apples originating in Chile, OJ L 98, 15 April 1988.

and No. 984/88 stipulated that applications for import licences pending on 18 April 1988 were to be rejected. Sofrimport then decided to bring an action under Article 173 of the EEC Treaty seeking the annulment of the regulations and compensation for the damages caused by the denial of its import licence application.

The Court acknowledged the existence of a general representation that created reasonable expectations. Sofrimport relied on a specific provision according to which traders of products in transit 'rely on a legitimate expectation that in the absence of an overriding public interest, no suspensory measures will be applied against him'.[39] The Court went on to explain that a legitimate expectation arises from a clear and specific representation (specific protection given to those importers) made by a public authority (the Commission) but could be legally frustrated in the presence of an overriding public interest.[40]

When addressing damages, the Court examined the merits of the nature of the change as well as the issue of overriding public interest. As a matter of principle, the enactment of protective measures fell within the Commission's powers, and Sofrimport might expect to suffer damage exceeding the *normal* risks inherent in economic activities. The contested regulations, however, are legislative choices of economic policy that violate a superior rule or law for the protection of individuals—legitimate expectations—without invoking any overriding public interest. As such, they were hardly foreseeable by a prudent trader, and the damage suffered by Sofrimport went beyond the limits of the economic risks inherent in the business at issue since the purpose of that provision was precisely to limit those risks concerning goods in transit. The point is reiterated in *CNTA*, where the Court explained that lost profits are not recoverable where based on legitimate expectations but where not suffered due to an unexpected change.[41]

The reasoning followed by the Court appears straightforward. Importers whose goods are in transit rely on a legitimate expectation that no restrictive measures will be applied against them, as provided by a sufficiently clear provision (Article 3(3) Regulation 2707/72). However, if, *before* shipping the goods, traders have been given a sufficiently clear indication of any suspension measures that might affect their goods in transit, those goods would not be immune

[39] The provision in question is Article 3(3) of Council Regulation (EEC) No 2707/72 of 19 December 1972 laying down the conditions for applying protective measures for fruit and vegetables. Case C-152/88, *Sofrimport v Commission*, EU:C:1990:259, paras 11 and 12.
[40] Ibid, para 16.
[41] Case 74/74, *CNTA v Commission*, ECLI:EU:C:1975:59.

from a restrictive measure and there would be no reason to protect traders' legitimate expectations.[42]

A few considerations arise from the above and are further reinforced by the broader case law of the Court of Justice of the European Union (CJEU). First, in the EU system, alterations at the policy level have to be expected. Disadvantages caused by changes in the law would not constitute a cause for complaint and are deemed to be foreseeable by a prudent trader. Economic agents would not develop a legitimate expectation that an existing situation, capable of being altered by a decision within the institutions' limits of their discretionary powers, will be maintained without limits.[43] Second, traders reasonably expect that alterations occur under certain conditions. Since legitimate expectations is a general principle of EU law that protects individuals and entities from changes in the legal environment when they have reasonably relied on assurances or established practices by EU institutions or Member States, the essential factor that can justify the frustration of such an expectation is the presence of an overriding public interest. This is accompanied by a reasonable warning and often, albeit not necessarily always, by appropriate transitional measures so that those affected get acquired with the changes.[44] The adoption of transitional measures may be precluded in respect of situations which arose before the new rules came into force but which are still subject to change as long as the attainment of the overriding public interest is not compromised.[45] It is for the defendant to show the overriding public interest and for the Court to balance the policy considerations in favour of the change against the legitimate expectations and interests of those affected. While it remains unsettled whether the test of significant imbalance[46] is in fact a proportionality test, on the whole it appears that the matter is more disciplined than in the investment regime. The last consideration and yet the one underpinning all the others is that EU law has to be sufficiently clear in terms of effects:

> [I]t must be recalled that [legal certainty is a] fundamental principle of EU law [which] requires, in particular, that *rules should be clear and precise*, so that individuals may ascertain *unequivocally* what their rights and obligations are and may take steps accordingly.[47]

[42] Case C-152/88, *Sofrimport v Commission* ECLI:EU:C:1989:590, para 26.

[43] Case C 69/89 *Nakajima v Council*, EU:C:1991:186, para 120.

[44] Case T-472/93, *Campo Ebro v Council*, EU:T:1995:35, para 52; *CNTA* (n 41).

[45] *CNTA* (n 41), para 44; *Sofrimport* (n 39), paras 16 and 19; Case 84/78 *Tomadini* EU:C:1979:129, para 20; Case C-51/95 P *Unifruit Hellas v Commission*, EU:C:1997:53, para 27.

[46] Schønberg Soren (2000), *Legitimate Expectations in Administrative Law.*

[47] Case C-72/15, *Rosneft*, EU:C:2017:236, para 161; Case C-308/06 *Intertanko*, EU:C:2008:312, para 69; Case C-344/04, *IATA and ELFAA*, EU:C:2006:10, para 68. Emphasis added.

C. The problem of balance and legal certainty

Unlike public international law systems where states face each other based on sovereign equality, in both the EU and investment regimes, individual rights and their legitimate expectations matter and must be protected. This protection forms part of the fundamental guarantees derived from the rule of law and it ensures stability, which, in turn, is derived from the foreseeability of the consequences a given action entails. In legal contexts, expectations refer to the anticipations or beliefs that parties hold regarding future actions, benefits, or rights based on existing laws, contracts, representations, or practices. These expectations shape the behaviour of individuals or entities, influencing their decisions and their reliance on the perceived certainty of outcomes. The connotations of expectations can vary across different areas of law. For example, in contract law, expectations are tied to the fulfilment of obligations and promises made within a contract, which parties anticipate will be honoured. In property law, expectations may relate to the continued enjoyment or use of property based on ownership rights or long-term leases. In administrative law, expectations arise when a public authority has made representations or established practices that individuals reasonably rely on, anticipating consistent treatment. In all these contexts, the legal system often evaluates whether these expectations are reasonable, legitimate, and supported by the circumstances, ensuring alignment with principles of fairness and predictability in the law. In international law, the International Court of Justice has clarified that general international law does not contain any principle that generates binding obligations solely based on a state's legitimate expectations.

A key point of divergence between the EU and investment regimes is the extent to which these expectations, derived from individual rights, can be violated. Seeking to uphold the guarantees specified in the agreements, investment treaties place significant emphasis on protecting investors' legitimate expectations of a predictable and stable investment environment. This finds its legal basis in the FET standard, albeit the provision does not explicitly prescribe that circumstances have to remain unchanged or that investor expectations have to be balanced against the host state's regulation of economic activities. Although the ongoing reform processes of investment arbitration indicate a reconfiguration towards the safeguarding of state regulatory flexibility at least in some form, investment agreements continue to suffer from double birth deficits of vagueness and asymmetrical configuration that accords investors high levels of protection in exchange for foreign capital attraction. This configuration provides for absolute protection of investors' rights with limited flexibility in case of policy change alterations and with no obligation upon investors (hence its absolute nature). As a consequence, it poses problems to the safeguarding of the state's regulatory flexibility and, more broadly, in terms of adaptation to changes in societal values or political choices. In the investment regime, the balancing line between investors' expectations and host state regulatory powers remains a moving target, with detrimental consequences on the certainty of the conditions on which the contracting parties are supposed to rely. EU law, instead, balances the legitimate expectation of a stable and secure legal environment with the necessity to adapt to policy changes which may not have been known previously or which have been subject earlier to different value judgments. According to EU law, an overriding public interest trumps the expectation, regardless of disadvantageous alterations at the economic level. Changes might be accompanied by complementary measures that are likely to mitigate their impact (e.g. transitional measures, reasonable warning), but legitimate expectations remain protected only in the absence of an overriding public interest that outweighs the interest in respecting such assurance.

The most prominent effect of this divergent protection of legitimate expectations between the EU and the investment regimes materializes with distorted effects on government actions and, consequently, on the overall balancing of the interests involved. In EU law, legitimate expectations cannot be used to push the administration into taking a specific course of action, particularly where that would imply allowing the enterprise concerned to substitute its own economic judgment for that of the EU institutions.[48] In EU law the boundaries are marked: economic agents know where they stand and what is legally reasonable to expect. In investment law, the matter is more complex and legitimate expectations may prevent the host state from taking a particular course of action to avoid incurring liability for a violation of investors' rights. Even the recent steer in favour of the state's right to regulate has not prevented arbitral tribunals from leaving the public interest prong almost entirely out of the discussion,[49] framing their analysis mostly in terms of proportionality between the pursuit of public policy objectives and the means necessary to meet and/or protect them. More often than not, arbitral tribunals have found themselves in the position of reviewing what constitutes a *normal* exercise of regulatory

[48] Sharpston, Eleanor (1990), 'European Community Law and the Doctrine of Legitimate Expectations: How Legitimate, and for Whom', Northwestern Journal of International Law & Business.

[49] Ortino, Federico (2024), 'The Public Interest as Part of Legitimate Expectations in Investment Arbitration: Missing in Action?' In *By Peaceful Means: International Adjudication and Arbitration: Essays in Honour of David D. Caron*, edited by Charles N Brower and Others; Ortino, Federico (2019), *The Origin and Evolution of Investment Treaty Standards: Stability, Value, and Reasonableness*.

powers according to investment treaty obligations. Only a handful of tribunals engaged in a (tepid) proportionality test grounded on the necessity and non-arbitrariness of the measures that rarely stretched to an exercise of balancing all interests involved. Thus far, one of the most distorting effects generated by the protection of legitimate expectation vis-à-vis the state's regulatory power is the well-known phenomenon of 'regulatory chill', according to which even the prospect itself of being hit with investment claims has the potential effect of deterring host states from changing their domestic regulatory framework and maintaining the status quo.

Balance and legal certainty stand in a relationship where from a logical standpoint the latter pre-dates the former. If the law is 'sufficiently precise' the subjects involved would reasonably foresee their legal rights and the possible consequences that their conduct generates. It is possible, in principle, to achieve legal certainty without reaching the perfect point of balance (assuming such things exist) among all interests involved. In EU law, assuming that there is no manifest imbalance between the interests of those affected by the measure at stake, an overriding public interest justifies the infringement of a right, and a public policy change would not be jeopardized in the name of economic judgments. On the contrary, achieving balance without legal certainty might prove harder in practice, as already displayed within investment law. The regime of international investments suffers from the absence of a regulatory framework apt to draw 'a judicious balance between the sometimes divergent interests and concerns of different entities'[50] because it has relegated legal certainty to a somewhat marginal position. More bluntly put, the obsessive insistence on balancing private and public interests[51] has overshadowed legal certainty. Unsurprisingly, investment tribunals have attempted to perform a balancing exercise on some occasions. However, they have rarely mentioned legal certainty as a rationale for protecting legitimate expectations,[52] which, in turn, could have led to some form of balancing insofar as legal certainty ensures that the protection of legitimate expectations does not constrain the exercise

[50] Kwakwa, Edward (2011), 'Regulating the International Economy: What Role for the State?' In *The Role of Law in International Politics*, edited by Michael Byers.

[51] Stern, Brigitte (2011), 'The Future of International Investment Law: A Balance Between the Protection of Investors and the States' Capacity to Regulate.' In *The Evolving International Investment Regime: Expectations, Realities, Options*, edited by Jose E Alvarez and Others; Geiger, Rainer (2011), 'Multilateral Approaches to Investment: The Way Forward.' In ibid; Barker, Paul (2015), 'Investor–State Arbitration as International Public Law: Deference, Proportionality and the Standard of Review.' In *Investment Treaty Arbitration and International Law*, edited by Ian Laird and Todd Weiler.

[52] Henckels, Caroline (2023), 'Justifying the Protection of Legitimate Expectations in International Investment Law: Legal Certainty and Arbitrary Conduct', ICSID Review—Foreign Investment Law Journal.

of regulatory stability. As things stand, legal certainty is almost absent in the investment regime and the protection of legitimate expectations is somewhat implied mostly through the FET interpretation. Without a clear understanding of the law, predicting how it will be applied in a given case becomes challenging, leaving individuals unable to plan their lives effectively with a full understanding of the legal consequences of their actions. The CJEU, instead, sets different boundaries because both legal certainty and legitimate expectations have been recognized among the general principles of EU law. According to EU law, the justification for the protection of legitimate expectations lies in legal certainty:[53] it is the certainty of the laws that by conferring rights and imposing obligations creates boundaries between competing interests and ensures the fulfilment of legitimate expectations and regulatory stability.

The search for balance presented an interesting opportunity for the EU to domesticate the investment regime (dis)order through the diffusion of its principle of legal certainty. In the next section, I explore whether and how this taming process is unfolding.

D. Greater balance through greater certainty: The EU's investment agreements approach

As outlined in the previous sections, in the investment regime one of the most critical issues pertains to how to protect investors without tying the hands of political and administrative decision-makers. The EU contributes to untangling this dilemma by mostly relying on its consolidated approach but also attempting to raise the bar across multiple lines of action. First, by clarifying the language of open-textured obligations that grant protections to foreign investors it refines the scope of legitimate expectations' protection. It then attempts to balance legal certainty with justice through the incorporation of stand-alone 'right to regulate' provisions. Lastly, it enhances the promotion of international labour, environmental, and sustainable development standards. Although this may not be explicitly aimed at achieving greater certainty, it nonetheless strengthens the foundation for states' regulatory authority and, more broadly, balancing. Let us now analyse each of these dimensions in greater detail.

[53] Ortino (n 49).

1. Language clarifications

Against the problem of open-textured provisions, like the FET standard, the refinements put forward by the EU have crystallized a progression towards more exacting requirements imposed on the host state.[54] This progression finds fulfilment in the FET standard envisaged in the Comprehensive Economic and Trade Agreement between Canada and the European Union (CETA). Article 8.10 CETA is labelled 'treatment of investors and of covered investments' and begins by stating that:

> [e]ach Party shall accord in its territory to *covered investments* of the other Party and to investors with respect to their covered investments Fair and Equitable Treatment and full protection and security in accordance with paragraphs 2 through 6.[55]

Except for the specification of 'covered investments', which is defined in the agreement,[56] at first glance the provision does not look particularly innovative. The first paragraph simply states that investors, with respect to their (covered) investments, are granted fair treatment, in addition to full protection and security. There is nothing new about this: it follows a generalized trend of the FET definition already included in many bilateral investment treaties (BITs). What is more interesting is what the provision does not say. No trace is found of the Minimum Standard of Treatment (MST), which, arguably, makes the CETA provision more liberal than the North American Free Trade Agreement (NAFTA) or the US model BITs, owing to the absence of an attempt to tie it to international or customary law. The provision then enumerates a detailed list of breaches of the standard and stipulates that:

> [a] Party breaches the obligation of Fair and Equitable Treatment referenced in paragraph 1 if a measure or series of measures constitutes:
> *denial of justice* in criminal, civil or administrative proceedings;
> fundamental *breach of due process*, including a fundamental breach of *transparency*, in judicial and administrative proceedings;

[54] Kaufmann-Kohler, Gabrielle (2007), 'Arbitral Precedent: Dream, Necessity or Excuse? The 2006 Freshfields Lecture', Arbitration International.

[55] Comprehensive Economic and Trade Agreement (CETA) between Canada, of the one part, and the European Union and its Member States, of the other part (entered into force provisionally on 21 September 2017), OJ L 11, 14 January 2017, Article 8.10(1).

[56] Ibid, Article 8.1.

> manifest *arbitrariness*;
> *targeted discrimination* on manifestly wrongful grounds, such as gender, race or religious belief;
> *abusive treatment of investors*, such as coercion, duress and harassment; or
> a breach of any further elements of the Fair and Equitable Treatment obligation adopted by the Parties in accordance with paragraph 3 of this Article.[57]

Despite the remarkable improvement, doubts persist as to which actions might violate the provision.[58] In this sense, one might wonder whether this list should be interpreted exhaustively or if the listed elements are merely descriptive and serve as guiding examples among (many) others. In the former hypothesis, the application of the standard would be more restrictive and less protective, whereas in the latter case, a free-floating provision would still leave space for broader interpretations. Given that the list can be modified by the parties through a regular review of the content of the obligation to provide fair and equitable treatment (Article 8.10(3)), the option of broader interpretations is more likely to prevail, even at the expense of legal certainty. Further confirmation of this can be found by looking at the functions attributed to the Committee on Services and Investment, which may recommend the adoption of further elements of the FET obligation.[59]

The list does a good job of identifying some of the most recurring elements that arbitral tribunals have considered in the determination of a breach of the FET standard,[60] as well as in introducing new components. Concerning the first two elements (denial of justice and due process), the approach is consistent with the US model BITs. Due process is dealt with together with the denial of justice,[61] with the underlying intention to consider the claim of the denial of justice as a profitable tool available when domestic remedies have been exhausted without a good result. Other components of the list make their appearance in an investment agreement for the first time. A breach of transparency is one of those and now features due process violations. Already addressed by several tribunals, which believed that a lack of transparency falls under the treaty's FET standard,[62] the inclusion of transparency is an

[57] Ibid, Article 8.10(2). Emphasis added.
[58] Lester, Simon (2015), 'Rethinking the International Investment Law System', Journal of World Trade.
[59] CETA (n 55), Article 8.44(3)(d).
[60] Klager, Roland (2010), 'Fair and Equitable Treatment: A Look at the Theoretical Underpinnings of Legitimacy and Fairness', The Journal of World Investment & Trade.
[61] Valenti, Mara (2014), 'The Protection of General Interests of Host States in the Application of the Fair and Equitable Treatment Standard.' In *General Interests of Host States in International Investment Law*, edited by Giorgio Sacerdoti and Others.
[62] *Maffezini v Spain* (Award, 13 November 2000), para 83.

additional attestation to the EU commitment towards greater transparency in investment matters. Despite being the most recurrent element recognized as a clear violation of the FET standard,[63] manifest arbitrariness is another component that makes its first appearance in an investment treaty as a stand-alone condition, rather than being paired with unreasonable and discriminatory conduct, as is often the case. In CETA, discriminatory conduct encompasses 'targeted discrimination on manifestly wrongful grounds', which for the first time are articulated in writing as 'gender, race or religious belief'. A vigilant observer would not find the specification particularly original given that it echoes the 'local sentiment, racial or class-based prejudice' of the *Loewen v US* case,[64] as well as the *Waste Management v Mexico* decision.[65] Protection against the abusive treatment of investors, such as 'coercion, duress and harassment'[66] wraps up the list.

Taken together, the first three paragraphs of the FET provision incorporated in the investment chapter of CETA are reproduced almost identically in all the EU investment protection agreements (IPAs) or investment chapters.[67] Another point of convergence across EU agreements is the exclusion from the FET scope of invoking other breaches (either from provisions of the same agreement or of a different one) as a breach of the treatment to be granted to investors.[68]

What a meticulous observer could not miss is the ground-breaking novelty enshrined in paragraph 4 of CETA Article 8.10, which reads:

> When applying the above fair and equitable treatment obligation, a Tribunal *may* take into account whether a Party made a specific representation to an

[63] See, among others, *Mondev v United States* (Award, 11 October 2002), para 127; *SAUR International SA v Argentina* (Decision on Jurisdiction and Liability, 6 June 2012); *Electrabel v Hungary* (Award, 25 November 2015).

[64] *Loewen v United States* (Decision on Hearing of Respondent's Objection to Competence and Jurisdiction, 5 January 2001).

[65] *Waste Management v Mexico* (Award, 30 April 2004), para 98.

[66] A couple of tribunals have already considered coercion and harassment as a breach of the standard. Specifically, *Lemire v Ukraine* (Decision on Jurisdiction and Liability, 14 January 2010), para 284; and *Binder v Czech Republic* (Final Award (Redacted), 15 July 2011), para 447.

[67] EU–Chile Interim Trade Agreement (entered into force 1 February 2025), OJ L 2953, 20 December 2024, Article 10.15; EU–India Investment Protection Agreement (EU textual proposal as of September 2022) Article 2.6; EU–Indonesia FTA (EU textual proposal as of December 2016) Article 2.6; EU–Mexico Economic Partnership, Political Coordination and Cooperation Agreement (EU–Mexico 'Global Agreement) (signed 17 January 2025), Article 15; EU–Vietnam Investment Protection Agreement (signed on 30 June 2019, pending Member States ratifications) (IPA), Article 2.5; EU–Singapore Investment Protection Agreement (signed on 13 February 2019, pending Member States ratifications) (IPA), Article 2.4.

[68] CETA (n 55) Article 8.10(6); EU–Vietnam IPA (n 67) Article 14(7); EU–Singapore IPA (n 67), Article 9.4(6).

investor to induce a covered investment, that created a *legitimate expectation*, and upon which the investor relied in deciding to make or maintain the covered investment, but that the Party subsequently frustrated.

This provision marks a radical point of departure from the traditional drafting of FET clause as it is the first instance where legitimate expectations have been explicitly included in the FET provision. This inclusion is likely to guide arbitral tribunals in interpreting legitimate expectations, which have traditionally been framed in terms of failing investors and thus indicating a clear potential breach of the standard. Paragraph 4 does not actually say that, but the perspective is radically different as transformed by the power of a single word: may. Frustrations of legitimate expectations may, and are likely to happen (to the detriment of the investor) but the tribunal is no longer bound to read into this a violation of the FET obligation. Legitimate expectations can be considered, but this 'giving thought to' is not as compelling as it has to be for the other elements listed in paragraph 2. The change of perspective lies in the fact that the tribunal is released from considering the legitimate expectations component as binding, nor should investors expect the tribunal to do so. CETA Article 8.9(2) is seminal in insisting on the same point: even in those instances where state regulatory powers negatively affect an investment or interfere with investors' expectations, they do not amount to a breach of investment protections. The point is reiterated also in the CETA Joint Interpretative Statement, where both Canada and the EU clarify that 'governments may change their laws, regardless of whether this may negatively affect an investment or investor's expectations of profits'.[69] The novel approach features many EU agreements and textual proposals as well.[70] The EU–Vietnam and EU–Singapore IPAs, for example, echoed the interpretive statement punctually, and both stipulate that investors' rights (like the FET) should not be interpreted as a commitment from a party to freeze its legal and regulatory framework.

The clarifications introduced in the EU investment agreements mark bold steps in the achievement of legal certainty and, implicitly, in rebalancing investors' expectations with states' regulatory autonomy. They are clearly inspired and firmly anchored in EU law, which recognizes the pursuit of a legitimate regulatory objective as a condition sufficient to frustrate investors'

[69] Joint Interpretative Instrument on the Comprehensive Economic and Trade Agreement (CETA) between Canada and the European Union and its Member States, OJ L 11, 14 January 2017.

[70] EU–Chile Interim Trade Agreement (n 67), Article 10.15(3); EU–India Investment Protection Agreement (n 67) Article 2.6(3); EU–Indonesia FTA (n 67), Article 2.9(2).

expectations. The insertion of stand-alone right to regulate provisions makes the EU imprint even more noticeable, as I posit in the following section.

2. The right to regulate

Following the concerns expressed in the public consultations, EU investment agreements have introduced elements, either *de novo* or that build on other states' experiences, to redress the potential limitations to governments' regulatory authority to regulate in the public interest. Beyond language clarifications, the EU IPAs contain a more detailed articulation of legitimate policy objectives, both in the preambles and in brand new right to regulate measures, which make their first appearance in CETA.

Largely recognized as crucial elements in treaty interpretation,[71] the 'object and purpose' assume even greater significance in contexts like the investment regime, where the purpose of investment agreements somehow fluctuates between capital attraction and host state development. Borrowing from Ortino, 'the object of a treaty is the substantial content of the treaty, that is the provisions, rights, and obligations created by the treaties', whereas the 'purpose is the reason for establishing the substantial content of the treaty'.[72] The object comprises those 'things' inside the treaty, and the purpose comprises the intention(s) that have driven the treaty-makers towards that specific content. As applied to investment agreements, the object has corresponded, often exclusively, to a listing of investors and investment protections, while the purpose has manifested a broad desire to intensify economic cooperation for the mutual prosperity of both parties, with various nuances in the intentions depending on the agreement and the parties in question.

This distinction is particularly relevant for treaties like CETA, whereby the parties commit to strengthening their economic relationship through *mutually advantageous* rules to govern trade and investments.[73] The assumption is that the law would, or rather should, be equally beneficial to both contracting sides, without favouring specific interests. One can interpret the equality of interests as a balance between the pursuit of economic growth and the safeguard of 'legitimate policy objectives, such as public health, safety, environment, public morals and the promotion and protection of cultural diversity'.[74]

[71] Vienna Convention on the Law of Treaties (23 May 1969), UNTS 1155.
[72] Ortino, Federico (2017), 'Investment Treaties, Sustainable Development and Reasonableness Review: A Case Against Strict Proportionality Balancing', Leiden Journal of International Law.
[73] CETA (n 55), Preamble.
[74] Ibid.

Be this as it may, the inference is not wrong but remains confined to the soft law ambit. A more assertive stand to strengthen this understanding comes from the explicit recognition that domestic authorities are entitled to regulate within their own borders matters concerning investment protection standards.[75] This recognition materializes in the novel form of right to regulate provisions, in part included under the FET obligation and more extensively as brand new stand-alone obligations.

A provision granting states a right to regulate made its first appearance in the CETA investment chapter that vested the obligation with binding force and that read as follows:

> For the purpose of this Chapter, the Parties reaffirm their right to regulate within their territories to achieve *legitimate* policy objectives, such as the protection of public health, safety, the environment or public morals, social or consumer protection or the promotion and protection of cultural diversity.[76]

The phrase 'such as' indicates the illustrative nature of the ensuing list and implies that additional elements are admissible. The proposed approach recognizes a state's right to regulate across different policies and grants them a greater margin of regulatory manoeuvrability. The margin of manoeuvre is quite broad in scope, and read in combination with Article 8.31 CETA stretches up to a point of shielding domestic autonomy from the review activity of arbitral tribunals. Indeed, violations of domestic law (and therefore of EU law) do not automatically amount to a FET violation,[77] and are dismissed from the tribunal's review as a 'matter of fact'. CETA accords no competence to a tribunal to rule upon domestic law because it does not possess the jurisdiction to determine the legality of a measure that is alleged to constitute a breach of the agreement in question.[78] If necessary, the only legally admitted understanding of domestic law and its eventual application has to be made following the prevailing interpretation given by domestic authorities. The tribunal interprets the text of the agreement in question and relies on international law principles, but refrains from any interpretation that is inconsistent with those already issued by national courts or authorities.

[75] European Commission (2015), 'Concept Paper Investment in TTIP and Beyond—The Path for Reform', 6.

[76] CETA (n 55), Article 8.9. Emphasis added.

[77] Ibid, Article 8.10(7).

[78] Ibid, Article 8.31.

The recognition of a right to regulate in the context of investment protection is a commendable effort but requires adequate levels of legal certainty to be fully effective. One first problem that Article 8.9 left open is whether a breach of the FET standard is invocable just when the pursuit of a policy objective lacks legitimacy, and/or whether said breach occurs because the conduct of the host state is inconsistent with the obligations in Article 8.10(1). CETA does not specify if the two conditions are exclusive or cumulative. Unsurprisingly, the risk is to deflect the determination of what constitutes a legitimate public policy objective to the adjudicators, again. At this point, one might wonder how this could be any different from the work carried out so far by arbitral tribunals in assessing what constitutes a *normal* exercise of the state's regulatory powers.

Another problem arises from the application, or rather non-application, of domestic law. The most enthusiastic would read it as a laudable attempt to increase legal certainty in case of conflicts of law. The most sceptical, instead, would not miss the opportunity to see behind this choice the perils of open strategic autonomy acting on self-interest motivations to preserve the autonomy of the EU legal system, and in particular to safeguard the primacy of the CJEU. Be this as it may, what happens if there is no 'prevailing domestic interpretation' on which to base a decision, or if existing interpretations are ambiguous or conflicting? CETA, as well as other EU IPAs, does not speak directly about such a situation and opens the provision to different, albeit equally plausible, interpretations of tribunals reviewing the government's action in question. But wait: haven't we heard this story already, in the first pages of this chapter? The issue is indeed complex and raises several questions: could an arbitral tribunal apply the investment agreement to review a domestic provision that is crucial for the delivery of the final award? Would that amount to a de facto interpretation of a domestic provision? In so doing, would the tribunal overstep its boundaries and exceed its interpretative powers? Could the tribunal's interpretation be classified as an abuse of power? And what kind of consequences would this action entail? Would the tribunal's interpretation be admissible in certain (but at present unknown) cases? Even admitting that the arbitral tribunal applies (and does not interpret) domestic law, there might be situations where said application is in conformity with EU law but violates investment obligations, or vice versa, situations where compliance with the investment treaty obligations would constitute a breach of EU law, as have already emerged in practice.[79]

[79] In essence, there is a potential risk of ending up with a 'catch 22' situation where following EU law might result in a violation of investment law (e.g. *Micula*), or vice versa, where following investment law means violation of EU law (e.g. *Vattenfall*).

The attempts at balancing are laudable but present some limitations that if left unaddressed make one wonder how the outcomes are so different from those delivered by arbitral tribunals.

3. Labour, environmental, and sustainable development standards

While the preservation of the parties' right to regulate amounts to a great deal in the EU rebalancing of competing interests, this analysis would be incomplete without recognizing the efforts made by the EU agreements to the advancement of sustainable development, environmental, social, and labour commitments. Although these commitments may not be explicitly aimed at achieving greater certainty, they nonetheless strengthen the foundation for states' regulatory authority and, more broadly, provide additional grounds for balancing public and private interests. The insertion of such instruments is part of a broader promotional approach developed throughout the Trade and Sustainable Development (TSD) chapters included by the EU since its FTA with Korea (2011).

TSD chapters are quite illustrative of the EU's value-based approach to balance competing interests and use trade, even investment but to a lesser extent, as vehicles for promoting sustainable development worldwide,[80] rather than, for example, imposing greater obligations on investors. Different sets of obligations made up the bulk of these chapters. The first set includes obligations derived from existing international standards, like the International Labour Organization (ILO) Declaration on Fundamental Principles and Rights at Work. They largely correspond to a 'minimum level' of commitment to be respected and implemented, although in practice, they remain close to a 'best-effort' obligation of some form with no precise level of compliance:

> Each Party shall make continued and sustained efforts to ratify the fundamental ILO Conventions if they have not yet done so.[81]

The most recent obligation to implement the Paris Agreement effectively belongs to this group—for example, the proposed EU–Chile FTA, EU–Mercosur

[80] Marin Duran, Gracia (2020), 'Sustainable Development Chapters in EU Free Trade Agreements: Emerging Compliance Issues', Common Market Law Review, 2.

[81] EU–India FTA (EU textual proposal as of September 2022) TSD Chapter, Article X.3(3); Free Trade Agreement between the European Union and New Zealand (entered into force 1 May 2024), OJ L 2024/866, 25 March 2024, Article 19.3(5).

FTA, EU–Japan FTA, EU–Mexico FTA, EU–Angola facilitation agreement, and EU–New Zealand FTA. The case initiated by the EU and subsequently won against Korea clearly demonstrated that such provisions provide a basis for challenging bilateral policies under an FTA. Furthermore, it highlighted that the nature of the commitment is likely to result in a binding obligation.[82]

The other set of obligations pertains to domestic legislation. This legislation should neither derogate from FTA commitments nor fail to enforce domestic environmental and labour laws in a way that affects trade or investment. These provisions are also known as non-regression clauses and are explicitly linked to bilateral trade and investment:

> A Party shall not waive or otherwise derogate from, or offer to waive or otherwise derogate from, its environmental or labour law in order to encourage trade or investment.
>
> A Party shall not, through a sustained or recurring course of action or inaction, fail to effectively enforce its environmental or labour laws in order to encourage trade or investment.[83]

The condition for establishing a violation is to demonstrate that the derogation or non-enforcement of domestic environmental or labour laws impacts trade or investment. The language is firmer than in the Korea agreement ('in a manner affecting trade or investment') but the intent remains consistent—prevent any weakening in the environmental and labour regulations in the name of greater liberalization and maintain a 'level-playing field'.[84]

The third set of obligations is more aspirational in nature and serves to ensure that parties aspire towards 'high levels' of environmental and labour protection:

> Each Party shall strive to ensure that its relevant law and policies provide for, and encourage, high levels of environmental and labour protection, and shall strive to improve such levels, law and policies.[85]

[82] Panel of Experts Proceeding Constituted Under Article 13.15 of the EU–Korea Free Trade Agreement (25 January 2021).

[83] EU–India FTA(n 81), Article X.2(4) and (5). The same provision is included in CETA (n 55); EU–Mexico FTA (n 67); EU–Mercosur FTA (signed on 6 December 2024); EU–New Zealand FTA (n 81) Article 19.3(5) and (6).

[84] Marin Duran (n 80), 6.

[85] EU–India (n 81), Article X.2(2).

This set is broader if compared to the scope of the first two sets of obligations but is legally weaker given that best efforts would allow for different levels of compliance.

A particularly critical point of the EU TSD chapters is the enforcement. The EU has comparatively made a more assertive use of dispute settlement provisions than the US and Canada in enforcing labour and environmental commitments, but the compliance-inducing effect remains questionable. The EU TSD chapters[86] provide for a self-contained system of dispute settlement that is separated from disputes arising under other FTA chapters and is articulated in two main phases. The first phase consists of consultations during which the parties seek a mutually satisfactory resolution. In case of an unsatisfactory consultation process, in the second phase, the matter can be deferred to a Panel of experts, whose deliberations and recommendations shall be taken into account by the parties. The implementation of the Panel's report is carried out by the Joint Committee (consisting of representatives of both contracting parties) and stakeholders can submit their observations. There is no formal follow-up on any submissions or coercive mechanisms in place to ensure compliance. This last aspect is particularly revealing of the EU's non-confrontational approach to the enforcement of the TSD chapters. The EU–India proposal might bring a new perspective on the issue. At the conclusion of the TSD chapter, a disclaimer states: 'Provisions on dispute settlement applicable to the Trade and Sustainable Development Chapter have been incorporated in a revised EU proposal for the Dispute Settlement chapter.' While the dispute settlement chapter includes certain exceptions, no cross-references are provided (as of the September 2022 version). If TSD commitments were to be incorporated under the trade liberalization dispute framework and thereby enforced through the extension of the standard state-to-state dispute settlement mechanism to the TSD chapter, the implications would be significantly different:

> The final report shall be binding on the Parties and shall be accepted *unconditionally* by the Parties.[87]

The language is stronger ('unconditionally') than in other agreements but the absence of effective means to enforce compliance is not altogether removed. The EU–India TSD chapter proposal references 'compliance measures' aimed

[86] With the exception of the EU–CARIFORUM Economic Partnership Agreement (provisional application from 29 December 2008), OJ L 51, 25 February 2011.

[87] EU–India FTA (n 81), Article X.3(3). Emphasis added.

at restoring conformity with the Agreement.[88] In cases of non-compliance due to impossibility, time constraints, or inconsistency, the proposal introduces the option of temporary remedies, including temporary compensation and the suspension of obligations.[89] This marks a point of rupture with the EU's traditionally softer approach towards violations of sustainability obligations. This approach is already adopted in the EU–UK Trade and Cooperation Agreement, where either party can take 'rebalancing measures' in the form of trade or investment-related sanctions[90] to induce the non-compliant party to comply.

As often the case with EU intentions, however sound on paper it remains to be seen whether this approach would materialize and ultimately be extended to other commercial partners. The pondering over the improvement and enforcement of sustainability provisions has gained particular prominence over the last few years. In October 2020, Commissioner for Trade Dombrovskis announced the proposal to consider the Paris Agreement an 'essential element'. This would imply that a serious and substantial violation of the agreement amounts to the suspension or termination of the entire FTA. This signals the importance the EU attaches to climate change and its aspirational approach but appears too far-fetched, more symbolic than practical, and, perhaps more importantly, cannot substitute the need for regular and proportional sanctions in respect of less fundamental violations.[91]

In the name of stronger enforcement and implementation of TSD commitments, the Commission launched a review of the TSD approach (2021 Trade Policy Review). The review was then followed by a communication aimed at strengthening the implementation and enforcement of TSD chapters. This included extending the standard state-to-state dispute settlement to the TSD chapter and introducing the possibility of applying trade sanctions as a last resort for material breaches of the Paris Climate Agreement and the fundamental labour principles of the ILO (June 2022).[92] The Parliament and many stakeholders advocated for reflecting the new approach in all EU trade agreements currently under negotiation and future trade agreements, as well as FTAs that are in force, by using the review clause included in existing agreements or other

[88] Ibid, Article X.14.

[89] Ibid, Article 17.

[90] Trade and Cooperation Agreement between the European Union and the European Atomic Energy Community, of the one part, and the United Kingdom of Great Britain and Northern Ireland, of the other part (entered into force 1 May 2021), OJ L 149, 30 April 2021, Article 411.

[91] Gruni, Giovanni and Bronckers, Marco (2021), 'Retooling the Sustainability Standards in EU Free Trade Agreements', Journal of International Economic Law, 49–50.

[92] COM(2022)409 final.

appropriate procedures. The EU–New Zealand FTA (entered into force in May 2024) is the first agreement to integrate the new TSD approach.

The evidence indicates that the EU is indeed making bold moves towards the implementation and enforcement of sustainability commitments. Nonetheless, one may be tempted to question the integrity and consistency of the EU's commitment to improving the environmental and social conditions in partner countries. TSD chapters epitomize the EU's ideal aspirations towards a desired state of environmental and social affairs but fell short of trade or investment conditionality, possibly overshadowed by the preservation of a more liberalized approach for EU traders and investors. This is not to say that the EU is undermining its commitment to reach more balanced agreements or that its policy changes are not that assertive but rather that there can be economic interests in pursuing environmental and labour ideals hard to ignore. Despite an undeniable commitment to sustainable development, eradicating a vision of justice intrinsically oriented towards the preservation and maintenance of the Common Market is gruelling to alter. Opinion 2/15 corroborates the point:

> The objective of sustainable development henceforth forms an integral part of the common commercial policy.[93]

> [TSD chapters] are intended ... to govern trade between the European Union and the Republic of Singapore by making *liberalisation* of that trade subject to the condition that the Parties comply with their international obligations concerning social protection of workers and environmental protection.[94]

TSD chapters are incorporated under the Common Commercial Policy (CCP) and, as such, have not been categorized as merely ancillary to the predominant trade aims of the EU FTAs—reference is made to the one with Singapore in the quotation in question but can broadly extend to other agreements. Albeit there is no trade conditionality based upon non-compliance with social and environmental obligations, the Opinion signals a marked willingness towards a value-based external policy ('sustainable development forms an integral part')[95] through exclusive EU powers; hence the inclusion under the CCP. While the presence of an idealistic developmental dimension is undeniable, it remains shaped by the nuances of the quest for liberalization which ultimately mediated a more utilitarian approach.

[93] Opinion 2/15, *EU-Singapore FTA*, EU:C:2017:376, para 147.
[94] Ibid, para 166.
[95] Marin Duran (n 80), 14.

An interesting exception to the generally broad nature of the EU's approach to incorporating separate chapters or annexes on the environment or sustainable investment can be found in the agreement with China. The EU–China Comprehensive Agreement on Investment (CAI) provides for environmental protection through non-derogation clauses, introduces corporate social responsibility clauses, and imposes a duty of effective implementation of multilateral environmental agreements. China undertook to make 'continued and sustained efforts' to ratify the fundamental ILO conventions and agreed to a neutral and open scrutiny of labour abuses. Section IV of the agreement focuses on sustainable development and provides for an obligation devoted to 'Investment and Climate Change'.[96] Regrettably, the agreement has not entered into force given that the ratification process has been paused since March 2021 as a consequence of the evolving dynamics of the wider EU–China relationship.[97] Considerations as to its effectiveness are thus overshadowed by questions as to whether the EU's ability to propel its values is ultimately defensible through hard power means (sanctions) only.[98]

One last development worth mentioning is the adoption of a Directive on corporate sustainability due diligence in May 2024.[99] This Directive aims to foster sustainable and responsible corporate behaviour and to anchor human rights and environmental considerations in companies' operations and corporate governance. The Directive imposes a duty of due diligence on companies that are required to ensure that their business strategy is compatible with climate commitments under the Paris Agreement. Failures to comply could result in sanctions proportionate to the non-compliance act(s) in question,[100] and could be pecuniary and civil liability, or could result in a requirement from the supervising authority to cease or not repeat the infringement. The Directive applies to EU companies but, perhaps more intriguingly, also to non-EU companies having a direct link to the Single Market and turnovers above a certain threshold. This means that it delivers an extra-territorial application of EU standards, in line with the EU's inclination to extend what it stands for (its standards) outside its borders.[101] Albeit its application is confined to

[96] EU–China Comprehensive Agreement on Investment (Agreement in Principle 22 January 2021).

[97] In March 2021 the EU imposed sanctions on four Chinese officials for human rights abuses in Xinjiang. In response, Beijing sanctioned ten individuals and four entities in the EU, including Members of the European Parliament and the Council's Political and Security Committee.

[98] See Chapter 7.

[99] Directive (EU) 2024/1760 of the European Parliament and of the Council of 13 June 2024 on corporate sustainability due diligence, OJ L, 2024/1760, 5 July 2024.

[100] Ibid.

[101] Sattorova, Mavluda (2023), 'EU Investment Law at a Crossroads: Open Strategic Autonomy in Times of Heightened Security Concerns', Common Market Law Review, 710.

the EU border, it would be interesting to survey whether and how arbitral tribunals will treat the Directive as a matter of domestic law in the ambit of foreign investments.

E. Do the clothes have an emperor?

In an attempt to provide more balance, the EU IPAs insisted on preserving the state's regulatory autonomy through more detailed language and the insertion of right to regulate provisions. These intentions are laudable as the EU rebalancing is timidly and slowly evolving from the amelioration of the status quo towards a more comprehensive systemic altering.

One aspect that surprised me is the comparatively limited utilization of the public interest approach in EU IPAs. I am puzzled as to why the EU has not advocated more strongly for the inclusion of a comprehensive overriding public interest clause, potentially accompanied by transitional measures, in the evaluation of investors' legitimate expectations and, consequently, in the determination of breaches. It is remarkable that the EU has not taken a more assertive stance in affirming that an overriding public interest should take precedence over investors' expectations, even when such prioritization leads to adverse economic consequences for investors. While considering the protection of public interests, the EU typically constrains the scope of investors' expectations rather than explicitly allowing for their violation. This approach is further supported by Opinion 1/17, which affirmed that EU law can coexist with international investment law, provided arbitral tribunals do not undermine the level of public interest protection set by the Union. Nevertheless, it seems that the EU focuses more on defending its policy competence than actively advancing the protection of public interests. In more direct terms, why has the EU not shifted its perspective from a somewhat passive right to regulate (where modifications in law do not breach investor protection obligations) to an active right to protect public interest (where public interest justifies potential restrictions on investor protection)?

Legal certainty was a compelling starting point. However, if it remains unclear what is legitimate to expect from a government in a given situation, how can all interests be balanced effectively? The absence of clarity regarding what constitutes a failure to meet these expectations leaves open the question of whether investor rights should prevail over public interests, subjecting such determinations to circumstantial judgments.

I cannot help but wonder why the EU has not emphasized legal certainty as the cornerstone for safeguarding legitimate expectations. Under such a framework, tribunals would evaluate whether a given legitimate expectation merits protection by assessing the strength of the claim through the lens of legal certainty. This perspective allows for categorizing situations where legitimate expectation claims arise in international investment law along a continuum—from strong claims involving retroactive revocation of legal rights and formal administrative decisions, to weaker claims related to prospective regulatory changes. Accordingly, the stronger the claim based on legal certainty, the more compelling the government's justifications for its actions must be, and the higher the burden to justify any actions that fail to protect these expectations.[102] In conjunction, a balance between overriding public interest and legal certainty could have served as a foundation for a more balanced investment regime. As things stand, significant adjustments are still necessary in how these principles are applied under EU IPAs to effect substantial change.

Although the EU accelerates the opportunity to make the reorientation of investment (and trade) towards balance more likely than in the past, this is not done exclusively in the name of social justice but rather serves to shield the internal market and EU nationals from competitive distortions. The adoption of labour and environmental standards, in fact, may be economically burdensome for developing host countries and instead of contributing to their development risks impeding economic progress. Labour and environmental aspirations ultimately respond to a logic of shielding the internal market and EU nationals. The developmental dimension is problematic in countries that can be threatened by the use of liberalizing provisions by EU investors to enter and operate their markets.[103] Violations may even be economically beneficial given that those affected are not provided with effective means of enforcement. Stricter coercive measures like sanctions or retaliation, however, are likely to penalize small countries even more, given their unlikeness to inflict meaningful economic harm to the most economically powerful countries.

In this respect, the EU approach, albeit value driven, presents some ambiguities. EU IPAs grant governments to determine their public policies, yet they contained no mechanisms to ensure that those affected by standards' violations are provided with the necessary means of enforcement, as is the case with TSD-related issues, or that those potentially affected by the decision-making process have standing in the process, as is the case with investment-related

[102] Henckels (n 52), 11–12.
[103] See Chapter 7.

issues. Regarding the former, the enforcement of TSD chapters, the EU has recently launched a process of systemic reconfiguration aimed at improving the implementation and enforcement of sustainability commitments. Regarding the latter, third parties standing in arbitral proceedings, the EU has done little to correct these imbalances and continues to invest more in the means (prosperity through capital attraction at expenses of development) than in the ends (prosperity through economic development for all). This mindset would be hard to eradicate in a system where governments conceived the Single Market in purely economic terms and where claims of general interest and proportionality are handled almost exclusively by the CJEU. As a result, while balance remains an ideal part of the EU ethos, it is profoundly shaped by long-standing focus on economic justice. From this standpoint, the balancing exercise must be carried out by the judicial authority, which reflects both legal and, inevitably, political considerations in the decisions it delivers. This is problematic as it would ultimately subject balancing and, therefore, public policy determinations to the scrutiny of other judicial bodies, as discussed in the following chapter.

6

Judicializing investment arbitration

A. Overview

Chapter 5 explored the concept of balance, an ideal that is integral to the ethos of the EU but that requires systemic support to ensure effective judicial protection. Balance refers to a system in which all actors are proportionally bound by, and entitled to benefit from, the laws to which they are subject. This proportionality—a term more commonly associated with the EU than balance—emerges from a mutual sacrifice of a degree of freedom and power by both those subject to the law and the law-makers themselves.[1]

For this proportionality to be functional it has to operate in a context of impartial and independent justice, in the absence of which all the other precepts included in the rule of law would be deprived of almost any legal effect. Independence and impartiality are essential standards for the respect of the rule of law and constitute the means to ensure effective judicial protection. This configuration is deeply rooted in the EU, provides the foundation to ensure effective judicial protection internally, and is potentially suitable for extending its reach internationally.[2] From this perspective, judicialization stands out as a persuasive strategy for fostering a rules-based, procedurally just, and legally structured reorientation of any legal regime. In the context of the investment arbitration system, this approach could effectively address some of

[1] This definition has been largely inspired by the rule of law definition provided by the Rt Hon. the Lord Bingham of Cornhill KG:

> *all persons* and *authorities* within the state, *whether public or private*, should be *bound by and entitled to the benefit of laws* publicly and *prospectively* promulgated and *publicly administered* in the courts. . . .
>
> There has been much debate whether the rule of law can exist without *democracy*. Some have argued that it can. But it seems to me that the rule of law does depend on an unspoken but fundamental bargain between the individual and the state, the governed and the governor, by which both sacrifice a measure of the freedom and power which they would otherwise enjoy. The individual living in society implicitly accepts [. . .] the constraints imposed by laws properly made *because of the benefits* which, *on balance*, they confer. The *state* for its part accepts that it *may not do*, at home or abroad, *all that it has the power to do* but only that which laws binding upon it authorise it to do.

Bingham, Tom (2006), *The Sixth Sir David Williams Lecture—The Rule of Law*. Emphasis added.

[2] Case T 288/15, *Ezz and others v Council*, EU:T:2018:619, paras 59–61.

EU Values in Investment Law And Policy. Maria Laura Marceddu, Oxford University Press.
 DOI: 10.1093/9780191986208.003.0006

the most pressing systemic dysfunctions that sustain imbalances. Moreover, it aligns with the goal of providing a judicial pathway for advancing political objectives that may not have gained traction in majoritarian decision-making arenas, even if this necessitates a degree of compromise between the EU and international law.

As this chapter explores, judicialization has evolved from being primarily concerned with upholding the rule of law to becoming the EU's favoured mechanism for guiding other countries towards adopting what the EU perceives as the appropriate 'rules of the game'. These rules can privilege certain interests, shape modes of conduct, and, even through litigation, influence the development of precedent.[3] Under the banner of judicialization, the EU has not only advanced integration but, perhaps more intriguingly, also driven political change—particularly in situations where politics and politicians were reluctant to act.[4]

The chapter is divided into three main stages. It begins by outlining the demands that have arisen within the investment system (Section B). Following this, it provides background on the evolution of the EU's judicialization narrative and examines the responses it has proposed (Section C). Finally, Section D concludes the analysis by questioning whether the EU's responses represent a genuine effort to address the imbalances within the investment regime or if they instead reflect a strategy to exert control over EU Member States.

B. Investment arbitration, arbitrators' powers, and legitimacy

It is fair to acknowledge up front that the investment arbitration order displays a significant degree of judicialization, of which the fair and equitable treatment (FET) doctrine constitutes an important illustration. The FET is an incomplete provision par excellence and offers a solid example of how arbitrators' progressive law-making has fleshed out its meanings in ways that have transformed the underlying law and politics of the regime.[5] Thanks to the absence of any explicit indication in investment treaties, arbitral tribunals had sufficient

[3] Sandholtz Wayne (2023), 'Is Winter Coming? Norm Challenges and Norm Resilience.' In *Tracing Value Change in the International Legal Order: Perspectives from Legal and Political Science*, edited by Heike Krieger and Andreea Liese, 54; Pelc, Krzysztof (2014), 'The Politics of Precedent in International Law: A Social Network Application', American Political Science Review.

[4] Weiler, Joseph (1999), *The Constitution of Europe 'Do the New Clothes Have an Emperor?' and Other Essays on European Integration*, 10–101.

[5] Stone Sweet, Alec and Grisel, Florian (2017), *The Evolution of International Arbitration: Judicialization, Governance, Legitimacy*, 171–217.

leverage progressively to construe the doctrine of legitimate expectations[6] as one of the major components[7] of the standard, if not the 'dominant' element,[8] albeit nowhere mentioned in a FET provision. Legitimate expectations, in turn, also propelled arbitrators towards a balancing posture[9] that attempts to take into consideration the rationale behind public policy choices along with the legitimate reliance on particular investment-backed expectations.

Truth be told, arbitrators have not concealed their law-making, and their interpretative reach into sensitive domains has grown proportionally to the state's involvement with the system. After all, states voluntarily entrust arbitral tribunals to substantiate their commitment to respect investors' rights, and arbitrators derive their inherent authority from investment treaties. This system worked relatively undisturbed and dormant for decades. The peculiar nature of the controversies to be resolved, however, eventually put the procedure under pressure and states' lingering doubts[10] over investment tribunals' law-making rapidly escalated into a matter of concern. While the arbitral procedure remains legitimized by the parties through an act of express delegation (from the contracting states to the tribunal), the act itself is implicated in political governance. As such, political legitimacy cannot be presumed but has to be scrutinized.[11]

When exposed to scrutiny, the arbitral procedure—that is, the process of assessing investors' entitlements in relation to what is prescribed by the investment agreement—reveals shortcomings in terms of both legitimacy and accountability. This type of critique is frequently derived from one of the historically distinctive features of arbitration that accords the disputants power to select their own adjudicators. Claimants and respondents, in fact, have the right to appoint one arbitrator each, in case of a three adjudicator tribunal, or to jointly designate one sole arbitrator. Unsurprisingly, it has often been argued that the parties' right of appointment fails to provide the same guarantees of independence and impartiality as a state court. The appointment connection between those subject to judgment and those in charge of judging instils the suspect of inappropriate bias in investment arbitration and questions the lack (whether real or perceived) of the institutional safeguards of independence and impartiality, which are otherwise present in the adjudicative function.

[6] See Chapter 5.

[7] *EDF (Services) Limited v Romania* (Award, 8 October 2009), para 216.

[8] *Saluka Investments BV v The Czech Republic* (Partial Award, 17 March 2006), para 302.

[9] *Thunderbird v Mexico* (Separate opinion of Thomas Wälde, 1 December 2005).

[10] Stone Sweet and Grisel (n 5), 218–52.

[11] Van Harten, Gus (2007), *Investment Treaty Arbitration and Public Law*; van Harten, Gus (2010), 'Five Justifications for Investment Treaties: A Critical Discussion', Trade, Law & Development.

Beyond the 'moral hazard'[12] underpinning arbitrators' appointment process, a further concern resides in the fact that the same individuals are not precluded from acting as counsel in different cases—that is, the so-called double-hat phenomenon. As Crawford has put it, the problem is that there exist

> situation[s] in which one day you are presenting an expert opinion on a particular point, the next day you are acting as counsel on the same point of investment law, and the day after you are sitting as an arbitrator in a case which raises that very point, [and this] undoubtedly give[s] rise to difficulties, however much personal integrity the individuals display.[13]

But there is more. The legitimacy problem is furthermore amplified by the nature of the controversies at stake and the powers bestowed upon arbitrators to resolve them. Tribunals are entrusted with the ascertainment of whether the host state's conduct constitute (or not) a *normal* exercise of its regulatory powers according to what is prescribed by the investment agreement invoked, and to award compensation to the investor where the state's liability is found. Unlike other dispute settlement systems, investment arbitration enables the claimants (investors) to seek direct enforcement of their substantive rights and, in case of violations of those rights, to obtain monetary compensation rather than invalidation or performance orders. It is not hard to read into this the neoliberalism prioritization of wealth creation, preservation, and economic efficiency as primary goals of policy. This is furthermore corroborated by the fact that the main purpose of investment agreements tends to remain (as it has been since their very beginning) the protection and promotion of investment, as clearly stated in their title, which generally reads as 'agreement between the Government of the state X and the Government of the state Y on the reciprocal *promotion* and *protection* of investments'.

These characteristics are problematic for many reasons. While it is undeniable that investment agreements seek to attract and protect foreign direct investments (FDIs), it would be too shortsighted to constrain their potential reach only to a utilitarian output legitimacy that would focus one-sidedly on investor interests and neglect all other non-economic interests. Yet, as things stand, there is liability and compensation for states' wrongdoings but no

[12] Brower, Charles N and Rosenberg, Charles B (2013), 'The Death of the Two-Headed Nightingale: Why the Paulsson—van den Berg Presumption that Party-Appointed Arbitrators are Untrustworthy is Wrongheaded', Arbitration International, 7.

[13] Hofmann, Rainer and Tams, Christian J (2011), *International Investment Law and General International Law: From Clinical Isolation to Systemic Integration?*, 21.

obligations upon investors or sanctions to offer remedies in case of investments that fail to perform efficiently. Even in the presence of failed investments, investment arbitration operates as a meaningful constraint on politics with tribunals questioning whether states' behaviours conform to what is prescribed by the investment treaty and whether such behaviours are ultimately the cause for the investment's failure.[14]

This configuration that accords discretion to arbitrators in the name of investment protection sits uncomfortably with the deference owed to states and since no non-market-based solutions are set to hold investors liable, the system is unavoidably exposed to the criticism that it creates imbalances and is inattentive to alternative social values. Overall, these imbalances undermine the regime's ability to deliver the promised material prosperity.[15] This becomes even more concerning when considering that the negative economic consequences of an investment are often borne disproportionately by citizens and consumers—potentially twice. First, because of the negative impact a failed investment may have locally, for example, because of its impact at the environmental level; second, arbitrations argued upon failed investments risk penalizing states that deviated from the standard rational model prescribed by investment agreements. As a matter of practice, failed investments and, more broadly, the negative effects on the investment's outcomes are often framed and sanctioned as consequences of changes introduced by the state to the investment environment, rather than being attributed to any wrongdoing on the part of the investor.

More bluntly put, the rationale behind this approach would appear to be a punitive logic that sanctions deviant governments with damage awards in case of unusual commercial behaviours impacting the investment negatively—where 'unusual behaviours' potentially include also legitimate political choices. Here is the point where the problem emerges more vividly: arbitrators possess inherent powers to determine applicable standards of review mainly in light of effective protection of foreign investments, which, incidentally, is derived from a certain reading of the treaty's purpose.[16] From this standpoint, how can arbitrators effectively balance a state's commitments to investors, as outlined

[14] A case in point is *Biwater Gauff (Tanzania) v Tanzania* (Award, 24 July 2008). See also Chapter 5 and the disputes emerged against Spain (as well as the Czech Republic, Italy) in the renewable energy context.

[15] Lang, Andrew (2013), *World Trade Law after Neoliberalism: Reimagining the Global Economic Order*, 1–7.

[16] Stone Sweet and Grisel (n 5), 218–52. Pelc posits that the record of investment disputes is consistent with the view that the regime is increasingly been used to challenge domestic regulation. Pelc, Krzysztof (2017), 'What Explains the Low Success Rate of Investor-State Disputes?', International Organization.

in the investment treaty, against its legitimate public policy obligations to its citizens in pursuit of a legitimate public objective? Despite the lack of reference in many investment agreements, especially those of the first generation, *Saluka* was one of the first tribunals that recognized that there were more factors to consider when interpreting investment agreements:

> The protection of foreign investments is not the sole aim of the Treaty, but rather a necessary element alongside the overall aim of encouraging foreign investment and extending and intensifying the parties' economic relations. That in turn calls for a balanced approach to the interpretation of the Treaty's substantive provisions for the protection of investments, since an interpretation which exaggerates the protection to be accorded to foreign investments may serve to dissuade host States from admitting foreign investments and so undermine the overall aim of extending and intensifying the parties' mutual economic relations.[17]

The interpretative approach has evolved from being primarily centred on the protection of investors to recognizing, though not always accommodating, the need for economic relations that are mutually beneficial for both investors and host states. As a matter of practice, arbitral tribunals have attempted to engage in some form of balancing, but these attempts are not uniform and proceed on a case-by-case basis. On their part, states have endeavoured to instil more proportionality in arbitral law-making in a way that would alter the determinants of arbitrators' decision-making. So far, the most common states' responses to curb arbitral law-making have been the insertion of state's right to regulate provisions, more detailed provisions,[18] and exception clauses that allow states to derogate from their treaty obligations when pursuing relevant policy interests—for example, health, environmental, social, and labour issues. None of these novelties comes without controversy. Nor they are applied and interpreted unreservedly.

The insertion of general exceptions in international investment agreements (IIAs), for example, safeguards the state's right to regulate by including a list of situations in which the state is allowed to enforce certain measures, under certain conditions, without falling under liability. In practice, however,

[17] *Saluka v Czech Republic* (n 8), para 300.
[18] See Chapter 5

tribunals interpretations have significantly narrowed[19] their scope of application, diminishing[20] and redefining[21] the state's margin of manoeuvre.

Arbitrators do not entirely disregard the public interest or dismiss the sovereign prerogatives of states. However, tribunals have consistently demonstrated a tendency to limit the impact of states' strategies to curtail their reach. States, in turn, find themselves trapped between the potential financial obligations owed to investors and their public policy commitments to citizens. This tension makes it increasingly difficult for states to justify the legitimacy of arbitral law-making to the public, particularly when its added value appears unclear in the context of well-established and well-functioning domestic legal systems.[22]

As a result, this created a demand for greater accountability, particularly regarding the legitimacy of arbitrators. The EU responded by emphasizing key rule of law principles, such as judicial impartiality and independence. These principles are embedded within a judicialized approach that embodies a modus operandi deeply valued by the EU, as explored in the following section.

C. The EU remodelling of investor–state arbitration's legitimacy: A story of judicialization

Arguably, judicialization is, or rather has become, one of the EU's preferred methods to induce systemic change, with a view to advancing economic and political integration.

Broadly speaking, the phenomenon of judicialization characterizes the growing role of international tribunals in global governance since the end of the twentieth century.[23] It refers to a two-sided process by which courts and

[19] In *Bear Creek v Peru*, a Canadian investor (Bear Creek) was barred from pursuing the exploitation of significant silver ore deposits due to the violent protests and social unrest of the local population toward the project and the investor, which culminated in a revocation from the government that ultimately shuttered the mining project. Despite the Peruvian invocation of the general exception, the tribunal read the presence of wording 'such as' in the provision narrowly and concluded that the general exception could be understood as exemplary and the list, therefore, must be understood to be an exclusive list. *Bear Creek Mining Corporation v Republic of Peru* (Award, 30 November 2017), para 473.

[20] Even assuming the applicability of the general exception (as an exemption from liability), compensation for expropriation to the claimant might be due anyway. *Eco Oro Minerals Corp. v Republic of Colombia* (Decision on Jurisdiction, Liability and Directions on Quantum, 9 September 2021), paras 830–833.

[21] Tribunals have insisted that reliance on other treaty provisions, such as the right to regulate, would give states more margin of manoeuvre and that would be redundant to include regulatory autonomy also in the ambit of a general exception. Especially if this is explicitly provided by the agreement. See in this sense, Canada FIPA model (2021), Annex B-13.

[22] *Saluka v Czech Republic* (n 8).

[23] Basedow, Robert (2021), 'Why De-judicialize? Explaining State Preferences on Judicialization in World Trade Organization Dispute Settlement Body and Investor-to-State Dispute Settlement Reforms', Regulation and Governance, 1.

judges increasingly dominate politics and policy-makers,[24] and policy-makers increasingly rely on the judiciary to address contentious legal issues of a political nature and significance.[25] Judicialization can be seen as a process of infusion of judicial decision-making that progressively shapes the strategic behaviours of the political actors engaged in interactions with one another.[26] Depending on the judicial setting, judicialization might express certain normative aspirations and generate the conditions necessary for reconfiguring the system accordingly, as illustrated by the ambitious constitutional reimagining of EU law driven by the Court of Justice of the European Union (CJEU).

The EU project can be depicted as the result of a process of judicialization in motion. Its entire unfolding is a story of economic integration through law, which was made possible because of early constitutional choices that rejected the 'ancient idea of the sovereignty of States in international law' to give life to 'a "true new legal order [*ordre juridique nouveau*]", with its own existence and organization, functioning with a minimum of autonomy from the Member States'.[27] The EU was established with a strong judicial foundation and a legal framework designed to safeguard its economic structure—most notably the Single Market—dating back to the European Economic Community and European Coal and Steel Community treaties. The judicialized configuration highlights the remarkable efforts of the CJEU in diligently protecting the EU's economic architecture, particularly its autonomy and prerogatives. By relentlessly supplying interpretative understanding of the binding nature of European obligations, the Court audaciously forged new legal configurations that bestowed upon EU law direct effect and supremacy,[28] and that furthered economic prosperity, peace, and the EU's influence.

In the EU project, the legal was coupled with the economic since the very beginning, whereas the political always remained somehow stuck in a state of tension. While judicialization emerged as a necessary strategy for the CJEU to progressively liberalize intra-community trade, its political dimension, at least initially, appeared more as a spillover effect than a deliberate choice. The global preferences for free markets and free trade provide a fertile soil also within the EU to advance liberalization by (i) preventing states' protectionism,[29] and,

[24] Tate, Neal and Vallinder, Torbjrn (1997), *The Global Expansion of Judicial Power*, 27.

[25] Hirsch, Ran (2009), 'The Judicialization of Politics.' In *The Oxford Handbook of Law and Politics*, edited by Keith E Whittington, Daniel Kelemen, and Gregory A Caldeira.

[26] Shapiro, Martin and Stone Sweet, Alec (2002), *On Law, Politics, and Judicialization*, 71–3.

[27] P Gori (1967) cited in Phelan, William (2019), *Great Judgments of the European Court of Justice*, 28.

[28] Phelan (n 27), 29, 83.

[29] See Case 120/78, *Rewe-Zentral AG v Bundesmonopolverwaltung für Branntwein* ('*Cassis de Djon*') EU:C:1979:42; Case 6-64, *Costa v Enel*, EU:C:1964:66.

more generally, (ii) fostering the pursuit of commerce in individual Member States.

What then distinguished the EU approach from the rest is a transition from correcting market failures to correcting regulatory failures. The Court did not impose its particular constitutional conception or model of the Single Market. Nor did it seize the opportunity to regulate supranational norms. The Court undertook a gradual process of evaluating and harmonizing the diverse economic models of Member States, rejecting those that failed to align with an ideal balance of all Member States' interests—what it identified as regulatory failures—even when these models were not inherently protectionist (i.e. market failures). The persistent institutional inefficiencies and largely overlooked political shortcomings that had characterized the Community since its inception, coupled with the inability of national markets to achieve self-integration, placed the Court in a unique position to exert broader control over national regulations within the Common Market, all in pursuit of greater harmonization.

The Court navigated the delicate balance between public intervention and free market principles, gradually defining the permissible scope of public regulation. In doing so, it effectively assumed the role of a *législateur de substitution*, as Maduro aptly described it.[30] Consequently, the Court increasingly perceived itself as 'authorized' to advance economic integration through judicial means whenever it deemed such intervention necessary.[31] Having acquired control over regulatory powers, the Court gradually guided the Community towards a deeper Europeanization of state policy-making regulation, shaping Member States' behaviours and exercising control over their escape mechanisms, unilateral safeguards, derogation mechanism, and retaliatory suspension of obligations.

The Court's contribution to construing a judicializing mindset for the advancement of the economic, and to a lesser extent political, integration, is undeniable, yet judicialization *à la* EU is not about how the judiciary has used its power, or at least cannot be entirely explained by that. After all, it is not as if the Court hunted policy-makers,[32] but rather because some institutional malfunctions[33] prevented other institutions from taking the lead. Judicialization was set in motion by policy-makers (especially the Commission) who believed that

[30] Maduro, Miguel Poiares (1998), *We the Court.*

[31] Ibid, 68.

[32] On the activism of some international courts see: Zarbiyev, Fuad (2012), 'On the Judge Centredness of the International Legal Self', European Journal of International Law, 247.

[33] Maduro (n 30).

the judiciary should participate in policy-making and resolve troublesome issues. On their part, EU technocrats and policy-makers alike did not miss the occasion to twist policy disputes into matters of rights[34] so as to avoid controversial decisions being left to the foolish (or wise) discretion of other institutions or Member States.[35]

This ideological approach is generated by a broader increase in the role of the regulatory state and the corresponding need to correct regulatory failures instead of market failures only. As Majone explains, the failure of regulation by public ownership led to a shift towards alternative models of control, with privatization standing as the most prominent example. Public utilities were transferred into private hands but remained governed by rules established by specialized agencies. These agencies, while operating independently of central government, maintained a connection to it, ensuring a balance between autonomy and accountability. It is only in Europe, however, that this transferred into the hands of the Court in Brussels and assumed a new breed and new modus operandi. In a system where the economic and the legal are intrinsically connected, this comes as no surprise. What originated as an enhancement of the power of rule-making to correct 'market failures' within the Single Market quickly became an issue of 'regulatory' failure necessary for the EU multilevel system to be operational. Regulatory failures provide ground for the consolidation of a constitutional structure that is supranational in nature, very much independent from the domestic (Member States) level,[36] but that became heavily reliant on the Court's involvement to harmonize different national regulations across the Member States. The more the need to correct regulatory failures, the more the power shifted towards the Court, which, in turn, built up a progressive harmonization of national misalignments and made sure that EU law had precedence over national laws.

Once set in motion, judicialization not only consolidated the EU legal order but also disciplined—if not outright tamed—Member States' behaviours. Bolstered by the Court's decisions, this normative approach functioned primarily as a safeguard against Member States' escape mechanisms, inter-state retaliation,[37] and internal disagreements. However, judicialization quickly evolved beyond these initial purposes. The EU's ability to generate and enforce rules through the CJEU, even without multilateral cooperation among

[34] Tate and Vallinder (n 24), 515–28.
[35] Ibid, 33.
[36] Majone, Giandomenico (1997), 'From the Positive to the Regulatory State: Causes and Consequences of Changes in the Mode of Governance', Journal of Public Policy, 144.
[37] Ibid.

Member States, was largely driven by the goal of advancing economic integration within the Single Market. To a lesser extent, it also aimed at safeguarding the broader political Community. Unsurprisingly, the EU's approach remained predominantly focused on strengthening the Single Market and ensuring seamless transactions among its members.

Lacking the traditional tools of state power, the EU swiftly recognized that norms, along with judicial mechanisms to enforce them, were among the most effective means of safeguarding its social preferences without undermining the competitiveness of the Single Market, particularly in the face of external threats.[38] The monopoly of the CJEU, along with its associated legal safeguards, was specifically designed to shield the EU from such external challenges.[39] This explains why the expansion, replication, export, and sometimes 'imposition' of the EU judicializing mindset in global economic governance rapidly became a condition to safeguard the competitiveness of European industries, albeit often advanced as a desirable, if not necessary, rule-based systemic feature to harmonize differences.

The tendency to emphasize the universal benefits of EU norms and values gained traction especially in the span of the last couple of decades, in the course of which judicialization materialized more solidly as a by-product of EU internal policies.[40] The Lisbon Treaty clearly played a role in accelerating the replication of norms (Article 2 TEU) outside EU borders, with a view to promoting and projecting EU values abroad (Article 3(5)TEU) and to contributing to the achievement of global good governance (Article 21 TEU). Under the Lisbon Treaty, 'normative power Europe'[41] becomes a fait accompli and expands into other, mostly the international, legal contexts, in a way that transforms and shapes while also defending EU values. Accordingly, the EU's transformative powers become even more prominent in its external action to project its normative choices externally, while safeguarding its interests.

It is not an exaggeration to posit that the EU retains an aspiration (read the power) to transform the global system by 'regulating' and fixing regulatory failures rather than simply preserving the existing standards of behaviour

[38] Bradford, Anu (2020), *The Brussels Effect*, 23.

[39] De Abreu Duarte, Francisco (2019), 'But the Last Word is Ours: The Monopoly of Jurisdiction of the Court of Justice of the European Union in Light of the Investment Court System', European Journal of International Law, 1187.

[40] Zielonka, Jan (2008), 'Europe as a Global Actor: Empire by Example?', International Affairs; Bradford (n 38).

[41] See among others: Manners, Ian (2009), 'The Concept of Normative Power in World Politics', Danish Institute for International Studies; Manners, Ian (2010), 'The Normative Ethics of the European Union', International Affairs.

for the rest of the world, especially whenever they cross EU vital interests.[42] The presumption is that the EU is prepared to propose normatively desirable principles that have universally applicable value for global governance[43] and are attractive to other countries.[44] The underlying assumption is that the EU embodies a 'desirable norm'—a set of values and principles that transcend the particular interests of individual parties (initially the Member States and ultimately the global community). These norms are presented as universally beneficial and something others should adopt. In reality, however, the EU's efforts are driven by economic interests tied to the Single Market and political processes with social implications. These interests necessitate the alignment of other legal regimes to ensure the EU can preserve and protect its prerogatives.

The EU is not entirely unique in its aspirations. Other norm-setters, albeit with important limitations, share with the EU a vocation to exercise democratic control over economic life,[45] if not even a predisposition to set the standards of review. One might well read similar judicializing aspirations in the investment arbitration order too. What is lacking in the latter and distinguishes the EU instead is the undeniable success attributed to its enforcement mechanism—that is, a powerful court that enjoys compulsory jurisdiction, autonomous decision-making, and legitimacy to exercise authority and ensure adherence to the EU norms.

When the EU began to navigate the investment arbitration regime it was inspired by its own story of judicialization, which evidently succeeded in harmonizing and levelling up the rules across Member States, often generating legitimacy and obedience internally. External judicialization followed, furthered by a favourable conjunction of global disquiet. Initially overlooked, the 'chaos of legal multiplicity' within the investment regime, coupled with

[42] Shared Vision, Common Action: A stronger Europe - A Global Strategy for the European Union's Foreign and Security Policy (2016), 39, emphasis added; Bradford (n 38), 24.

[43] Barbé, Esther, Herranz-Surrallés, Anna, and Natorski, Michal (2014), 'Contending Metaphors of the European Union as a Global Actor', Journal of Language and Politics, 18.

[44] Aggestam, Lisbeth (2012), 'Global Norms and European Power.' In *Routledge Handbook on the European Union and International Institutions*, edited by Knud Erik Jørgensen and Katie Verlin Laatikainen.

[45] It may be argued that trade (WTO) and investment adjudicators (e.g. NAFTA panels) were genuinely inspired by a sense of the 'greater good' and were acting as 'the guardians' of the underlying trade and investment values: liberalizing trade and protecting foreign investment. Marceddu, Maria Laura and Ortino, Federico (2021), 'Intersections Between Trade and Investment Law and Policy.' In *Yearbook on International Investment Law and Policy 2019*, edited by Lisa Sachs, Lise Johnson, and Jesse Coleman. Harrow considers that the same capitalist, market, economic ideology of the EU forms the background values of the WTO and also, with important reservations, the World Bank and International Monetary Fund, though the scope for action and dissemination of values has so far been less than is the case with the EU. Harrow, Carol (2006), 'Global Administrative Law: The Quest for Principles and Values', European Journal of International Economic Law, 196.

states' growing dissatisfaction with arbitral tribunals' law-making, created a vacuum that the EU was quick to exploit to address political and legitimacy challenges. Much like its approach to democracy, the EU recognized that the imbalanced relationship between arbitration law-makers and the deference owed to states presented a unique opportunity to pursue a dual strategic objective: address legitimacy issues on the global stage while continuing to refine them domestically.

In the name of greater coordination and harmonization of controversial matters, avoidance of deadlock, and blame deflections,[46] the EU advanced a set of judicializing solutions that are much more than a simple answer to legitimacy problems of investment arbitration, but pave the way for the EU to impart its standards of behaviour and drag others into its normative orbit. Building on this premise, one could argue that judicialization could help address legitimacy concerns. However, the EU's approach—framed around the idea of 'good legal decisions applied by good countries'—seems to be obscured by a broader commitment to establishing a rule-based international order, one that is inspired by and structured according to its own standards and interests. Perhaps ironically, it looks as if arbitrators' law-making poses problems in terms of legitimacy, whereas its replacement with an EU *legislateur de sustitution* suddenly would not. While judicialization may help resolve the legitimacy and imbalance issues affecting investment arbitration, furthering this process is likely to allow the EU to assert its normative orientations—or, more directly, impose its own law-making style. In practice, the situation is more granular and the EU approach oscillates between these two extremes. To assess whether this approach effectively balances investors' entitlements with host states' right to regulate, let us now examine the EU's key actions aimed at reshaping investment arbitration: (i) ensuring the independence and impartiality of adjudicators, and (ii) establishing an Investment Court System (ICS) and a Multilateral Investment Court (MIC).

1. Independence and impartiality of adjudicators

One of the most contentious aspects of investment arbitration concerns its adjudicators; specifically, what is often questioned is the impermeability of arbitrators to external influences and, therefore, their legitimacy. These concerns are aggravated by arbitrators' appointment configuration which makes

[46] Hirsch (n 25).

them reliant on prospective claimants,[47] and thus unlikely to possess a 'psychological attitude of initial indifference'. This (perceived) lack of legitimacy threatens to undermine the trust that justice is expected to inspire in a democratic society.[48] Public confidence in the independence and proper functioning of the judiciary is crucial not only for ensuring systemic legitimacy but also for safeguarding the very foundation of the rule of law,[49] which rests on independence and impartiality as its cornerstones. Without guarantees of judicial independence, the judiciary risks being unable to effectively constrain power and remain vulnerable to external pressures. Indeed, effective judicial protection depends on independent and impartial courts; in the absence of these attributes, the fundamental rights to judicial protection and a fair trial are severely compromised.

In EU law, independence and impartiality are the two complementary dimensions of judicial protection. Independence *strictu sensu* is the external dimension and implies protection against external constraints that would cloud an independent judgment. Independence imposes a duty to exercise adjudicating functions fully autonomously, 'without being subjected to any hierarchical constraint' and 'without taking orders or instructions from any sources'.[50] Impartiality, instead, refers to the internal dimension and requires objectivity and absence of any interest in the outcome. The adjudicators are expected to possess a 'psychological attitude of initial indifference' and appear equidistant from the litigant parties,[51] so as to ensure a level playing field for the parties to the proceedings and their respective interests as regards the subject matter of the proceedings.[52]

In investment arbitration, impartiality and independence mostly surface during arbitrators' disqualifications. In this context, independence is referred to the lack of a relationship with a party that might influence the arbitrator's decision and, more broadly, to the absence of external control.[53] Impartiality is defined as the absence of bias or predisposition towards one of the parties.[54]

[47] Van Harten, Gus (2013), *Sovereign Choices and Sovereign Constraints*, 163.

[48] Case C-508/19, *Mf v Prokurator Generalny*, ECLI:EU:C:2021:290, para 29.

[49] Case C-791/19, *Commission v Poland*, ECLI:EU:C:2021:596.

[50] Case C-503/15, *Margarit Panicello v Hernández Martínez*, ECLI:EU:C:2017:126, para 37.

[51] Case C-17/00, *De Coster v Collège des Bourgmestre et Échevins de Watermael-Boitsfort*, EU:C:2001:366, para 93 citing Calamandrei fn 117.

[52] Case C-685/15, *Online Games and others v Landespolizeidirektion Oberösterreich*, EU:C:2017:452, para 60–61; Case C-748/19, *Prokuratura Rejonowa*, EU:C:2021:403, paras 172–174.

[53] *Blue Bank v Venezuela* (Decision on the Parties' Proposals to Disqualify a Majority of the Tribunal, 12 November 2013), para 59; *Burlington v Ecuador* (14 December 2012), para 66; *ConocoPhillips v Venezuela* (Decision on the proposal to disqualify a Majority of the Tribunal, 5 May 2014), para 51; *VM Solar v Spain* (Decision on Respondent Proposal to disqualify all members of the tribunal, 18 October 2022), para 72.

[54] *Blue Bank v Venezuela* (n 53).

Both qualities provide the parties with protection against 'arbitrators being influenced by factors other than those related to the merits of the case'.[55] Independence and impartiality have been described as 'a state of mind' that can only be 'inferred from the conduct of the arbitrator in question or those connected to them'.[56] For this reason, the burden of proof lies with the challenging party that is required to indicate what leads to a manifest and evident lack of independence and impartiality (Article 57 International Centre for Settlement of Investment Disputes (ICSID) Convention).[57] In the last decades states have increasingly specified the arbitrators' requirements in their investment treaties and arbitral tribunals have begun to insist on treating independence and impartiality as fundamental rules of procedure,[58] the departure from which would amount to a violation of the international law minimum standards.

Under both EU and investment law, independence and impartiality serve to ensure a fair trial, but while in investment arbitration these are (or at least have long been) presumed, in the EU they are implied. The difference is more noticeable from an output perspective: legitimate doubts as to an adjudicator's independence and impartiality threaten the very existence of the rule of law and prejudice the foundational structure upon which EU values and norms are built and which should be promoted externally. In the investment regime instead, the lack of either component equates to a matter of procedure violations,[59] which could be rectified by an annulment but would not put the system's existence in question.

Against these shortcomings, current reform processes have called for a retooling of certain institutional design aspects, mainly to rectify the absence of characteristics like tenure, fixed remuneration, prohibition of concurrent work, etc. in the arbitrator's profile. UNCITRAL and ICSID, for example, have devised a code of conduct for arbitrators, which was formally adopted in the course of the UNCITRAL 56th annual session.[60] The code constitutes

[55] Ibid.

[56] *Suez v Argentina* (Decision on the Proposal for the Disqualification of a Member of the Arbitral Tribunal, 22 October 2009), para 30.

[57] Ibid.

[58] *Lemire v Ukraine II* (Decision on Annulment, 8 July 2013), para 263; *Impregilo v Argentina* (Annulment, 24 January 2014), para 163-5; *Quilborax v Bolivia* (Decision on Annulment, 18 May 2018), para 114; *Eiser v Spain* (Decision on Annulment, 11 June 2020), para 239.

[59] One exception, albeit the language remains soft, is *Infinito Gold v Costa Rica* that considered independence and impartiality as 'indispensable to the proper administration of justice', albeit no mention of the fulfilment of the rule of law is found. *Infinito Gold v Costa Rica* (Award, 3 June 2021), para 445.

[60] UNCITRAL Working Group III, 'Draft code of conduct for arbitrators in international investment dispute resolution and commentary. Note by the Secretariat (28 April 2023)', UN Doc A/CN.9/1148 (for discussion purposes only).

a remarkable attempt to enhance confidence and even the appearance itself of confidence.[61] As the commentary explains, an arbitrator must remain vigilant and be proactive in ensuring that he or she does not instigate an impression of bias and should make continued efforts to not create a perception of bias. The Code marks an interesting turning point in tackling the concern of double hatting of arbitrators (external dimension) and the risk it poses to their independence and impartiality. Despite the positive impact this type of reform might generate on perceptions, it is an exercise in discipline that remains focused on an individual level, hence the emphasis on appearances, and largely continues to ignore 'the foundational role of safeguards of adjudicative independence in domestic courts, international courts, and some other systems of arbitration'.[62]

The added value of the EU approach lies precisely in providing a more foundational role to procedural safeguards. In this sense, independence and impartiality as institutional safeguards would shield litigant parties from particularly restrictive interpretations that have, at times, imposed constraints on their policy-making and regulatory functions in ways not intended or desired. In the long term, this is likely to yield consistent and potentially balanced outcomes, especially if supported by additional tools that would scrutinize independence and impartiality as foundational, and not merely procedural, components. The new method of arbitrators' appointment and the establishment of a structured and permanent judicial process with tenured adjudicators are all elements that corroborate this line of action, as discussed in the following part.

2. The investment court system and the multilateral investment court

Rather obviously, the imparting of any normative orientation requires an effective enforcement mechanism, in the absence of which any obligation is likely to lose much of its relevance. An enforcement mechanism like the CJEU—firmly established, deeply rooted in EU principles, and widely recognized as an authoritative body—perfectly aligns with the judicialization objectives underpinning the EU project. However, it has no parallel within the ad hoc investment arbitration system.[63]

[61] Ibid, Article 3 provides for the obligation not to: '[t]ake any action that creates the *appearance* of a lack of independence or impartiality'. Emphasis added.
[62] Van Harten (n 47), 131–2.
[63] Weiler (n 4), 188–218.

In investment arbitration, the EU judicializing response took the form of the so-called Investment Court System (ICS). The ICS features in a number of international investment agreements—notably, in the Comprehensive Economic and Trade Agreement (CETA) between Canada and the European Union (2017), the EU–Singapore Investment Protection Agreement (2019), the EU--Vietnam Investment Protection Agreement (2020), and the agreement with Mexico (2025).[64] The ICS is a two-tier system that comprises a first-instance tribunal and an appellate tribunal. It still combines elements typical of investment arbitration as we have known it hitherto, especially as far as enforcement is concerned, with some significant adjustments such as (but not limited to) the standing status of the tribunal, the imposition of a code of conduct on its members, the members' tenured position and their appointment, which is no longer at the discretion of the litigating parties, that is, the claimant investor and the respondent host state.

The first-instance tribunal represents a hybrid entity, functioning as a distinct sub-category within the broader 'trustee' framework, striking a delicate balance between an arbitral tribunal and an international court. It is a last resort option in case of a dispute, available only in case of a failing consultation phase. The tribunal's jurisdiction is narrowed to claims concerning either breach of non-discriminatory treatment or violations of investment protection provisions.[65] The tribunal is composed of a number of members, proportionally being nationals of a Member State of the EU, of the other contracting state, and third countries.[66] It is far from clear which third countries members will feature in the tribunal; perhaps the idea is to opt for a broad participation that encompasses both developed and developing countries, so as to amplify the EU's impact at a diplomatic level and diffuse the 'EU values' on a global scale.[67] On the whole, the heterogeneous composition is likely to bring different perspectives to the adjudication table (although much will depend on

[64] Comprehensive Economic and Trade Agreement (CETA) between Canada, of the one part, and the European Union and its Member States, of the other part (entered into force provisionally on 21 September 2017), OJ L 11, 14 January 2017; Free trade Agreement between the European Union and the Republic of Singapore (entered into force 21 November 2019), OJ L 294, 14 November 2019; Free Trade Agreement between the European Union and the Socialist Republic of Vietnam (entered into force 1 August 2020), OJ L 186/1, 12 June 2020; EU–Singapore Investment Protection Agreement (approved on 13 February 2019, pending Member States ratifications); EU–Vietnam Investment Protection Agreement (approved on 12 February 2020, pending Member States ratifications); EU–Mexico Economic Partnership, Political Coordination and Cooperation Agreement (EU–Mexico 'Global Agreement) (signed 17 January 2025).

[65] CETA (n 64), Article 8.18.

[66] Ibid, Article 8.27(2).

[67] WTO, 'Communication from the European Community and its Member States to the WTO Working Group on the Relationship between Trade and Investment' (16 April 2002), WT/WGTI/W/115.

which countries are considered for these roles) while safeguarding EU law in cases of clashes with investment law obligations. It seems plausible to expect that the presence of at least one EU adjudicator on the Tribunal would guarantee a more appropriate application of EU law, or at least ensure that EU law is not applied wrongly. The members of the Tribunal are tenured, with a staggered extension for a number of them to be determined by lot, and will be paid a monthly retainer fee. Cases will be heard by a three-member panel, whose composition reflects the geographical division of the tribunal. The members of the panel are selected by rotation, ensuring that the composition of the divisions is random and unpredictable, while also giving equal opportunity to all members to serve. Independence and impartiality are listed as compulsory requirements for members of the tribunal, who are also expected to possess specific expertise 'in international investment law, in international trade law and the resolution of disputes arising under international investment or international trade agreements'.[68]

A particularly interesting novelty introduced with the ICS is the different mode of appointment of adjudicators. Instead of leaving the litigant parties the right to appoint their own adjudicators, the appointment process is deferred to a third mechanism, known as the Joint Committee and composed of representatives from the EU and its treaty contracting partners. The Joint Committee is a treaty party instrument co-chaired by the Minister for International Trade (of the EU treaty partner in question) and the European Trade Commissioner, or their respective designees. The Joint Committee is responsible for determining the number and the nomination of the members of both the first-instance tribunal and the appellate tribunal upon the entry into force of the agreement, as well as their retainer fees. Shifting the appointing authority from litigants to a third party is expected to:

> insulate the adjudicator from influence by powerful private interests, so as to ensure that no one can say that the judge was predisposed to decide a case or interpreted the law in a way that would increase his or her prospects for future income and career advancement.[69]

One might argue that the new mode of appointments and the 'tenure track' status do not automatically lead towards more impartial or balanced

[68] Ibid, 5.

[69] Van Harten, Gus (2008), 'A Case for an International Investment Court', Society of International Economic Law (SIEL) Inaugural Conference.

individuals, especially considering there is no tangible evidence to demonstrate that tenured judges always reach unbiased decisions, even assuming there were a way to measure it, or that an absence of security of tenure would not lead to careerism.[70] A more compelling counterargument is that the third-party appointment system detaches individuals from the influence of parties' interests, which may sway after their appointment—especially given evidence of arbitrators exhibiting bias toward the party that nominated them.[71] Passions and emotions, such as the anger or indignation of litigants driving the selection of individuals perceived as most likely to rule in their favour,[72] are effectively eliminated from the designation process.

Those who see in this new method of appointment a deprivation of a (legitimate) party autonomy right operating only against investors[73] are not completely wrong, given that states, through their representatives, still have access to the designation procedure. The gap between those who hold the rights (the investors), and those in charge of appointing the tribunal (the treaty parties, i.e. states) is mitigated in two ways. First, a code of conduct ensures that individuals of high calibre are selected to perform interpretative tasks independently and impartially. The code of conduct responds to the temptation to appoint adjudicators for political or other reasons, such as their likelihood to support the public interest, and not for their qualifications and experience.[74] Second, while investors do not generally take part in the negotiation process,[75] they might be in a position to influence the content of the treaty anyway. The prominent role played by state representatives within the Joint Committee framework can thus be explained and justified by the fact that governments are supposed to represent all the diverse interests at stake, including those of their investors investing in a foreign country.

[70] Waibel, Michael and Others (2010), *The Backlash Against Investment Arbitration. Perceptions and Reality.*

[71] Puig, Sergio (2016), 'Blinding International Justice', Virginia Journal of International Law.

[72] Investment Treaty Working Group of the International Arbitration Committee, American Bar Association Section on International Law (2016); Waibel, Michael and Wu, Yanhui (2012), *Are Arbitrators Political?*

[73] According to De Brabandere, 'the equality of arms is a fundamental principle of arbitral procedure in public international law, as it is in commercial arbitration'. De Brabandere, Eric (2012), 'Individuals in Advisory Proceedings Before the International Court of Justice: Equality of the Parties and the Court's Discretionary Authority', The Law & Practice of International Courts and Tribunals, 253.

[74] Zuleta, Eduardo (2015), 'The Challenge of Creating a Standing International Investment Court.' In *Reshaping the Investor–State Dispute Settlement System*, edited by Jean Kalicki and Anna Joubin-Bret, 422.

[75] Magraw, Kendra (2015), 'Investor–State Disputes and the rise of Recourse to State Party Pleading as Subsequent Agreements or Subsequent Practice under the Vienna Convention on the Law of Treaties', ICSID Review—Foreign Investment Law Journal, 142.

Even outside the EU, there is agreement around the idea of appointing tribunal members through an intergovernmental body voting from a list of nominated candidates to ensure diversity of legal expertise, gender, regional representation, and language. UNCITRAL, for instance, insists on flexibility in the establishment of the tribunal depending on geographical representation, following any variation in the number of participating states, as well as in caseload.[76]

One final point to consider is the reasonable expectation of consistency. When the same individuals are charged with interpretative tasks it is likely to expect a certain normative orientation, regardless of the specifics underpinning each claim. While the outcomes would probably vary depending on the underpinning agreement and the factual scenario, it seems plausible to expect that EU adjudicators would resolve different disputes influenced by the same EU normative mindset and interpretative style. What could follow is a judicialization through discourses of normality—that is, a 'desirable normal' (*the* norms) that goes beyond the particularistic interests of the parties, as enshrined in EU values for the benefit of a larger number of beneficiaries.

The judicializing process is completed by an appeal facility that would increase the acceptance and legitimacy[77] of the investment arbitration system. Unlike the ICSID annulment that can rectify procedural errors only (Article 52 ICSID Convention), the EU appeal is concerned with the legitimacy of the process as well as the correctness of the decision. As such, it is empowered to conduct a *de novo* review to analyse legal (errors of law) and factual (errors in the appreciation of the facts) issues.

In principle, there is a possibility that an appeal tribunal operates in favour of addressing imbalances left unresolved in the first instance. However, even assuming that the EU appeal body is compatible with the ICSID system,[78] the potential coexistence of multiple appeal bodies, one for each of the EU agreements, raises doubts as to its effectiveness. If each EU investment agreement grants the possibility to create its own appellate mechanism, then the risk is to end up with multiple bodies, a separate one for each treaty, with divergent

[76] UNCITRAL Working Group III, 'Possible Reform of Investor–State Dispute Settlement (ISDS) Standing Multilateral Mechanism: Selection and Appointment of ISDS Tribunal Members and Related Matters, Note by the Secretariat (8 December 2021)', UN Doc A/CN.9/WG.III/WP.213, para 18.

[77] Warner and Sheppard, (2005), 'Appeals and Challenges to Investment Treaty Awards: Is It Time for an International Appellate System?–Editorial Note', Transnational Dispute Management.

[78] Lévesque, Celine (2016), 'The European Union Commission Proposal for the Creation of an "Investment Court System": The Q and A that the Commission Won't Be Issuing', Kluwer Arbitration Blog <https://arbitrationblog.kluwerarbitration.com/2016/04/06/the-european-union-commission-proposal-for-the-creation-of-an-investment-court-system-the-q-and-a-that-the-commission-wont-be-issuing/>.

understandings about possible outcomes. It sounds rather obvious that one appeal facility would be more effective in bringing coherence than several mechanisms. Uniformity would be maximized if there were a 'European Appellate Body' that, despite treaty language differences, exercises persuasive authority over other adjudication facilities, albeit other countries might be so unwilling to embrace EU law influences unreservedly.

The problem of having multiple tribunals is potentially resolved by the establishment of an MIC, the long-term proposal vehemently advanced by the EU in the context of the ISDS reform process carried out by the UNCITRAL Working Group III. Modelled after the ICS tribunal, and clearly inspired by the World Trade Organization (WTO) Appellate Body, the MIC is composed of permanent adjudicators and aims to provide a *judicial* procedural framework for investor–state dispute settlements without intervening in the underlying substantive laws (e.g. bilateral investment treaties), which remain part of the investment agreements the court is called to interpret and apply.[79] The MIC crystallizes the judicializing approach initiated with the ICS, and increases reliance on judicial bodies, rather than on treaty makers.

Both instruments—the ICS and the MIC—are indications of the EU's path towards greater judicialization, which, in turn, is likely to supply the applicable standards of review as shaped by the EU vision of justice. Delegating judicial authorities for strengthening certain normative orientations holds potential to restore balance and thus achieve greater legitimacy in a field as politically sensitive as investment arbitration. One can't help but notice, however, some resemblances between the EU approach and investment arbitrators' law-making and wonder whether the former is that different from the latter in terms of output. One problem common to both approaches lies in the balancing powers bestowed upon the judiciary called to weigh incommensurable values like environmental protection and legality. Would the appetite for balancing generate fewer problems if delivered by a court rather than arbitral tribunals? Would the risk of investment decisions reflecting the adjudicator's personal preferences be that different from ICS or MIC (or CJEU) judges? Any judicial authority that admits it is balancing admits it is out of its assigned territory in a democracy[80] and risks infusing potentially destructive political implications with the law. As the WTO paralysis revealed, states (Member States included)

[79] UNCITRAL Working Group III, 'Possible Reform of Investor–State Dispute Settlement (ISDS): Submission from the European Union and its Member States' (24 January 2019)', UN Doc A/ CN.9/ WG.III/WP.15.

[80] Shapiro, Martin (2020), 'Judicial Power and Democracy.' In *Judicial Power—How Constitutional Courts Affect Political Transformations*, edited by Christine Landfried, 21–35.

appear quite reluctant to extend courts' reach into the political or embrace degeneration into a type of 'juristocracy', albeit it may be too late to dismiss the latter altogether, as pointed out in the following section.

D. Does the EU balance investment arbitration or tame its Member States?

Barely a handful of the EU FTAs—and none of the Investment Protection Agreements (IPAs)—have entered into force (at the time of writing, and arguably for some time afterwards). Yet the Commission and its Member States have already felt the urge to seize the Court twice: first to resolve political deadlocks over issues of competence allocation (Opinion 2/15), and second for problems of ICS compatibility with EU law (Opinion 1/17). In Opinion 2/15, the Court, upon the Commission's request,[81] clarified that in the context of the EU–Singapore FTA, portfolio investment and ISDS provisions fall outside the exclusive competence of the EU.[82] In Opinion 1/17, the Court resolved the dispute brought by the Belgian government by recognizing the compatibility of ICS with EU law, given that CETA provided enough safeguards to EU law autonomy. What might not readily transpire from the Opinions is the extent to which judicialization has become part of the Member States' DNA. Even from their perspective, the legal realm is the most appropriate port of call to address problems that are framed in legal terms (issues of competence and compatibility) but carry significant political implications (Member States' reluctance to accept the Commission's expansion of exclusive competence, or public opposition and protests in the Wallonia region against the perpetuation of a certain neoliberal approach). A perceptive observer would not miss that Opinion 1/17 is somewhat receptive to public opinion, especially if combined with (or disguised under) the Commission's pressure. But there is more. When judicialization falls short from a policy perspective, the political sphere is often compelled to resort to alternative strategies—which may prove even more problematic.[83] In such cases, the remedy can end up being worse than the problem it seeks to address. For example, the Commission, after the setback of Opinion 2/15, chose to split investment chapters from the core trade provisions, introducing two independent agreements—the FTA and the IPA—thus

[81] Opinion 2/15, *EU-Singapore FTA*, EU:C:2017:376.
[82] Ibid, para 305.
[83] See Chapter 7.

shaping the dangers of mandatory mixed competences rather than face the Court once again.

If these Opinions are read alongside the analysis carried out in Section B, one plausible inference to make is that the EU judicializing approach goes beyond how the adjudicators decide. Instead, it appears to be conceived as a tool for shaping and embedding a particular orientation that is both legal and inherently political. From this perspective, judicialization serves to legitimize a specific interpretative style, even if implicitly. However, even assuming that weaker forms of judicial review are insulated from adjudicators' individual preferences, there are inherent limits to how effectively this process can function.

While it is hardly deniable that from an output perspective judicialization may ensure obedience to the rules, and it is congenial to keep a united front between Member States, blind faith in judicialization may not play out in multilateral settings. The WTO Appellate Body paralysis quite bluntly proved that there may be limits to the extent that the international community accepts judicial decisions particularly intrusive in the domain of policy-making. By placing significant reliance on judicial powers to deliver law-making (and not just interpretations), one first risk is to generate discriminations or imbalances among the interests worth protecting. Being granted significant amounts of power, including some forms of law-making authority, the judiciary finds itself in the position of determining the values and, albeit to a lesser extent, balancing the rights that need protection, like investors' protection over regulatory authority or vice versa. Harrow describes this process as the 'juridification of values',[84] whereas Spieker frames it in terms of an EU 'juristocracy' from Article 2 TEU.[85] One first point could be to consider that since the 'EU rule of law' concept is very much aligned with the international vision, as well as with that of many domestic legal systems, the risk of juridification of rights/'juristocracy' of values appears relatively low. Different considerations flow, however, with respect to the choice and/or balancing of values and interests that are worth protecting according to the EU vision of justice and may not be shared and accepted globally or multilaterally. If values and interests like human rights, climate change, but also the neoliberal preservation of the Single Market, come into play, the imposition of a certain vision through judicialization risks

[84] Harrow (n 45).

[85] Spieker, Luke Dimitrios (2023), *EU Values Before the Court of Justice: Foundations, Potential, Risks*, 260–2.

creating selective forms of law-making by those who claim to possess the authority to weigh which interests are worth protecting.

This is precisely what has already happened with investment arbitration: accepting forms of judicial review and law-making has exposed systemic deficits, especially in terms of accountability towards those affected by such decisions—that is, societies bearing the costs of arbitral awards delivered by adjudicators assessing the 'normality' of legislative actions. Replacing law-making with judgments emanated from the unelected representatives of the socio-economic and political elite for that of majoritarian political institutions[86] creates, in fact, significant accountability deficits. This disconnect arises between those who have delegated their power to elected officials (citizens and governments) and the arbitrators, who, despite being entirely detached from the electorate, wield authority over them. The EU counter-argument to this reasoning is that under certain circumstances, international courts can correct some problems, especially if a judicial system lacks independence and cannot provide effective remedies (in this case it would be investment arbitration). While there may be merit in this argument, the delegation of important law-making powers to independent institutions (like courts) is democratically justifiable only in the name of efficiency, in those instances where reliance on expertise and a problem-solving style of decision-making is more important than reliance on direct political accountability.[87] If such conditions of efficiency are met, the expansion of judicial power and the increasing reliance on judicialization is likely to strengthen the majoritarian democratic institutions.[88]

This is admittedly too far-fetched for investment arbitration, which displays independence and, albeit questionable, remedies. From a political standpoint, what could be particularly problematic with a judicialization process is whether it aims to expand *certain* normative orientations only. Take the WTO Appellate Body paralysis. Its judicializing approach was praised by the EU for the enhancement of systemic integration and the consolidation of coherent normative orientations. The same judicializing expansion, however, was perceived by the United States as a threat to its policy-making sovereignty. While other WTO members, including the European Union, Canada, Brazil, India, and China, were not necessarily in disagreement with some US concerns about 'the activist approach of the Appellate Body on substantive interpretations' (or, at least, not all of them), they have been content to let the Appellate Body and,

[86] Tate and Vallinder (n 24).
[87] Majone (n 36), 162.
[88] Tate and Vallinder (n 24), 527.

more generally, the WTO dispute settlement system continue to operate unchanged. They probably underestimated the frustration of the United States and remained confident that the system would survive.[89] History proved them wrong and demonstrates that the EU's and other WTO members' blind trust in judicialization has clear limits, especially if the impression, whether real or perceived, is of having imbalanced interpretations. Replace the frustration of the United States with the lingering doubts of many host states, and the WTO reliance on judicialization with arbitrators' law-making—whether belonging to the original form of investment arbitration or the modernized version with the EU corrections—and the resemblance between the Appellate Body's and the investment system's crises is even more noticeable. One possible explanation could be the following:

> The 'harder' the law in terms of its binding effect both on and within states, the less willing states are to give up their prerogative to control the emergence of such law's 'opposability' to them. When the international law is 'real,' when it is 'hard' in the sense of being binding not only on but also in states, and when there are effective remedies to enforce it, decision-making suddenly becomes important, indeed crucial.[90]

Interestingly, Weiler was referring to the European integration process, yet the limits encountered by too much expanded judicialization within investment arbitration fit the same frame. Law is a source of rights and remedies but if it is stretched to create and sustain certain (political) inclinations it may become problematic. For the same reasons, judicialization risks becoming problematic if it expands *certain* normative orientations only, as the balancing problem affecting investment arbitration already showed. However, as long as the manner in which the EU judicializes recognizes the due deference owed to states without imparting a direction that serves the EU's interests only or destroys the protections attached to investments, there is potential for this approach to advance.[91]

The more judicialized the investment arbitration order becomes, the more the need for rules that protect from the arbitrary exercise of power.[92] Since it

[89] Perezcano Díaz, Hugo (2019), 'The WTO Appellate Body's Impending Paralysis', CIGI online, <https://www.cigionline.org/articles/wto-appellate-bodys-impending-paralysis/>.

[90] Weiler (n 4).

[91] It is interesting to note that some EU like-minded countries, like Canada and other EU treaty partners (Vietnam, Mexico) that endorsed, for example, the establishment of a multilateral investment tribunal in their investment agreements with the EU, have not stood out as a strong proponent of the same mechanism within the UNCITRAL meetings.

[92] Lang (n 15), 6.

remains unlikely that the European adjudicator sitting on the first-instance tribunal will impose an interpretation *à la* EU only, some sort of compromise with international law, rather than supremacy over it, would become unavoidable, as already displayed by Opinion 1/17. In what may have seemed an ironic twist of fate to many, the Court validated the brand new ICS after the system was somehow already in place. It would seem that the Court endorsed the Commission's ambition to judicialize political objectives that might not have advanced through majoritarian decision-making arenas both internally (because of Member States) and externally (because of other countries' prerogatives). The unusually strong acceptance of the EU legal order's coexistence with international (investment) law of Opinion 1/17 is the price to pay to overcome the ontological constraints between the EU and its Member States[93] almost as if authority over international law would enhance EU legitimacy internally.

In the course of a WTO meeting, the EU delegate told the following fable:

> If a frog is put suddenly into boiling water, it will jump out, but if the frog is put into tepid water which is slowly brought to boil, it will not realise the danger and be cooked to death. Apparently, however, it has been demonstrated that this story is false. The frog will jump when the water gets too hot. Let us draw inspiration from the frog.[94]

The frog seems to be a fitting metaphor for EU judicializing aspirations. Judicialization per se is not malicious. On the contrary, it is often congenial to ensure adherence to rules and maintain unity in the face of divergent interests. In such scenarios, states may find judicialization advantageous, particularly when little attention is given to the mechanisms by which tribunals themselves are subjected to oversight. In investment arbitration, where states aim to be in a position to supervise how investors' protections are balanced against regulatory autonomy, judicialization may be an effective strategy to level up the rules and legitimize decision-making processes. Nevertheless, the extent to which the international community is willing to tolerate judicial interference in policy-making has its limits. If such interference becomes—or is perceived as—excessively invasive, the frog will inevitably jump out. Achieving a balance between the discretion afforded to protect investments and the deference owed to states is thus a key metric for the success of judicialization. Emphasizing

[93] See Chapter 7.

[94] WTO, Minutes of the Dispute Settlement Body Meeting (23–24 July 2019), WT/GC/M/179, para 126; see also https://youtu.be/O0HYnCW4Mio.

'new' standards of review, such as the rule of law principles of independence and impartiality, is likely to produce more equitable outcomes. While states may remain unable to exert direct control over how tribunals strike this balance, these enhanced standards of review should sufficiently address lingering concerns about the legitimacy of judicial processes.

PART III

UNKEPT PROMISES, MISPLACED PREMISES, OR ENTRENCHED INTERESTS?

This Part comprises Chapters 7 and 8, which conclude the book by critically recognizing the limitations of the EU project and the ambitious rhetoric that often permeates the EU external action.

Chapter 7 synthesizes the analysis from Chapters 3 to 6, investigating whether, and to what extent, the EU has succeeded in embedding its core values—democracy and the rule of law—into the international investment regime. While the EU is undeniably established and influential in the international legal order, it is debatable whether its actions prioritize these values or primarily pursue economic and political interests, particularly in investment law. The EU frequently encounters resistance both from treaty partners hesitant to fully adopt its positions and from its own Member States, forcing it to make compromises. As a result, the EU faces growing pressure to accommodate demands for protections that transcend purely market-driven considerations. It strives to balance the wealth created by liberalization with social values such as environmental protection, public health, and sustainable development, all while safeguarding its own interests. After all, the EU's standing within the international legal order depends on its ability to preserve the openness and competitiveness of its Single Market.

Despite commendable efforts, the EU's actions have unveiled three critical challenges rooted in the foundational assumptions of its Europeanizing promises. First, an enduring identity problem continues to surface within the international investment regime. Second, deep-seated ontological constraints persist in the EU–Member State relationship. Third, the EU's approach to international law and governance is marked by inherent ambivalences. These challenges arise from the misplaced legitimacy the EU assumes in positioning itself as a great multilateral power. In this context, embracing open strategic autonomy could offer the EU an optimal path forward, albeit at the expense of its image and coherence.

Chapter 8 concludes the analysis by framing the EU's evolving role in investment law and policy as a dynamic and ongoing journey. As the EU has expanded, the world has become increasingly complex, interconnected, and global, thus becoming less Eurocentric. EU values have sometimes significantly influenced investment policy, but often their impact has been minimal, overshadowed by bureaucratic intricacies.

The book's fundamental question—can democracy and the rule of law extend from EU borders to the realm of international investments— continues to seek a definitive answer, and the tensions between 'spreading values' and 'pursuing interests' continue to underscore the limitations of the EU as a global actor. These constraints are evident in the various systems the EU engages with, particularly following the judicial development of Article 2 of the Treaty on European Union (TEU). Ultimately, the analysis reveals a lack of a clear and compelling purpose in the EU's agenda, primarily because the core objective of the EU Treaties remains centred on establishing and maintaining a Common Market. However, it remains uncertain what direction this market should ultimately evolve towards, leaving the future of the EU's economic and political integration somewhat ambiguous. In the context of international investment, this agenda reflects a broader struggle to balance EU's ideals with pragmatic realities in an ever-changing world.

7
Limits of the EU action: Misplaced premises or entrenched interests?

A. Overview

This chapter concludes the analysis presented in Chapters 3 to 6, aiming to determine whether, and to what extent, the EU has succeeded in fulfilling its promises to diffuse the values it professes to hold most dear—democracy and the rule of law—into the international investment regime. The answers are mixed and reveal inherent limits in the EU line of action that might jeopardize its globalizing expectations to shape investment law and policy according to its own vision of justice.

Three main problematic aspects emerged quite vividly, all of which can be derived from the premises upon which the 'Europeanizing' promises have been forged. First, there is a problem with the EU identity in the regime of international investments (Section B). Then, there exists a long-standing issue with the ontological constraints affecting the relationship between the EU and its Member States (Section C). Third, there are ambivalences in the EU approach to international law and governance (Section D). All these aspects compromise the diffusion of the EU values and raise doubts as to whether the EU attempts to reform the regime of international investments are genuine. The Euro-idealists would argue that a certain degree of flexibility would not pose particular problems for a system like the EU, whose actual and potential influence in the world resides in its non-military and non-coercive character.[1] The most sceptical or cynical, however, would be tempted to see the EU normative influence as a disguise to purse the EU's (predominantly economic) interests and needs, all while taming the Member States through the shaping of binding international norms in the field of foreign investments. The chapter concludes on a bittersweet note arguing that from the perspective of outputs,

[1] Manners, Ian (2002), 'Normative Power Europe: A Contradiction in Terms?', Journal of Common Market Studies.

EU Values in Investment Law And Policy. Maria Laura Marceddu, Oxford University Press.
 DOI: 10.1093/9780191986208.003.0007

the EU ambivalences could be a potentially successful strategy. However, using its normative power as a means to an end (a 'carrot and stick' approach) rather than an end in itself, undermines the EU ambition to craft a particular identity as an international actor (Part E).

B. EU's identity ambiguity in international investment law

One first problem aggravated by the EU's entry into the regime of international investments concerns the ambit of its identity. More specifically, this is a problem that pertains to the premises upon which the EU had (and to a certain extent still has) built its identity in external relations, with consequent reverberations into the investment regime. The EU identity's construction predominantly operates from the inside and is inspired by a 'messianic vocation' to promote and project its values abroad, and contribute to the achievement of global objectives (as per Article 3(5) of the Treaty on European Union (TEU)). The interactions with the outside play a role in its shaping too, especially in the realm of concrete foreign policies, with their burden of values, principles, and interests[2], as well as through its interaction with others who project their own representation of the EU and interact with it accordingly.[3] Without a univocal characterization, however, the EU has often hesitated in carving out a particular identity for itself and it still fluctuates across multiple personalities.

The EU has undeniably often aspired to position itself as a global standard-setter or, at the very least, as a global role model. In modern society, legal rules serve as the quintessential form of authority, offering the structure and predictability needed to navigate complex governance frameworks effectively.[4] This ambition is evident in its experience with public consultations and, more broadly, in its efforts to create new channels for gathering democratic inputs before, during, and after the negotiation processes of free trade agreements (FTAs), with the ultimate aim of engaging society as a whole.[5] Other commendable initiatives include codifying the advancements made over the past two decades in investment law-making, as well as the established practices of

[2] Lucarelli, Sonia and Manners, Ian (2006), *Values and Principles in European Union Foreign Policy.*

[3] Lucarelli, Sonia (2008), 'European Political Identity, Foreign Policy and the Others' Image.' In *The Search for a European Identity—Values, Policies and Legitimacy of the European Union*, edited by Furio Cerutti and Sonia Lucarelli; Cederman, Lars-Erik (2001), 'Nationalism and Bounded Integration: What it Would Take to Construct a European Demos', European Journal of International Relations.

[4] Weber, Max, Guenther, Roth and Claus, Wittich (eds) (2013), *Economy and Society: An Outline of Interpretive Sociology.*

[5] See Chapter 3 and Chapter 4.

arbitral tribunals, into clearer and more precise provisions—such as those addressing the fair and equitable treatment (FET) standard.[6] While these efforts are praiseworthy, the EU stops short of embracing a more ambitious approach, particularly in recognizing public participation as a normative principle. This reluctance undermines the pursuit of democratic values in the EU's external relations, revealing a disconnect between its rhetoric of promoting democracy and its willingness to institutionalize mechanisms that genuinely reflect this commitment.[7] By failing to prioritize public engagement as a foundational principle, the EU risks missing a critical opportunity to reinforce the legitimacy and inclusivity of its external investment framework.

One can detect 'Europeanizing' attempts also in the Commission's approach towards sustainability issues.[8] Indications of the EU's aspirations as a global standard setter are in the extension of the standard state-to-state dispute settlement to the Trade and Sustainable Development (TSD) chapter,[9] the adoption of a Directive on corporate sustainability due diligence,[10] and the inclusion of corporate social responsibility clauses.[11] With respect to the last point, it is important to acknowledge that the discourse around the implementation of corporate liability is not an EU phenomenon but has gained traction globally.[12] The EU's direction nonetheless appears promising especially as far as the advancement of sustainable development in trade matters is concerned. It remains to be seen whether the EU is willing to be as audacious in investment matters as well.

[6] See Chapter 5.
[7] See Chapter 4.
[8] See Chapter 5.
[9] Free Trade Agreement between the European Union and New Zealand (entered into force 1 May 2024), OJ L, 2024/866, 25 March 2024; Trade and Cooperation Agreement between the European Union and the European Atomic Energy Community, of the one part, and the United Kingdom of Great Britain and Northern Ireland, of the other part (entered into force 1 May 2021), OJ L 149, 30 April 2021.
[10] Directive (EU) 2024/1760 of the European Parliament and of the Council of 13 June 2024 on corporate sustainability due diligence and amending Directive (EU) 2019/1937 and Regulation (EU) 2023/2859, OJ L 2024/1760, 5 July 2024.
[11] EU–China Comprehensive Agreement on Investment (CAI) (Agreement in Principle 22 January 2021).
[12] Albeit in a limited number, some states have begun to clarify in their investment agreements that investors of both contracting parties will uphold corporate social, business, and human rights responsibilities, and have drafted clauses that explicitly create treaty obligations for investors in the context of sustainable development. For example, the 2016 Morocco–Nigeria BIT requires compliance with environmental impact processes and imposes upon investors the duty to apply the precautionary principle in the context of the environmental impact assessment and its implementation (Article 14). The agreement also contains post-establishment obligations for investors to maintain an environmental management system, honour core labour standards, and specifies specific standards for resource exploitation (Article 18). Morocco–Nigeria BIT (signed 3 December 2016, not yet entered into force).

At other times, the EU has worn its problem-solver hat, often disguising its entrepreneurial attitude towards setting norms. Examples of this attitude are several and diverse. Opinion 2/15 is a case in point, having the Commission chosen to split investment chapters from the core trade provisions to streamline the ratification process and enhance the 'EU only' conclusion of trade agreements. Rather than face the Court once again, the Commission introduced two independent agreements—the FTA and the Investment Protection Agreement (IPA)—thus shaping the dangers of mandatory mixed competences.[13] A more marked indication of the Commission's entrepreneurial skills can be found in the process of judicialization advanced to reform investment arbitration.[14] While conceived as a procedural safeguard for the rule of law, judicialization has provided the EU with a channel for steering other countries towards what the rules of the game *should* be (according to the EU vision, of course), especially when politics (and politicians) were in deadlock.[15] The Investment Court System (ICS) is the short- to medium-term solution advanced by the EU vision to address the problems affecting investment arbitration and appealing to other countries seeking to develop economically. Mandatory competence mixing and judicialization are two sides of the inclination of the EU to solve problems.

A slightly different characterization of this role as problem-solver would consider the EU as a mediator between various interests of the developing and the developed worlds. Efforts in this direction can be detected in the FTA chapters on sustainable development. In this respect, it remains questionable whether the EU is driven by the satisfaction of moral demands such as the development of truly democratic and sustainable economic growth through its foreign policies. Even so, however, the mantra 'peace through trade' might not apply uniformly anywhere, and compliance with EU higher standards has already generated inequalities and challenges for developing and less developed countries. It would appear, therefore, that the inclination to solve problems subsides in the face of the broader reaffirmation of the EU's own 'Promethean' vision of, and advantages within, the international legal order, to ensure openness and competitiveness (or protectionism depending on the circumstances) of the Single Market. This is furthermore consistent with the EU's choice of International Investment Agreement (IIA) partner countries, which suggests

[13] See Chapter 2.
[14] See Chapter 6.
[15] Weiler, Joseph (1999), *The Constitution of Europe 'Do the New Clothes Have an Emperor?' and Other Essays on European Integration*, 10–101.

that the intent to channel FDI in developing countries is not the leitmotif behind the EU's investment policy.[16]

A more flexible characterization has insisted on the EU identity as a 'power'. From this perspective, the EU has displayed a significant capacity to direct or influence the behaviour of others or the course of events (the classic definition of power). Duchêne rightly framed this in terms of civilian power, as an alternative to military power, in exerting influence in international relations.[17] The EU's power in fact predominantly emerged through non-military means, of which trade and investment constitute prominent modes of its action. This characterization has given the EU enough leverage to engage in a more subtle diffusion of its norms and values, which, in turn, has gradually revealed the EU's interest in replicating 'the EU way' globally. Framing the EU identity in terms of power is congenial to include both its 'imperialistic' attitudes to generate global standards as well as its softer inclination to resolve problems. Somewhere in between the two, Manners introduced the idea of a 'normative power Europe' that reflects the EU's ability to define what passes for normal in world politics, as construed upon the EU's perception of itself as a force for good.[18] This is ideologically exercised through the EU's resource and structural powers that penetrate and shape those of its recipients. However, resource and structural powers are fundamentally peculiar in the EU system because of their different political forms, which originated in a context of hybrid polity and political-legal constitutionalism. As a result, power is exerted by placing universal norms (democracy, rule of law, social justice, and human rights) at the centre of its relationship with the Member States internally, and with the rest of the world externally:

> The EU has gone further towards making its external relations informed by, and conditional on, a catalogue of norms which come closer to those of the European convention on human rights and fundamental freedoms (ECHR)

[16] Basedow, Robert (2020), 'The European Union's New International Investment Policy and the United Nation's Sustainable Development Goals: Integration as a Motor of Substantive Policy Change?' In *International Trade, Investment, and the Sustainable Development Goals: World Trade Forum*, edited by Cosimo Beverelli, Jürgen Kurtz, and Damian Raess, 60. A notable exception to this trend may be the Facilitation Agreement with Angola, which prioritizes environmental, social, and governance (ESG) standards while excluding investor–state dispute settlement mechanisms. Sustainable Investment Facilitation Agreement between The European Union and The Republic of Angola (entered into force 1 September 2024), OJ L 2024/830, 8 March 2024.

[17] Duchêne, François (1972), 'Europe's Role in World Peace.' In *Europe Tomorrow: Sixteen Europeans Look Ahead*, edited by Richard Mayne.

[18] Solana, Javier (2006), *The Sound of Europe Conference*.

> and the universal declaration of human rights (UDHR) than most other actors in world politics.[19]

Norms are diffused in several ways. First, by transference of goods, aid, and financial assistance; second as a result of the physical presence of the EU in third states and international organizations; third, by unintended contagion (e.g. the General Data Protection Regulation); and last, norms are diffused through the procedural institutionalization of a relationship with a third party often in the form of an agreement, as it is the case with investment agreements and FTAs. Normative power in multilateral settings alludes to the power emanating from imposing concepts and identities upon others through discourses of normality. Speaking about normative multilateralism thus implies a certain representation of the world order and the establishment of criteria of inclusion/exclusion and standards of legitimacy which are rooted in what the EU embodies.[20]

Regardless of certain nuances characterizing the EU's exercise of power,[21] what epitomizes the EU's normative multilateralism is a contradiction between the aspirations to employ power multilaterally while often proceeding with one bilateral agreement at the time, especially in the realm of international investments. However, this should not come as a surprise: exerting power bilaterally comes naturally to the EU. The most powerful instance to exercise power bilaterally is accession to the EU, but other forms like trade conditionality are not used less frequently in order to promote democratization, the rule of law, or good governance. Bilateralism allows the EU to contain the disciplining effects of transnational legality insofar as they do not go beyond domestic consensus or law, or at least not beyond those that the EU has set. However, the power wielded on the basis of its economic clout, the fear of exclusion from its market, and the membership perspective would qualify as very tangible sources of hard power, which are likely to function

[19] Manners (n 1), 241.

[20] Barbé, Esther, Herranz-Surrallés, Anna, and Natorski, Michal (2014), 'Contending Metaphors of the European Union as a Global Actor', Journal of Language and Politics.

[21] Ibid. Barbé, Herranz-Surrallés, and Natorski identify three distinctive traits that define the EU's global engagement. First is the 'model' trait, wherein the EU promotes its own rules and practices as a benchmark for other countries and international institutions to adopt. Second is the 'player' trait, reflecting the EU's active role in shaping global rules through engagement with major powers, often via bilateral partnerships or exclusive club settings. Lastly, the 'instrument' trait underscores the EU's function as a facilitator for broader global rule-making processes within universal international institutions such as the United Nations. These traits collectively illustrate the EU's multifaceted approach to global governance and its aspiration to influence international rule-making in diverse capacities.

in certain settings (e.g. with prospective members)[22] but not in others. The regime of international investments belongs to the latter. It displays a bilateral asymmetric configuration of power where the far-reaching implications provided by investment agreements are safeguarded by arbitral tribunals that sanction states deviating from the standard rational model prescribed by said investment agreements. This form of judicial review interferes, if not strikingly clashes, with the EU sensitivities. Yet the EU has done little to rectify the inherent asymmetry that permeates the investment arbitration order and by proceeding with one bilateral agreement at a time is likely to continue to generate old results.[23] Like 'traditional' investment arbitration, the newly branded ICS and, as things stand, the Multilateral Investment Court (MIC) proposal, assign only rights to investors and only obligations to states. This approach retains social injustices and raises questions as to access to justice for those parties that have no standing in the process, despite their rights or interests being affected by the decision-making underpinning an investment project. Procedural and substantial refinements that expand regulatory capacities can be saluted as positive changes, but as long as the dispute settlement system continues to operate to the advantage of one side alone, it would leave public policy determinations to the scrutiny of judicial bodies that might (or might not) 'give thought' to third parties instances and would question the EU power—whether hard or normative—to defend what it professes to hold most dear, like the rule of law and access to justice.

Disregarding which identity should prevail or relying on the law of unintended consequences would challenge the EU when it comes to identifying the most appropriate means and successful strategy to influence other legal systems. As a result, the lack of identity, or rather the heterogenic approach to the definition of its identity, has weakened the 'Europeanization' of the investment regime, and is further amplified by the ambivalences that more broadly permeate EU relations with international law and governance.

Beyond reputational costs, one might wonder what the use is of these identities and under which one the EU has accomplished the most. The answers are mixed. As for its standard-setter aspirations, in the realm of international investments, the EU has not yet gained a role as prominent as it has in trade.

[22] Hyde-Price, Adrian (2008), 'A "Tragic Actor"? A Realist Perspective on "Ethical power Europe"', International Affairs.

[23] Alschner, Wolfgang (2021), *Investment Arbitration and State-Driven Reform—New Treaties, Old Outcomes.*

This is furthermore exacerbated by the ambivalences that characterize the EU relationship with international law, as discussed in Section C. The problem-solver identity has yielded some positive results, for example in the ambit of clearer interpretations, albeit doubts over the EU's coherence in external relations persist, as epitomized by Opinion 1/17.[24] Characterizing the EU as a power gives merit to the EU's efforts to build an unprecedented network of bilateral agreements across different fields (from aid to diplomacy), in which trade and investment amount to a great deal. Trade and investment agreements are congenial for the EU to use in order to export, at least, its mode of values and governance to its external relations[25] if not its normative mindset in entirety. This export, however, might work through a passive power of attraction but is likely to encounter resistance from other norm-makers, as well as the constraints imposed by international law, particularly by investment law. The lack of a strong identity could weaken the EU's influence on other countries and, for the sake of political consideration, mediate its normative powers with those of its commercial partners. This does not mean the EU has lowered its values and principles but that it had to embrace a compromise of some form, depending on the commercial partner. This explains why the EU has been successful in imposing its norms and values on countries in a weaker bargaining position (Vietnam) or in drawing like-minded countries (Canada) towards shared values convergence, but it has failed to convince countries in stronger bargaining positions (Japan, US) to embrace its normative mindset and ethics. The impression is that the EU has adjusted its response depending on the negotiating party rather than seizing the chance to exercise normative leadership more audaciously and defend its vision of values strenuously. One partial justification could be that compromise paves the way for future refinements, whereas a too strict approach might end up with no agreement at all.

The ambiguous foundations of the EU identity show that its stance in relation to the global investment regime is often impregnated with bold rhetoric, and that, in practice, the EU does not retain a monopoly on legal norms and values. One factor to consider at this point is the long-standing conflict that features the relationship between the EU and its Member States, as discussed in the following section.

[24] De Abreu Duarte, Francisco (2019), 'But the Last Word is Ours: The Monopoly of Jurisdiction of the Court of Justice of the European Union in Light of the Investment Court System', European Journal of International Law.

[25] Lavenex, Sandra (2004), 'EU External Governance in "Wider Europe"', Journal of European Public Policy.

C. The ontological constraints between the EU and its Member States

While the EU is regarded as an economic power with significant leadership potential, its image appears somehow weakened, or less assertive, in certain multilateral settings. In negotiations with less developed countries, the EU leadership potential is less contested, probably because it is perceived as a unitary actor.[26] In other contexts, however, its internal fragmentation prejudices its effectiveness. This fragmentation transpires, for example, at a military level, not only because the EU has never been a 'traditional' military power but also because its Member States are differently equipped and inclined to respond to global threats with hard power. Even at the economic level, the Euro crisis has further exacerbated the divisions across the Member States, displaying a fragmented confidence in the European way.

Internal fragmentation is a long-standing issue that has characterized the Union since the outset because the fundamentals of its relationship with the Member States have remained unaltered throughout the unfolding of the EU project.[27] The tensions underlying the decision-making process stem from the EU's original configuration as a 'new legal order', which necessitates Member States limiting their sovereign rights across increasingly broad areas, ostensibly for their collective benefit.[28] In the EU systemic configuration, these limitations materialized as a double level of aggregation, given that before becoming decisions, interests need to be aggregated twice, at the Member States' level and then at the Union level, each of which could potentially turn into a veto point.

In principle, the Union possesses 'only those powers which have been conferred on it by the Treaty' (principle of conferral),[29] limited exclusive competences,[30] and involves Member States through their representatives sitting in the Council in the decision-making process. Unlike the Member States that exist independently of the EU, the Union is not a self-authenticating order, its competences are conferred by the legal bases provided in the Treaties,[31] and any competences not conferred upon the EU rest with the Member States.[32]

[26] Lucarelli, Sonia (2014), 'The EU's Leadership in Global Governance: Perceptions from the Others.' In *Communicating Europe in Times of Crisis*, edited by Natalia Chaban and Martin Holland, 11.
[27] Dashwood, Alan (2004), 'The Relationship between the Member States and the European Union/ European Community', Common Market Law Review.
[28] Opinion 1/91, EU:C:1991:490.
[29] Opinion 2/94, EU:C:1996:140, para 23; Consolidated version of the Treaty on European Union, OJ C 326, 26 October 2012 (TEU), Article 5.
[30] Consolidated version of the Treaty on the Functioning of the European Union, OJ C 326, 26 October 2012 (TFEU), Article 3.
[31] Dashwood (n 27), 357–8.
[32] TEU (n 29), Article 5(1) and (2).

Along with the principle of conferral, the Union's action is guided by the proportionality principle, which restricts the Union to not going beyond 'what is necessary to achieve the objectives of the Treaties'.[33] Both principles (of conferral and proportionality) are clear attempts to assuage Member States' fears about the extension of exclusive competences, albeit, truth be told, the boundaries for exclusive competences are well marked and rarely put the Member States completely out of action in a given policy area, apart from few exceptions.

The Common Commercial Policy (CCP) is one of these exceptions.[34] It is a policy area markedly external in nature[35] and entails an even more marked exclusivity that demotes Member States' autonomous actions and confines them to pre-authorized activities. Once competences have been transferred under the Union exclusively, Member States are precluded from undertaking international obligations that could alter the scope of the EU rules[36] and that would run counter to the competence exercised by the Union. Trade and investment are exemplary manifestations of this category of *a priori* exclusive powers. International trade is a long-recognized area of exclusive competence, whereas for exclusivity in foreign direct investments (FDIs), the Union had to wait for the Lisbon Treaty to gain competence in this field. Article 207(1) of the Treaty on the Functioning of European Union (TFEU) provided the legal basis for *a priori* exclusivity and marked the shifting of investment negotiations from the Member States' domain to the Union's, thus reigniting long-term tensions between the two.

While the Council retains the power to instruct the Commission in the negotiating process (through the Council's negotiating mandates) along with the Parliament, it is the Commission that decides in more practical terms the

[33] Ibid, Article 5(4) TEU.

[34] Another notable exception is the fishery conservation. See Joined Cases 3/76, 4/76, and 6/76, *Kramer*, EU:C:1976:114:

> The Community has exclusive power to conduct negotiations and conclude agreements in connexion with measures intended to conserve the resources of the fishing industry and designed to limit quantitatively the catches or fishing.

The other areas in which the EU has exclusive competence are listed under Article 3 TFEU and comprise the customs union, internal market, and monetary policy.

[35] Wessel, Ramses and Takács, Tamara (2017), 'Constitutional Aspects of the EU's Global Actorness: Increased Exclusivity in Trade and Investment and the Role of the European Parliament', European Business Law Review, 105.

[36] Case 22-70, *Commission v Council*, EU:C:1971:32, para 31:

> these community powers exclude the possibility of concurrent powers on the part of Member States, since any steps taken outside the framework of the community institutions would be incompatible with the unity of the common market and the uniform application of community law.

direction to take, with a consequent magnification of the power bestowed upon the Union's exclusivity in the international investment affairs.

In the initial phases of the EU investment policy, the Commission conceded to consider the Member States' pre-Lisbon Treaty bilateral investment treaties (BITs) in conformity with EU law—that is, grandfather them[37]—only in return for the Member States acceptance that their BITs with third states will be automatically replaced by EU investment agreements with those respective states. Nonetheless, Member States' autonomous action was restricted by the imposition of an explicit authorization to be obtained from the Commission to negotiate new or amend old investment treaties with countries that have not yet entered into negotiations with the EU.

In the eyes of the Commission, the continual integration of foreign economic policy is seen as one of the key factors contributing to the success of the Single Market and European integration. The Commission traditionally keeps fighting for larger areas of exclusive competence in external affairs to justify its teleological narrative of speaking with 'one single voice' proportionally commensurate with the EU's role in the world. In the eyes of the Member States, however, the Commission's extension of the CCP reach to FDIs continues to be seen as a usurpation of their competences to regulate international investment flows.

A moment of arrest of the expansion of EU exclusive powers in international investment matters came from Opinion 2/15. The Court clarified that the Union has to share its competence over issues concerning agreements that include an investor-state dispute settlement (ISDS) clause and cover portfolio investments.[38] For those with ears to hear, shared competence in this area provides reassurance that, as a matter of practice, the Union's competences were not 'absolutely' exclusive.[39] The recognition of certain shared competence brought the ball back into the Member States court, given that any investment agreements containing an ISDS clause and covering portfolio investments would now require the EU's ratification as well as those of the Member States. In an exercise of damage control, the Commission advanced the bifurcation option and split FTAs into two distinct treaties: an 'EU only' FTA, and a separate mixed protection investment agreement that would require the ratification of the EU and all its Member States. The Council quickly seized the

[37] Regulation (EU) No. 1219/2012 of the European Parliament and of the Council of 12 December 2012 establishing transitional arrangements for bilateral investment agreements between Member States and third countries, OJ L 351, 20 December 2012.

[38] See Chapter 2.

[39] Dashwood (n 27), 370–1.

opportunity to retain further prerogatives such as 'to decide, on a case-by-case basis, on the splitting of trade agreements'.[40] The case-by-case approach that resulted against the setback of Opinion 2/15 deliberately sought to reiterate the powers still retained by Member States, albeit in the form of shared competence. The bifurcation option has currently been applied to the agreements with Singapore and Vietnam and is likely to inspire the agreements with the Philippines, Indonesia, and India; conversely, other agreements will remain mixed agreements, like the Comprehensive Economic and Trade Agreement between Canada and the European Union (CETA) and those with Mexico, Mercosur, and Chile.[41] In the negotiations with Australia and New Zealand, the EU adopted a notably different orientation. The focus was on achieving mutual liberalization of goods and services, deliberately excluding investment protection and the resolution of investment disputes from the discussions. Similarly, in the agreement with Kyrgyzstan, investment provisions were incorporated within the broader framework of trade in services rather than addressed as a stand-alone issue. This approach reflects a strategic departure from traditional investment chapters, emphasizing trade liberalization while avoiding contentious elements of investment dispute resolution. The Investment Facilitation Agreement with Angola embodies a bold and innovative approach to sustainable development, potentially marking a departure from the traditional features of older generation IIAs. However, it remains a distinct instrument focused on facilitating rather than merely promoting or protecting investments. If not adopted as a model in other treaties, it may instead signal a case-by-case, incremental progression.

A more extreme option comes from Japan, with which the EU has concluded an FTA but has not been able to continue negotiations for a separate investment agreement. While some might read into this an expression of the EU's power over Member States, it would seem more likely that it signals a complex negotiation with a partner—Japan—particularly attached to investment arbitration. By preserving the power to choose whether and when to pursue the bifurcation route, the Council emphasized that the exercise of the EU's exclusive power is not unfettered but requires a decision by the Council. As a result, the Member States were able to retain leverage in a key domain of global economic governance and subjected foreign investments to their national political

[40] Council of the European Union (2018), 'Draft Council conclusions on the negotiation and conclusion of EU trade agreements', 8622/18, para 3.
[41] Ibid, see also Chapter 2.

review processes, thus diluting the idea of the EU as an ontologically unitary entity.

Despite the fact that even in the realm of FDIs, Member States do participate in the decision-making process through their representatives in the Council, the persistent tensions between the EU and its Member States remain problematic mostly because they risk jeopardizing the consistency of the EU's internal and external action, which is at the heart of its legitimate exercise of power.[42] As part of the broader CCP, international investments are not just a key exclusive policy in external relations but form part of the European integration process and constitute a manifestation of the interactions between internal and external developments.

The implication that Article 2 TEU values would be promoted externally (Article 21 TEU) rests on the foundation of internal democracy, which must navigate the inherent ontological constraints between the EU and its Member States. The key question is whether these constraints function as a democratic safeguard in the transfer of exclusive competences or whether they expose a deeper democratic ambivalence: on the one hand, the aspiration to project an imperfect yet functional vision of democracy for external promotion and replication, and on the other, a flawed internal conceptualization of democracy in the distribution of powers within the Union. If the former, despite some internal contradictions, the EU is likely to persuade other actors into the orbit of its values. If the latter, the mismatch between the aspirations imposed externally and those lacking internally would lead the system towards a progressive decline in influence. The analysis carried out in this book revealed that the answers are mixed and tend to be positioned between these two extremes.

Similar considerations pertain to the rule of law. The EU can only make progress in internal rule of law standards and the normative character of its foreign policy if it strives for a more rigorous application of the rule of law at the international level. However, the Member States too can only maintain and reinforce their internal rule of law standards if they strive for a more rigorous application of the rule of law at the level of the EU.[43] Member States have different visions on matters of foreign policy which are inherently part of their identities, and ceding ground to a truly common foreign policy even in the ambit of foreign investments would arguably require a 'more common identity composed of principles and values made concrete in aims'.[44]

[42] Meunier, Sophie and Nicolaïdis, Kalypso (2006), 'The European Union As a Conflicted Trade Power', Journal of European Public Policy.
[43] De Baere, Geert (2012), 'European Integration and the Rule of Law in Foreign Policy.' In *Philosophical Foundations of European Union Law*, edited by Julie Dickson and Pavlos Eleftheriadis, 379.
[44] Ibid, 381.

For a naive observer, the uneasy relationship between the Member States and the EU desire to act on the global stage would prejudice the spread of its values. From this standpoint, the heterogeneity of interests among Member States might generate unsurmountable obstacles that would prevail over the proliferation of EU values and would not render the EU particularly influential. Reality, however, is more complex and sometimes beats imagination. As Chapter 5 demonstrated, while the attainment of global sustainable goals like climate change is common to both the EU and its Member States, their pursuit does not have to be exclusive as the EU dictates but leaves the Member States a considerable margin of contribution, sometimes even in the form of opposition. A case in point is the modernizing efforts the EU put into renegotiating the Energy Charter Treaty (ECT) over three years and that the Member States deemed unfit for a genuine reorientation towards clean energies.[45] The Member States displayed coherence in ascertaining the limitations of the ECT modernized version. For example, they did not buy into the incorporation of a particular dispute settlement mechanism for sustainable development disputes. They were not wrong in not seeing radical differences from the self-contained system of dispute settlement that largely characterizes the TSD chapter in comprehensive FTAs and the limits this type of enforcement entails when protecting clean energy. Another particularly salient point that raised scepticism was the 'flexibility mechanism', which allows the contracting parties to exclude the protection of fossil fuels within their territories. Regrettably, the mechanism is only optional, and existing investments will continue to benefit from the protection of the treaty for ten years from entry into force of the new provisions. While the reluctance of Member States is likely to be influenced by the setbacks many experienced in energy sector investment arbitrations, it also highlights that opposition to the EU's primary approach may serve as a means to preserve systemic integrity and maintain high standards rather than compromising them.

On the other side of the spectrum, the line of action toward transparency in investment arbitration would appear to indicate an alignment of Member States to the EU's global aspirations. The tepid interest displayed initially by the Member States has been replaced by a more solid commitment to transparency, as attested, for example, by the growing number of their BITs that

[45] This is attested by the position endorsed in the Commission's Non-Paper, albeit unofficially, regarding a coordinated withdrawal from the Energy Charter Treaty (ECT) by the EU, Euratom, and Member States. This position is further reiterated in the recommendations for a Council decision to jointly exit the ECT, following the pledge of some governments (France, Germany, Italy, Poland, Portugal, and Slovenia) to leave the treaty due to climate concerns. COM(2023)446 final.

include the UNCITRAL Rules on Transparency. Despite these efforts, an uncomfortable truth persists as to the effects of the mismatch between the EU's global aspirations and its internal contradictions. The opposition of a few Member States has precluded the ratification of the Mauritius Convention for almost a decade and, more broadly, might preclude the affirmation of a general principle of transparency. In this stance, the absence of a unitary line of action questions the internal articulation of democracy and thus exposes the Europeanizing aspirations to an uncertain fate.

The issue becomes amplified in the ambit of the affirmation of values, as it is likely to undermine what the EU stands for if questioned from within. Perhaps surprisingly to some, a silver lining could be seen in the possibility that internal conflict can generate bargaining power.[46] Tying one's hand internally can confer strength in the negotiations. A prime example is the strong opposition to investment arbitration initially voiced by some Member States, followed by civil society, and ultimately supported by the European Parliament.[47] This resistance enabled the EU to secure more favourable outcomes—such as the establishment of the ICS—than might have been possible under a system where all decisions were made through majority voting.

One complementary observation in this respect pertains to the opposite scenario: the lack of universal appeal to the EU's line of action regardless of its internal fragmentation. The proposal of establishing an MIC, for example, has gained limited traction globally, despite a uniform front across the Member States favouring a two-tier mechanism as 'the only type of reform which can effectively respond to all the concerns identified'.[48] While the internal fragmentation between the EU and its Member States might compromise a unitary line of action, it is not the only factor that influences the effectiveness of the spread of EU values more widely.

Further developments on this front might occur if the Council endorses the Parliament's proposal to change the EU Treaties, as outlined in a historic resolution of November 2023.[49] If approved, the Resolution will strengthen the Union's capacity to streamline the conclusion of IIAs, bypassing the impediments raised by Member States within the Council. The shift from unanimity to qualified majority voting (QMV) could be welcomed as a way to facilitate

[46] Meunier, Sophie (2005), *Trading Voices*.
[47] European Parliament, P9_TA(2023)0427 (22 November 2023).
[48] UNCITRAL Working Group III (24 January 2019), 'Possible Reform of Investor–State Dispute Settlement (ISDS) Submission from the European Union and its Member States)', UN Doc A/CN.9/WG.III/WP.159/Add 1, para 40.
[49] European Parliament (n 47); see also Chapter 2.

the Union's decision-making, reducing the risks of political deadlocks invoked by recalcitrant Member States. It has to be recognized, however, that Member States would keep fighting to retain their prerogatives, especially considering that throughout the entire EU history, each Member State was granted a position of power brokerage.[50]

As for the values both the EU and its Member States claim to profess internally and externally, I have some concerns as to how these will possibly function under the new dispensation. An extreme and certainly unwarranted result of reinforcing the EU's exclusive powers could be that of further distortions in EU governance. If stripped of their shadow right of veto, the Commission's efforts to persuade the Member States that its measures are in the general interest and of sufficient importance to override the single interests might not be enough to justify the constraints placed on them. As a last resort, Member States might opt to lower their stance to the 'narrowest' or lowest common standard that is considered beneficial for the Community as a whole. Worse still, they could resort to blocking or rejecting measures that would undermine their pre-eminence, or form ad hoc alliances to achieve QMV, further complicating collective decision-making and undermining the EU's cohesion. A possible remedy against this downgrading could be offered by the Parliament, insofar as it gives voice and power to fragmented interests whose 'membership' is more difficult to channel under a qualified majority than unanimity. Yet the Parliament alone is unlikely to curb Member States powers, let alone overcome the Council's vetoes.

Depending on the legal basis, the Member States exercise a lesser or greater prominence in the formation and execution of international action in the relevant area. Conversely, the role of the EU and its supranational institutions expands or contracts depending on the policy area at issue. The relationship between the EU and international law is based on this ambiguity, which continues to make it difficult for the EU to live up to the demands of coherence and consistency in its external relations.[51] The challenge here remains to control the uncontrolled reflexes of national (even EU) interests in the international sphere,[52] which, on its part, already poses complex constraints on the capacity of the EU to act on a global scale, as discussed in the next section.

[50] Weiler, Joseph (2012), 'Deciphering the Political and Legal DNA of European Integration: An Exploratory Essay.' In *Philosophical Foundations of European Union Law*, edited by Julie Dickson and Pavlos Eleftheriadis.

[51] Wessel and Takács (n 35), 107.

[52] Weiler (n 15), 341–2.

D. The EU's ambivalence towards international law and governance

Another aspect to consider among the factors hindering the diffusion of EU values is the EU's ambivalent approach to international law and governance. The political values of the EU are exemplified in the promotion of democracy, multilateralism, and human rights, which stand as the most distinctive aspects of its normative approach to international affairs. The EU approach is grounded in the projection of its values to the rest of the world and the transformation of the international environment in its own image.[53] In this respect, the contestations and the crises affecting international regimes, like that of foreign investments, presented an opportunity for the EU to politicize its external actions and supply a framework for the affirmation of its principles in response to a global normative appetite. However, as I argue in the remainder of this section, the openness and friendly attitude of the EU towards international law and governance is more rhetorical than literal as the Union remains a closed system which opens itself to legal acts from the outside only after thorough scrutiny.

Despite choices of a spectacular manner fashioning a 'new legal order', and emphasizing its autonomy structure, the EU has conventionally displayed itself as a good international citizen committed to international law and institutions, defending multilateralism, regularly deploring the pursuit of self-interests and ad hoc exceptionalism. Yet the EU's history with international law remains as troubled as it is with any legal regime that threatens the primacy of its law.

From this standpoint, the EU does not look different from other standard-setter aspirators like the US and its ambitions to establish global rules. Similarly to the American approach, the EU combined 'domestic' (Community/Union) with international forces and negotiated bilateral agreements over reciprocal market access. What distinguishes the EU, however, is a pronounced rules-based character that, more often than not, trumps political choices. This markedly normative inclination implies a certain representation of the world order grounded in universal norms and governed by certain standards of legitimacy—or principles of conduct, to use Ruggie's words[54]—rather than exclusively by political processes. This inclination sits comfortably with the image of the EU as a civilian power whose force is derived from norms.

[53] Barbé, Esther and Morillas, Pol (2019), 'The EU global Strategy: The Dynamics of a More Politicized and Politically Integrated Foreign Policy', Cambridge Review of International Affairs, 757.

[54] Ruggie, John Gerard (1992), 'Multilateralism: The Anatomy of an Institution', International Organization, 561.

Perhaps unsurprisingly, these norms are expressed and modelled after what the EU stands for[55] and they constitute the building blocks primarily for a legal (but not necessarily political) system. The assumption here is, of course, that principles/values like democracy and the rule of law as intended within the EU are worth pursuing universally, or that, at least, they would not be overtly opposed. From this representation, the EU derives the intention to level up and/or harmonize the rules towards higher standards, often concealing this aspiration behind market access concessions.

In EU external relations, the EU's power in trade and investments is uncontested and particularly revealing of these EU levelling up aspirations (or 'imperial'[56] attempts, depending on who you ask) to extend its normative influence. The scale of the Single Market and the EU's extensive experience in negotiating trade and investment agreements establish it as one of the most powerful trading blocs in the world. As the largest global trader of services and a major force in the trade of goods, the EU holds a particularly strong position to expand its influence further *through* its trade and investment agreements.[57] In this sense, the EU has used its power to obtain changes in the domestic policies of its trading partners in exchange for market access and liberalization. The conditions attached to market access have ranged from labour and environmental standards to broader efforts at reshaping global governance patterns, largely reflecting the promotion of Western ideological priorities—particularly in developing countries—on issues like services and intellectual property.[58] In contrast, the EU has increasingly fallen behind in other critical areas, most notably the digital economy. Unlike global leaders such as the United States, China, and other nations that have nurtured the rise of major Internet-based businesses across diverse sectors, the EU remains confined to a secondary role. While the EU continues to focus heavily on regulation, these countries drive innovation and, through the dominance of their tech giants, shape international norms and redefine power dynamics in global affairs. This disparity underscores the EU's struggle to establish itself as a leader in one of the most dynamic and influential fields of the modern era.

At this point, the most sceptical would not miss the chance to question whether the EU aspirations are indeed about putting values like democracy

[55] This is the case with the neighbourhood policy and the conditions attached to it for prospective members as discussed further below.

[56] I borrow this terminology from Zielonka. Zielonka, Jan (2008), 'Europe as a Global Actor: Empire by Example?', International Affairs.

[57] Meunier and Nicolaïdis (n 42).

[58] Pollack, Mark and Shaffer, Gregory (2001), *Transatlantic Governance in the Global Economy.*

and the rule of law first or about concealing the pursuit of (economic, political) interests in the name of resolving the problems that the EU seeks to address by extending its normative influence on other legal regimes. A cynical observer would thus argue that what drives the EU may not be the satisfaction of moral demands such as the development of truly sustainable economic growth through its foreign policies of democracy and rule of law, but rather the affirmation of its own 'Promethean' vision of, and advantages within, the international legal order, so as to ensure openness of and competitiveness in the Single Market.

This is not an easy question to answer, especially in purely legal terms, and different layers of considerations should prevent trenchant conclusions. The growing interdependence that characterizes today's shifting geo-economic order[59] requires multilateral cooperation or collective action to address challenges affecting domestic systems and having implications that extend well beyond that—for example, climate change, energy supply, and health crises, just to name a few. In a world where many countries are powerful, and no country is powerful enough to get anything done alone, multilateralism may soon become an inevitable option. The EU is acutely aware of that, yet its approach towards international law and governance displays some incongruencies that question the effectiveness and genuineness of its normative projections in the world, as I outline in the remainder of this section. Two aspects are particularly interesting to consider. First, a recalibration and steering of global justice towards the EU's strategic autonomy, and second, an assessment of the EU conception of multilateralism in other legal orders.

1. Open strategic autonomy and institutionalism

One problem of the relationship between the EU and international law lies in the contradictory premise upon which the EU is forging a vision that is imbued with rules-based multilateralism but calibrated upon its strategic interests and values. There is a fundamental contradiction at the heart of the EU's identity[60] and role as an international actor because its pursuit of common or shared interests includes 'European' territorial integrity, political, and strategic security, and the prosperity and economic well-being of its Member States.

[59] Roberts, Anthea, Moraes, Henrique, and Ferguson, Victor (2019), 'Toward a Geoeconomic Order in International Trade and Investment', Journal of International Economic Law, 655.

[60] See Section A.

Different implications stem from considering the EU as an inspirational 'model' or an influencing 'power'. If the former, the EU could exemplify one approach (among others) and inspire others to be drawn into its orbit; if the latter, the EU more or less explicitly imposes a line of action, the deviation from which entails some costs. The problem with the EU is that it has often concealed the latter (power) behind the former (inspirational model). Unsurprisingly, it follows that the EU's characterization as an 'ethical' power championing values and principles having universal applicability and reflecting cosmopolitan norms fell short of its rhetoric:

> The problem here is obvious: no actor can effectively pursue its own interests in a diverse and pluralist international system, and claim to be 'doing good' by others, at the same time – unless one uncritically accepts liberal-idealist claims that there are cosmopolitan or universal values and interests that transcend those of individual political communities.[61]

Men come easily to believe that arrangements agreeable to themselves are beneficial to others and are tempted to clothe their aspirations and actions in the universal moral purposes of the universe.[62] The EU is far from being exempted from this belief. In response, it has recently recalibrated its ethical powers in more strategic terms. However, the shift toward what it has branded as 'open strategic autonomy' introduces a new set of challenges that shape the EU's relationship with international law.

The concept of 'open strategic autonomy' comes from defence/military planning and refers to the EU ability to chart its own course in line with its interests and values. Open strategic autonomy is a mindset whereby the EU prioritizes multilateral cooperation to safeguard its interests and uphold its values whenever feasible while acting independently in all other circumstances. Put more succinctly, it represents 'the EU's ability to make its own choices and shape the world around it through leadership and engagement, reflecting its strategic interests and values'. This implies accepting and 'managing interdependence in the best possible way'[63] while recognizing that the power of rights might not prevail over the rights of power when strategic interests are at stake and cannot be achieved otherwise. Here emerges another significant incongruence in the EU approach. Despite having made the normative levelling up of the

[61] Hyde-Price (n 22), 32.

[62] Morgenthau, Hans (1948), *Power Among Nations: The Struggle for Power and Peace*, 13.

[63] European Parliament (2023), 'What if Open Strategic Autonomy Could Break the Cycle of Recurring Crises?', EPRS_ATA(2023)747420_EN.

rules a cornerstone of its external relations and, consequently, the respect of EU values and norms in external relations a matter of principle (Article 3(5) TEU), the principle remains tied up with vital interests.[64] When the attractiveness of the EU model is not pervasive enough, the EU has to resort to other ways to validate the power of its rights, stretching its action up to a point of resorting to the right of its power. As outlined in Chapter 6, judicialization provides an effective channel for the enhancement of rights, insofar as others will abide by such decisions. In other instances, open strategic autonomy might come into play in the name of protection against practices that allegedly risk undermining the benefits of (economic and political) openness.[65] The need for protection is derived from a certain normative understanding of what is fair/free trade and what is not, which corresponds to the EU's belief of possessing arrangements that are beneficial to universal purposes.

Traces of tautology are not difficult to detect in this approach: the EU advocacy for the power of rights is ultimately protected by an appropriate level of ambition and strategic autonomy; open strategic autonomy ultimately serves to ensure the fulfilment of rights through 'stronger' means. At this point, one may wonder what degree of strongness is entailed and whether the EU acts in the name of making multilateral cooperation more effective globally or for its own benefit. Two examples—the agreement with China (CAI) and the Directive on corporate due diligence mentioned in Chapter 5—provide some answers to the first question.

The agreement with China provides for environmental protection through non-derogation clauses, introduces corporate social responsibility clauses, imposes a duty of effective implementation of multilateral environmental agreements as well as of the fundamental International Labour Organization (ILO) conventions, and focuses on sustainable development while committed to deal with 'investment and climate change'.[66] Many scholars and practitioners could read into this an indication of the EU's normative and taming influence on third countries, albeit time is proving them wrong, given that the ratification process has been paused since 2021 as a consequence of the evolving dynamics of the wider EU–China relationship. Specifically, in March 2021 the EU imposed sanctions on four Chinese officials for human rights abuses in Xinjiang, to which Beijing responded with its own sanctions on ten individuals and four entities in the EU, including Members of the European Parliament

[64] Bishop, Sven (2019), *European Strategy in the 21st Century*.

[65] Phol, Jens Hillebrand (2021), 'Strategic Autonomy as a Means to Counter Protectionism', ERA Forum, 183.

[66] CAI (n 11).

and the Council's Political and Security Committee. These developments unavoidably question the effectiveness of the EU's commitment to engage others in its normative vision while defending its own interests and values, especially as to whether the ability to propel its values is ultimately defensible through hard power means (sanctions) only.

Another example that questions the EU's multilateral intentions is the Directive on corporate sustainability due diligence. The Directive advances the EU's global vision of sustainability, not merely by promoting its principles as outlined in Article 3(5) TEU but through a more tangible and strategic extraterritorial application of EU standards. This approach bypasses reliance on voluntarily negotiated agreements which, while still considered an 'essential platform to engage' with international partners, are complemented by the EU's assertive push to extend its standards beyond its borders, ensuring greater alignment with its sustainability objectives. Perhaps unexpectedly, the Directive applies also to non-EU companies having a direct link to the Union market (and turnovers above a certain threshold) and epitomizes how the EU exercises leverage through its normative inclinations outside its borders.[67]

The Directive responds to the need to ensure responsible companies' behaviours and overcome the limitations that have so far characterized investment agreements in respect of the application of standards on human rights, the environment, and labour to foreign investors. This is open strategic autonomy in action: if cooperation on investors' accountability is not achievable through cooperative means—for example via international agreement—the EU overcomes the impasse and attains the same objectives through other instruments with limited forms of cooperation with others, like the directive in question. The strategic approach, however, is unlikely to hit the mark, as argued by Sattorova:

> While the proposed corporate sustainability due diligence Regulation is designed to prevent negative effects of foreign investment ('do no harm' obligations), what is still missing is a *discussion* of how investment policies can be redesigned to maximize the positive contribution that investors can bring to societies—how to 'do good' for the communities that host them.[68]

[67] Sattorova, Mavluda (2023), 'EU Investment Law at a Crossroads: Open Strategic Autonomy in Times of Heightened Security Concerns', Common Market Law Review, 710.

[68] Ibid, 729. Emphasis added.

While the approach of anchoring sustainability through internal market directives is less usual than through international agreements, the Commission bet on Member States, risking a disappointing result in cases where the Council's disagrees with the EU Directive. That is precisely what happened in February 2023: despite the Parliament and Council negotiators eventually reaching a political agreement in December 2023, the European Council did not reach a QMV and prevented its adoption. The Belgian Presidency of the Council issued a statement explaining that it had 'to consider the state of play and will see if it's possible to address the concerns put forward by Member States, in consultation with the Parliament'.[69] This configures the risks I identified in Chapter 2: the uncontrolled reflexes of national interests in the international sphere pose complex constraints on the EU as an actor on the global stage. Taking into account some concerns raised by some Member States, the Parliament and Council amended the text accordingly during a second reading, and, after four years of negotiations, the adoption process was completed in May 2024 upon the Council approval.

The most fainthearted would at this point find comfort in institutional persistence theories. From this standpoint, institutions persist, even when they generate consequences that are unintended or unreasonable (from a justice perspective), and actors will pursue transformative institutional changes rather than abandoning them. As explained by historical institutionalists, institutional stability is enhanced by a process of positive feedback that resists change and gradually builds deeper and more stable foundations.[70]

New hopes and a reality of new possibilities to change the horrors the war left in people's minds constitute this 'positive feedback' that the EU project triggered from its beginning, proceeded throughout its unfolding, and has become a fundamental pillar of the EU's entire story. Over time, EU policies and institutions created constituencies that developed and deepened preferences and resisted change. Institutions became the mechanisms through which these preferences are expressed, diffused, and consolidated (or contested).[71] The EU built its identity precisely on these mechanisms that, while consolidating certain preferences, required compromise and sacrifices on the part of the Member States, often with the help of a particular institution—the Court. It

[69] European Parliament, (2024) 'Press conference by Lara WOLTERS, rapporteur on corporate sustainability due diligence directive', 20240228-1600-SPECIAL-PRESSER.

[70] St John, Taylor (2018), *The Rise of Investor-State Arbitration—Politics, Law, and Unintended Consequences*, 235.

[71] Laatikainen, Katie Verlin (2012) 'EU multilateralism in a multipolar world'. In *Routledge Handbook on the European Union and International Institutions Performance, Policy, Power*, edited by Knud Erik Jørgensen and Katie Verlin Laatikainen, 476.

is the commitment—embodied in the willingness to sacrifice and compromise for a greater collective benefit—that makes exit unlikely and guides actors toward a gradual layering of change in the face of disagreements. Consequently, although not free from criticism, the EU's institutional foundations are seldom fundamentally questioned. Member States fight the Commission's attempts to extend its competences but questioning the unique constitutive foundation of EU multilateralism is rare. The EU's distinctive predisposition to institutionalized multilateralism appears to be as in-built or even reflective of the European 'soul'.[72]

Beyond taming effects within internal borders, institutionalized multilateralism presents competitive advantages for powers competing ideologically with other great powers. The more a norm becomes institutionalized, the greater the political and rhetorical resources available to defend it when challenged.[73] In the case of the EU, its supranational structure ensures that its institutions are enduring, capable of withstanding contestation, and designed to create decentralized commitments that make exit costly and logistically challenging. Yet unreserved reliance on institutions may not be enough. While adaptations and even contestations would not undermine the overall institutional stability, the prospect of exit represents a critical vulnerability. Brexit has precisely underscored this reality: although exit is undeniably complex and entails substantial costs, it remains feasible and, under certain circumstances, may appear more appealing than enduring the constraints imposed by EU membership. This highlights the delicate balance between institutional robustness and the necessity of maintaining the legitimacy and appeal of multilateral commitments.

2. EU multilateralism in other legal orders

One last point to consider is the question introduced a few paragraphs above—that is, whether the EU acts in the name of making multilateral cooperation more effective globally or for its own benefit. Beyond economic purposes, the EU is acutely aware of the potential of giving access to its market as a channel

[72] Jørgensen, Knud Erik (2006), 'Intersecting Multilateralism: The European Union and Multilateral Institutions.' In *The European Union at the United Nations*, edited by Katie Verlin Laatikainen and Karn Smith, 31.

[73] Sandholtz, Wayne (2023), 'Is Winter Coming? Norm Challenges and Norm Resilience.' In *Tracing Value Change in the International Legal Order: Perspectives from Legal and Political Science*, edited by Heike Krieger and Andrea Liese, 58.

to export its normative visions and ideals through laws and the conditions attached to them. The economic and normative dimensions stand in a state of tension and are not always separable from one another, given that the latter constitute a prerequisite of the former to obtain market access. By identifying a certain set of rights that deserve compliance more than others and are allegedly concealed behind economic reasons, the EU generates a process that Harrow describes as the 'juridification of values'[74] to assert its own interests.[75] The presumption is that the EU economic interests are articulated in normative values and principles that possess universal significance and *should* be widely applied. For the juridification of values to be operational, it has to rely on the use of international machinery—mostly through judicialization—to gain authority, not necessarily legitimacy. One preliminary problem is that the values and interests that are worth protecting for the EU may not be shared and accepted globally or multilaterally. Therefore, their imposition through judicial means risks creating selective forms of multilateralism by those who claim to possess the authority to weigh precisely which interests are worth protecting.

The risk is to shift competing visions of multilateralism from the political to the judicial arena.[76] While compromises and adjustments are more achievable within the political terrain, once framed in judicial terms the competition among visions is likely to generate disturbance in the rule of law. An extreme configuration of this disturbance could be that of having two judgments whose legal effects are mutually exclusive and, therefore, would lead to the negation of the effectiveness of the rule of law. The question is of particular relevance for the clashes between the EU and the regime of foreign investments and has so far materialized in situations where arbitral awards contradict EU law, or where compliance with EU laws happens to the detriment of international (investment) law obligations. From the Court of Justice of the European Union's (CJEU) perspective, this conflict produces disturbances of the rule of law, which are 'inherent in this incompatibility between the legal effects produced by the two judgments'.[77] This configuration is not particularly surprising in a globalized and globalizing world, where there are significant overlaps in jurisdictions that are not delineated in a way to avoid conflict or that prescribe how to manage conflicts.[78]

[74] Harrow, Carol (2006), 'Global Administrative Law: The Quest for Principles and Values', European Journal of International Law.

[75] Morlino, Leonardo (2010), 'The Two "Rules Of Law" Between Transition to and Quality of Democracy.' In *Rule of Law and Democracy*, edited by Leonardo Morlino and Gianluigi Palombella, 53.

[76] See Chapter 6.

[77] Case C-80/00, *Italian leather v Weco* EU:C:2002:107, paras 65–67.

[78] De Búrca, Gráinne (2009), 'The European Court of Justice and the International Legal Order after Kadi', Jean Monnet Working Paper, 6.

Treating domestic law as a matter of fact (Article 8.31(2) CETA)[79] is one way to prevent potential conflicts between EU and investment laws. It is unlikely, however, to generate definite answers, especially in the absence of a clear EU jurisprudence on any point in question or because of the reluctance of other judicial bodies to treat EU law differently from domestic law or accord it a superior status. Another possible approach to mitigate this permanent conflict would be to allow arbitral tribunals to request preliminary rulings from the CJEU where EU law issues are at stake. This solution is the one adopted by the Andean Community Court of Justice[80] but has, so far, been largely ignored within the investment regime. The risks posed by these conflicts are not limited to the ambit of investment matters and, as already proved by the *Kadi* case, sit uncomfortably with the traditional self-presentation of the EU as a committed multilateral actor and its political ambition to carve out a distinctive international role for itself as a 'normative power' committed to effective multilateralism under international law.[81]

In *Kadi*, the CJEU suggested that protecting the EU's values, including those regarding human rights, is a primary obligation that cannot be called into question, not even by a UN Security Council (SC) Resolution. While the annulment of the EC instruments implementing a UN Resolution did not call into question its primacy in international law, the Court argued that the risks posed by said Resolution, as by any other international law, could affect and possibly alter the primacy of the fundamental principles of EC law. Without diminishing the merits of protecting EU values,[82] the means to reach this goal appear questionable. While from an output perspective, the EU's ambivalence towards international law and governance is a potentially successful strategy to tame Member States, using multilateralism as a means to an end rather than an end in itself, undermines the EU's ambition to establish a particular identity as an international actor. I am persuaded by De Búrca's argument that the Court here missed an opportunity to develop a shared communicative framework[83] and enable the EU to act as the normative power it aspires to be.

[79] See Chapter 5.

[80] See Alter, Karen and Helfer, Laurence (2017), *Transplanting International Courts—The Law and Politics of the Andean Tribunal of Justice.*

[81] De Búrca (n 78), 2, 4.

[82] The dualistic approach taken here should be understood as a deliberate response to specific challenges that may arise in multilevel systems. Its primary aim is to ensure a higher level of protection deemed indispensable in such complex and layered governance frameworks. Kokott, Juliane and Sobotta, Christoph (2016), 'The *Kadi* Case—Constitutional Core Values and International Law—Finding the Balance?' In *The European Court of Justice and External Relations Law—Constitutional Challenges*, edited by Marise Cremona and Anne Thies, 213.

[83] De Búrca (n 78), 38.

> Had the ECJ [European Court of Justice], as the judicial branch of this important regional organization, invoked international law norms rather than only internal European standards in refusing to implement the SC Resolution without further due process guarantees, it would not only have provided a better example for other states and organizations contemplating the implementation of the UN sanctions regime, but it would also have added some substance to the rhetoric of 'normative power Europe'.

This judicial strategy is corroborated by Opinion 2/13 (concerning the EU's access to the European Convention on Human Rights), which strenuously insisted on preserving the EU's autonomy against any interferences from any judicial body and continued to eschew dialogues on international law norms belonging to and affecting a plurality of legal orders. This inward-looking tendency experienced an apparently radical change in Opinion 1/17. The Opinion posited that investment law coexistence with EU law is admissible as long as the arbitral tribunal does not call into question the level of protection of public interest determined by the Union following a democratic process.[84] This is a step forward if compared to *Kadi*, but a leap in the dark, if not an ironic twist of fate when compared to Opinion 2/13. In Opinion 1/17, it appears that the rule of law's condition of compatibility with EU treaties is a given (as per *Kadi*), and what needs to be preserved is the level of protection of public interest established by the EU measures, regardless of the adjudicating authority. It looks as if preserving the autonomy of the EU legal order has to pass through the protection of public interests, the degree of which is determined by the EU anyway. Despite recognizing that 'the EU's municipal legal order and the international legal order do not pass by each other like ships in the night',[85] the Court is once again missing an opportunity to let the EU contribute to discourses about the rule of law that would have relevance for the entire international community and not just for the EU circle.

Despite its apparent originality, Opinion 1/17 does not endorse any form of judicial dialogue among different judicial bodies. Rather, it is 'ratifying' the new ICS after the Commission has already included it in a handful of investment agreements or chapters. It displays acceptance of the EU legal order's coexistence with international (investment) law rather than supremacy over it. This, however, does not go as far as engaging in and developing discourses of

[84] See Chapter 6.

[85] Joined Cases C-402/05 P and C-415/05 P, *Kadi I v Council of the European Union and Commission of the European Communities*, EU:C:2008:11, para 22.

international dialogue that could have strengthened the EU as a global actor and benefitted other legal orders. It also reveals a significant paradox in the EU's relationship with the international legal order, which begs, in turn, the question of whether the EU is genuinely attempting to globally share its 'autochthonous values' (along with its conditions) in response to the investment regime deficits or whether the EU is using multilateralism and fidelity to international law and governance as channels to shape the system in ways more favourable to its own interests and needs.[86]

This brings to light another facet of the 'juridification' of values issue. Since adherence to EU values is realized through compliance with standards embedded in FTAs or IIAs, the normative prerogatives of the EU become inextricably intertwined with its economic interests. This conflation makes it challenging to separate the noble intentions ostensibly underpinning these values from the EU's overarching 'Promethean' vision of the international legal order—one that ultimately seeks to reinforce and safeguard its own economic priorities. Empirical evidence suggests a preference for the preservation of openness and competitiveness (or protectionism depending on the circumstances) of the Single Market. This is exemplified by the significant challenges and burdens that compliance with EU standards often imposes, particularly on developing and less developed countries, underscoring the tension between the EU's economic objectives and the global inclusivity it professes to champion.

Implementing sustainable development practices, improving environmental protections, and ensuring fair labour practices require substantial investments in infrastructure, technology, capacity building, and institutional strengthening that many less developed countries lack. Additionally, less developed countries may lack the expertise and administrative capacity to effectively enforce these standards, leading to challenges in implementation and monitoring, which, in turn, are likely to generate potential legal disputes over non-compliance. A related risk is that less developed countries would prioritize short-term economic gains over long-term sustainability objectives to attract foreign investment and avoid non-compliance liability. This can lead to governments prioritizing the attraction of investment over citizens and investment protection, and therefore to environmental degradation, exploitation of natural resources, and labour rights abuses. Despite the noble intentions, the standardized approach of FTAs or IIAs remains congenial to the economic

[86] Hyde-Price (n 22), 30.

interests of the Single Market but poses burdens of compliance that would require disproportionate efforts on less developed countries.

The EU's choice of IIA partner countries suggests that the EU is somewhat aware of these burdens and that the intent to channel FDI in developing countries is not the leitmotif behind its investment policy.[87] In fact, only a handful of the countries with which the EU is or has been negotiating IIAs (either as IPAs or as investment chapters in FTAs) qualify as middle- or low-income economies,[88] and many of them are evolving towards the status of emerging economies in lesser need of assistance. The recent empowerment to regulate FDIs is a further opportunity for the EU to enhance its performance as a good citizen who speaks the language of shared norms and seeks to advance its vision of justice. Its commitment, however, is not always the result of a truly multilateral vision but reflects self-serving considerations about a widespread aversion against investment arbitration, especially within Europe.

E. Conclusions

There is little doubt that the EU is firmly established within the international legal order and plays an active role in shaping its development, leveraging its normative influence and regulatory power to drive global governance and international rule-making. Yet it is questionable whether the 'EU way' is indeed about putting the values of democracy and the rule of law first, or whether it is primarily led by the pursuit of (economic, political) interests, especially in the realm of investment law. Disguised under the resolution of some of the investment regime problems, what truly drives the EU may not be the fulfilment of moral imperatives, such as fostering genuinely sustainable economic growth through its foreign policies. Instead, it may be the assertion of its own 'Promethean' vision of, and strategic position within the international legal order, ultimately aimed at safeguarding openness and competitiveness within the Single Market.

There is plenty which, in my eyes, is admirable in the EU spreading of its values. For example, the opening up of new channels to directly gather democratic inputs (like the experience of public consultations) is a laudable effort that would make the system more open and accessible. In these areas, the EU

[87] Basedow (n 16), 60.

[88] As of May 2025, the middle- or low-income countries involved in negotiations or agreements with the EU are Angola, China, Kenya, Kyrgyzstan, India, Indonesia, Myanmar, Philippines, and Vietnam.

approach is likely to leave an imprint on the investment regime's dynamics and will continue to contribute to strengthening and consolidating international trends. However, some incongruencies and ambiguities feature the translation of the values of democracy and the rule of law into the investment regime and have exposed the deficits in the EU's role as an actor on the global stage. Some of these are long-standing issues mostly related to the ambiguities that characterize the EU's identity. Some others, however, are aggravated by what would appear as an iatrogenic configuration of the EU line of action: the treatment for the problems sought to address causes further damages.

Clearly, a one-size-fits-all approach is unlikely to work. Yet one of the most uncomfortable aspects of the flexible approach that has characterized the EU investment policy concerns its ambivalence towards international law. Alarmingly, when vital European interests are at stake, ethical principles often take a back seat, with less influence on shaping the EU's foreign and security agendas. A plausible explanation is that since it takes two to tango there might be instances where EU treaty partners are unwilling to embrace the EU line unreservedly, and reaching a compromise is better than arriving at no agreement at all. A particularly sensitive point in this respect is the combination of liberalization with the social effects of market integration. The EU is increasingly facing demands for protection beyond the mere market logic and is attempting to balance the wealth potentially generated through liberalization and free trade with other social values like environmental protection, health, and sustainable development. To this end, the EU has made bold changes towards the clarification of ambiguous language provisions and has sought to mitigate the negative effects of liberalization on the state's regulatory capacity, further limiting foreign investment activity by preserving and expanding the state's right to regulate, subjecting investment provisions to exceptions (i.e. general and public security exceptions), and promoting international labour, environmental, and sustainable development standards.[89]

One can salute these changes as an opportunity to counter inconsistent case law. Yet one might also wonder whether the specifications introduced by the EU in its investment treaties only seek to avoid interpretations too restrictive of the state's regulatory autonomy,[90] or whether they could, more broadly, catalyse the attainment of balance and sustainable development. If the former, one

[89] See Chapter 5.

[90] Gehring, Markus and Tokas, Marios (2022), 'Synergies and Approaches to Climate Change in International Investment Agreements: Comparative Analysis of Investment Liberalization and Investment Protection Provisions in European Union Agreements', The Journal of World Investment and Trade, 793–4.

related question would inquire whether treaty language simply avoids regulatory conflicts, because of the state's fear of regulatory chill, or because it seeks to positively incentivize developments. One risk of devoting too much effort to expanding regulatory autonomy is that it may hinder third parties from acting as incidental enablers and enforcers. Admittedly, even investors could contribute positively to the communities that host them, fostering mutual benefit and cooperation rather than simply viewing them as external actors. The EU does not pursue this path, or at least not explicitly, but leaves open the option to enforce compliance with commitments undertaken for example under environmental agreements through state to state dispute settlement.[91]

This is where the iatrogenic configuration becomes even more evident. The linguistic clarifications introduced in agreements such as the CETA FET standard aim to address inconsistent case law on legitimate expectations, particularly by precluding such expectations when regulatory changes adversely affect investments (CETA Article 8.10(4)). While such clarifications serve as a corrective measure against ambiguous interpretations of states' regulatory rights and are not inherently detrimental to development goals, they also carry unintended consequences. By broadening the scope of regulatory autonomy, these clarifications risk disincentivizing other actors—particularly investors—from playing roles as incidental enablers or enforcers of developmental policies. Although the intention to reduce ambiguity is commendable, EU decision-makers must carefully consider a wider array of issues when weighing alternative policy approaches to ensure balanced outcomes.[92]

A problem of this sort could be mitigated by advancing alternatives with less impact, but it might be complicated by Member States prerogatives, as shown by the bumpy adoption of the directive of due diligence. In the end, entrenched interests (of both the EU and its Member States) inexorably overshadow the EU's role in the multipolar system. Although the EU has crafted a unique expression of a particular set of norms, values, and constrained sovereignty that have emerged wholly from its exceptional internal experience,[93] its external relations are not about embedding its generalized principles of multilateralism to support universalism.

From the outside in, systemic repercussions of the spread of EU values on international investment law materialized in missed opportunities for

[91] Tropper, Johannes and Wagner, Kilian (2022), 'The European Union Proposal for the Modernisation of the Energy Charter Treaty—A Model for Climate-Friendly Investment Treaties?', The Journal of World Investment and Trade, 840.

[92] Hyde-Price (n 22), 39.

[93] Laatikainen (n 71), 480.

projecting EU values through strategic and judicial dialogues with other great powers. This is largely due to the misplaced premises upon which the EU has derived its legitimacy to act strategically like a great power.[94] However, if seen from a completely different angle, the EU's failure to promote effective multilateralism in these partnerships could be a reflection of the EU learning to act like a great power. The EU sees strategic partnerships as a means to project its values, but 'for realist countries like China, Russia and India, strategic partnerships are essentially regarded as a tool to further their interests'.[95] Open strategic autonomy might precisely fit the purpose, albeit at the cost of diminishing the EU normative impact.

[94] Ibid, 481–2.

[95] Grevi, Giovanni and de Vasconcelos, Álavaro (2008), *Partnerships for Effective Multilateralism—EU Relations with Brazil, China, India and Russia*, 155.

8

Spreading values or pursuing interests? Some concluding observations on the EU's role in international investment law and policy

This concluding chapter synthesizes the book's exploration of the EU's evolving role in investment law and policy, highlighting it as an ongoing and dynamic journey. As the EU has expanded, the world has become more complex and has changed, becoming increasingly interconnected. It has, as a consequence, become less Eurocentric. There have been instances where EU values have prominently shaped investment policy, yet on many other occasions it fluctuated between leaving unimpressive marks and conducting business through the bureaucratic technicalities of its institutions. It would seem that at times the EU give the impression of being somewhat elderly, feeling less than a protagonist in a world which frequently regards it with aloofness, mistrust, and even, suspicion.[1]

In a world where cross-cutting identities and loyalties push people into more flexible networks of convenience, the narrative of EU multilateralism as a force of good has followed a predictable and understandably EU-centric trajectory. However, due to systemic changes in the international environment and the crises of European integration, its role in the world is becoming more contentious.[2] Nonetheless, for many the EU remains a remarkable example of multilateralism, even if it sometimes falters in its mission to engange in multilateral relationships. Some would continue to argue that the attractiveness of the European model of regional integration is unquestioned, as evidenced by the evolution of the African Union, Mercosur, and perhaps even China's cultivation of regionalism through ASEAN and the Shanghai Cooperation

[1] The Holy See (2014), *Address of Pope Francis to the European Parliament.*

[2] Barbé, Esther and Morillas, Pol (2019), 'The EU Global Strategy: The Dynamics of a More Politicized and Politically Integrated Foreign Policy', Cambridge Review of International Affairs.

EU Values in Investment Law And Policy. Maria Laura Marceddu, Oxford University Press.
 DOI: 10.1093/9780191986208.003.0008

Organization. The EU continues to be impressive, albeit often appearing oddly detached from the environment in which it operates. For many others, however, the EU's ambitions to serve as a role model are unrealistic, if not counterproductive, in a world where new non-Western powerhouses are emerging and tend to regard the EU as complicated, bureaucratic, and potentially unengaging for the broad public.[3]

The fundamental question posed by this book—is it possible that values like democracy and the rule of law can expand from EU borders to the realm of international investments?—continues to seek a definitive answer. Reality is more nuanced than simply providing binary answers, and while Europe remains the last politically effective utopia—at least in the eyes of most romantics—whether its promises to bring democracy and the rule of law to the investment regime are genuine or flawed remains blurred. As things stand, it appears unlikely that the EU will fulfil its aspiration of becoming a global standard-setter purely on normative terms. This is especially true given that not all its commercial partners are willing to embrace EU-specific approaches without reservations and that, in terms of innovation, the EU lags behind many of its competitors. Presumably, strategic considerations could ensure some alignment with EU standards, but this is likely to intensify the tension between spreading values, pursuing interests, and imposing regulation. Such a dynamic could further expose the limitations of the EU as a global actor, highlighting the inherent challenges in balancing these competing objectives. The resulting constraints are evident in many systems with which the EU interacts and have impacted the foreign investment regime, especially since the operational development of Article 2 of the Treaty on European Union (TEU).

The recently initiated judicial monitoring of Article 2 TEU[4] has given the EU's promotion of values an additional dimension, extending its political reach into the judicial sphere and adding a further layer of complexity and challenges. As long as values are seen as the product of Europe's cultural, religious, and humanist inheritance—endowed with symbolic significance that must be reflected in legal norms—they remain a matter of principle: highly valued reference points close to ideals, but not much more. When framed in judicial terms these values acquire more operational functions; they become legal norms and, as such, render political actions juridical and constrain them within legal boundaries. The complexity arises because neither

[3] Lucarelli, Sonia (2014), 'The EU's Leadership in Global Governance: Perceptions from the Others.' In *Communicating Europe in Times of Crisis*, edited by Natalia Chaban and Martin Holland, 7.

[4] Case C-64/16, *Associação Sindical dos Juízes Portugueses*, EU:C:2018:117.

conceptualization—principles as values and principles as norms—can maintain its original conditions. The result is a moving target oscillating between virtuous norms and normative principles, each carrying different expectations. For example, if sustainability in international investments is considered a matter of principle, compliance with EU standards might be sufficient to demonstrate best efforts in some form, albeit with no precise level of adherence. Conversely, if sustainability is regarded as a matter of norm, judicialization becomes a more powerful tool for ensuring compliance and enforcing a specific vision of justice.[5] In the former scenario, the creation of laws is politicized; in the latter, politics is legalized.

Depending on the poison one picks, the translation of values significantly influences the role of the EU as a global actor. In the former scenario (principles as values), the more idealistic component calls for a resolute understanding of the teleological underpinnings of the EU's messianic identity. Article 2 TEU provides the EU with a sufficiently capacious base for its own democratic legitimacy and for the generation of values of universal desirability and normalization. Such a broad foundation allows the EU to assume different roles as a global standard-setter, ranging from small-scale impacts, such as promoting global economic development through investment treaties, to intermediate-scale impacts, such as establishing forms of investors liability towards the host state, to large-scale impacts, such as extending remedies to domestic investors. The EU aspires to occupy a position somewhere between small- and medium-scale roles. However, it often falls short of its rhetoric and must resort to judicially oriented approaches to persuade others to follow its lead, particularly when it harbours large-scale aspirations.

Unsurprisingly, the latter perspective (principles as norms) has become increasingly suitable for maximizing the EU's role as a global actor. This approach is grounded in more realistic components, incorporating strategic visions and market-justice orientations. If policy-makers persist in identifying the EU primarily as a market leader, with a focus on maintaining competitive advantage, then the dissemination of values will largely emphasize norms that advocate for (investment) liberalization. The resulting impact on the EU's role as a global actor is aptly captured by the Brussels Effect, which largely confines the EU's role to the economic and, by extension, legal domains. While this

[5] The case that the EU initiated and subsequently won against Korea unequivocally demonstrates that even 'best effort' obligations towards sustainability, despite lacking a precise level of compliance, can result in binding obligations. Panel of Experts Proceeding Constituted Under Article 13.15 of the EU–Korea Free Trade Agreement (25 January 2021).

influence remains significant, its reach into other areas is limited but nonetheless persistent, creating subtle yet enduring spillover effects.

Both perspectives implicitly aim to empower the EU, yet they lead to distinct characterizations of its role as a global actor: the first frames the EU as a legal actor with constrained global influence, while the second depicts it as a market actor wielding regulatory power. While committed to preserve the Single Market, the EU appears unwilling to allow one perspective to dominate or to completely abandon the other. This self-inflicted conflict overshadows the EU's potential as global actor, constraining its role between a legal and/or market model and power.[6] The conflict has emerged quite vividly within the investment regime and in other areas, potentially jeopardizing the EU's ambitions to shape the global order according to its own vision. The failure to deliberately craft a specific stance—whether as a model or a power, and whether in legal or economic terms—has generated contradictions and frustrated expectations. For example, the EU advancement of transparency in investment arbitration follows the lead of other players. However, in instances where it could have demonstrated leadership, such as through public participation in consultations, the EU appears reluctant to set higher standards, possibly hindered by internal constraints on its democratic process of law-making. Similarly, although relatively unexplored by the EU, a more audacious approach would have pursued systemically radical reforms in other areas, such as redefining investors' liability or extending remedies to domestic investors. One possible explanation for this lack of boldness is that the EU, as a market leader driven by competitiveness, remains primarily focused on investment liberalization and promotion. Its strategy is inspired by the ultimate goal of unlocking the economic potential of the world's significant growth markets for EU trade and investment. Even at the economic level, the EU's envisioned model for sustainable development underscores the need for an internal binding instrument—a directive—to influence the behaviour of others, raising questions about the effectiveness of its power, reach, and persuasiveness. This is particularly notable in light of the agreement with Angola, which introduces significant innovations by fostering (rather than merely promoting) foreign direct investment (FDI) while integrating environmental and labour standards, transparency,

[6] Barbé, Esther, Herranz-Surrallés, Anna, and Natorski, Michal (2014), 'Contending Metaphors of the European Union as a Global Actor', Journal of Language and Politics; Aggestam, Lisbeth (2012), 'Global Norms and European Power.' In *Routledge Handbook on the European Union and International Institutions*, edited by Knud Erik Jørgensen and Katie Verlin Laatikainen; Manners, Ian (2013), 'Assessing the Decennial, Reassessing the Global: Understanding European Union Normative Power in Global Politics', Cooperation and Conflict.

and corporate social responsibility. However, this agreement stands out as a unique case within the EU's negotiation framework, leaving uncertainty about whether similar approaches will be adopted in the future and with which countries.

The unsatisfactory outcome is the EU's failure to translate its economic strength into hard political power,[7] combined with a lack of capacity and resolve (and lack of resolve to have that capacity) to defend and protect the values it professes to hold most dear. These values, though established, evidently lack the virtues necessary for vindication or have become the product of a culture in which it appears that nothing is worth making significant sacrifices for. It follows that both perspectives are at odds with the EU's global ambitions to shape the world according to its own vision, resulting in limited impact. In the realm of international investments, transforming the world according to the rules established in Brussels is problematic for at least two main reasons. First, and not particularly new, it leaves the EU vulnerable to charges of hypocrisy when it proclaims its ethical intentions (principles as values) but then pursues policies that favour European economic, strategic, or political interests (principles as norms and strategies). Second, defining EU foreign policy primarily through second-order normative concerns risks relegating the Union to a weak and ineffective role within an international system shaped by intense competition and the self-help logic of international anarchy, where states prioritize maximizing their power. This approach also leaves the EU vulnerable to the unchecked pursuit of national interests by its Member States on the global stage, further undermining its cohesion and strategic impact.[8]

One risk shared by the EU and the regime of foreign investment is the reduction of multidimensional interests into binary dichotomies: the law or the market, values or norms, investors or states, institutions or (Member) states. This issue is particularly sensitive because the pressure from multinational interests which are not universal weakens democracy and transforms it into a uniform system of economic power at the service of unseen empires. An important caveat, however, is that the EU empowerment to regulate FDIs and negotiate international investment agreement is relatively recent and progressing slowly. Consequently, the empirical scope of EU investment agreement remains fairly limited. So, while it may be premature to definitively assess the extent to which the EU is transforming the role of democracy and rule of law at

[7] Weiler, Joseph (2011) 'The Political and Legal Culture of European Integration: An Exploratory Essay', International Journal of Constitutional Law.

[8] Weiler, Joseph (1999), *The Constitution of Europe 'Do the New Clothes Have an Emperor?' and Other Essays on European Integration*, 341–2.

a systemic level, this 'adolescent' empowerment nonetheless provides a foundation for tentative conclusions and potential trajectories.

To date, EU investment policy has had modest overall impact on the regime of foreign investments. The EU entered the global investment system during a period of significant re-evaluation, leaving long-standing issues surrounding standards—issues that are likely to have pre-dated the Investor-State Dispute Settlement (ISDS) mechanism—largely unaddressed or only partially resolved within the legal framework. While all legal processes inherently represent simplified versions of more complex social realities, it appears that the EU has contributed to the flattening of multidimensional disputes into a binary relationship between investor and state, often rendering local perspectives invisible.[9] To reinforce this dynamic, the judiciary has become an inexhaustible source of new developments, accumulating disproportionate influence, which may result in a potential tyranny of values and the emergence of neo-colonialism tendencies. However, placing too much emphasis and reliance on the judiciary may not yield the expected outcomes and could expose the EU system to further backlash. The regime of foreign investments already exhibited signs of resistance to EU claims on multiple occasions, especially as a matter of principle. For instance, in the *Eskosol v Italy* case, the tribunal noted that EU law does not hold a privileged place but exists 'side-by-side with other sub-systems, including those created by various multilateral treaties', such as the Energy Charter Treaty (ECT). This implies that while EU law certainly has primacy over the national laws of its Member States, it does not hold the same supremacy over independent rules of international law.[10]

What transpires from this is a lack of a compelling purpose in the EU's agenda that binds together and coherently aligns different policies. As asserted by the Tribunal in *Oostergetel v Slovakia*, the objective of EU Treaties is primarily to establish and maintain a Common Market, whereas bilateral investment treaties provide 'specific guarantees for the investor's investment'.[11] This highlights the absence of a long-term vision across policies that can sustainably advance growth without compromising either economic or social components. This is particularly surprising in light of the EU's moral imperatives (morals, if

[9] Perrone, Nicolás (2019), 'The "Invisible" Local Communities: Foreign Investor Obligations, Inclusiveness, and the International Investment Regime', American Journal of International Law (AJIL) Unbound.

[10] *Eskosol v Italy* (Decision on Termination Request and Intra-EU Objection, 7 May 2019), para 182. On the same point, the Tribunal in *Vattenfall v Germany* noted that EU law also contains internal rules that are not part of international law. *Vattenfall v Germany* (Decision on the Achmea issue, 31 August 2018).

[11] *Oostergetel v Slovakia*, (Decision on Jurisdiction, 30 April 2010), para 75.

you wish), which aimed to provide timely and appropriate responses, as demonstrated by their transformation of the devastation of war into a new reality filled with hope for a better future and new possibilities. While the EU maintains a clear normative agenda, it increasingly resembles a comprehensive to-do list of regulations based on universally appealing ideas rather than fostering any genuine sense of belonging or attachment. Consequently, it supports functioning markets and economic integration, albeit not flawlessly, but it fails to contribute to the deeper formation of the EU as a cohesive entity. While values are operational within a legal framework, they exhibit limitations in achieving broader goals such as peace or development, which extend beyond mere economic utility. Without a psychological, emotional, and transcendental identification, citizens are likely to feel more like consumers, making legitimacy hard to achieve.

The foreign investment regime, for its part, is undergoing a growing sense of fluidity, opportunity, and uncertainty. This evolving landscape seems to make a shift towards a more balanced framework—one that emphasizes transparent public participation and accommodates public interests—more attainable than in previous years. The EU is well positioned to provide effective solutions in those areas. Indeed, the trajectory established by the EU indicates movement in this direction: its approach 'breathes the right spirit: to transform investor–state arbitration into a truly public, fully transparent, more predictable, and balanced system of global adjudication'.[12] The signing of the Mauritius Convention in July 2024, after remaining on the Council's table for almost a decade, marks the first UN treaty signed by the EU since *Gabon-EU FPA*[13] and exemplifies this commitment. However, for the EU to be more ambitious, it needs to develop a clear understanding of the teleological foundations of its identity in investment law and policy. Is spreading its values the reason and the mission for which the EU was created? Or has it gradually become the purpose the EU intends to exploit to fulfil its interests?

Beyond the actions of individual EU institutions, it is incumbent upon all Europeans to uphold shared values such as democracy, the rule of law, and fundamental rights. As President Lenaerts emphasized, these values are crucial for reinforcing that 'what brings us together remains stronger than what pulls us apart'. Therefore, in order to ensure that the EU continues to be a 'Union of

[12] Schill, Stephan (2016), 'Editorial: US versus EU Leadership in Global Investment Governance', The Journal of World Investment & Trade.

[13] Case 551/21, *Commission v Council (Signing of International Agreements)*, EU:C:2024:281.

democracies, a Union of rights, and a Union of justice', integration through the rule of law is the only way forward.[14]

I hope that the EU will live up to its values and will not, in Brecht's words, 'grub first, then ethics'.

[14] Lenaerts, Koen (2019) 'Upholding the Rule of Law through Judicial Dialogue', Yearbook of European Law, 34.

Bibliography

Aggestam L, 'Global Norms and European Power' in KE Jørgensen and KV Laatikainen (eds), *Routledge Handbook on the European Union and International Institutions* (Routledge, 2012). DOI 10.4324/9780203083642.

Alexy R, 'Constitutional Rights, Balancing, and Rationality' (2003) 16 *Ratio Juris* 131. DOI 10.1111/1467-9337.00228.

Allott P, ' European Governance and the Re-branding of Democracy' (2002) 1 *European Law Review* 60.

Allott P, 'The Crisis of European Constitutionalism: Reflections on the Revolution in Europe' (1997) 34 *Common Market Law Review* 439.

Alter K and Helfer L, *Transplanting International Courts—The Law and Politics of the Andean Tribunal of Justice* (Oxford University Press, 2017). DOI 10.1093/acprof:oso/9780199680788.001.0001.

Alschner W, *Investment Arbitration and State-Driven Reform—New Treaties, Old Outcomes* (Oxford University Press, 2021). DOI 10.1093/oso/9780197644386.001.0001.

Aman AC Jr, *The Democracy Deficit: Taming Globalization Through Law Reform* (New York University Press, 2004).

.Barbé E and Morillas P, 'The EU Global Strategy: The Dynamics of a More Politicized and Politically Integrated Foreign Policy' (2019) 32 *Cambridge Review of International Affairs* 753. DOI 10.1080/09557571.2019.1588227.

Barbé E, Herranz-Surralés A, and Natorski M, 'Contending Metaphors of the European Union as a Global Actor' (2015) 14 *Journal of Language and Politics* 18. DOI 10.1075/jlp.14.1.02bar.

Barker P, 'Investor–State Arbitration as International Public Law: Deference, Proportionality and the Standard of Review' in I Laird, I Sabahi, F Sourgens, and T Weiler (eds), *Investment Treaty Arbitration and International Law* (Juris Publishing, 2015).

Basedow JR, 'Why De-judicialize? Explaining State Preferences on Judicialization in World Trade Organization Dispute Settlement Body and Investor-to-State Dispute Settlement Reforms' (2021) 16 *Regulation and Governance* 1362. DOI 10.1111/rego.12431.

Basedow JR, 'The European Union's New International Investment Policy and the United Nation's Sustainable Development Goals: Integration as a Motor of Substantive Policy Change?' in C Beverelli, J Kurtz, and D Raess (eds), *International Trade, Investment, and the Sustainable Development Goals: World Trade Forum* (Cambridge University Press, 2020). DOI 10.1017/9781108881364.004.

Basedow JR, *The EU in the Global Investment Regime: Commission Entrepreneurship, Incremental Institutional Change and Business Lethargy* (Routledge, 2017). DOI 10.4324/9781315112282.

Bellamy RP, Bufacchi V, and Castiglione D (eds), *Democracy and Constitutional Culture in the Union of Europe* (Lothian Foundation Press, 1995).

Bingham T, *The Rule of Law* (Penguin, 2011).

Bishop S, *European Strategy in the 21st Century* (Routledge, 2019).

Bjorklund A, 'Improving the International Investment Law and Policy System: Report of the Rapporteur' in J Alvarez, KP Sauvant, KG Ahmed, and GP Vizcamno (eds), *The Evolving International Investment Regime: Expectations, Realities, Options* (Oxford University Press, 2011).

Blackaby N, 'Public Interest and Investment Treaty Arbitration' (2004) 1 *Transnational Dispute Management* 1. DOI: www.transnational-dispute-management.com/article.asp?key=36.

Blockmans S and Russack S, *Representative Democracy in the EU* (CEPS, 2019).

Bongiovanni G, Sartor G, and Valentini C (eds), *Reasonableness and Law* (Springer, 2009). DOI 10.1007/978-1-4020-8500-0.

Bonnitcha J, Poulsen LS, and Waibel M, *The Political Economy of the Investment Treaty Regime* (Oxford University Press, 2017). DOI 10.1093/law/9780198719540.001.0001.

Bradford A, *The Brussels Effect* (Oxford University Press, 2020). DOI 10.1093/oso/9780190088583.001.0001.

Brower CN and Rosenberg CB, 'The Death of the Two-Headed Nightingale: Why the Paulsson—van den Berg Presumption that Party-Appointed Arbitrators are Untrustworthy is Wrongheaded' (2013) 29 *Arbitration International* 7. DOI /10.1093/arbint/29.1.7.

Brown CM, 'A Multilateral Mechanism for the Settlement of Investment Disputes: Some Preliminary Remarks' (2017) 32 *ICSID Review—Foreign Investment Law Journal* 673. DOI 10.1093/icsidreview/six018.

Bungenberg M, Reinisch A, and Tietje C (eds), *EU and Investment Agreements Open Questions and Remaining Challenges* (Dike, 2013).

Calamita JN, 'Dispute Settlement Transparency in Europe's Evolving Investment Treaty Policy' (2014) 15 *The Journal of World Investment & Trade* 645. DOI 10.1163/22119000-01504014.

Calamita JN, 'The Making of Europe's International Investment Policy: Uncertain First Step' (2012) 39 *Legal Issues of Economic Integration* (2012) 301. DOI 10.54648/leie2012019.

Cardwell PJ, 'Mapping Out Democracy Promotion in the EU's External Relations' (2011) 16 *European Foreign Affairs Review* 21. DOI 10.54648/eerr2011002.

Cederman LE, 'Nationalism and Bounded Integration: What it Would Take to Construct a European Demos' (2001) 7 *European Journal of International Relations* 139. DOI 10.1177/1354066101007002001.

Cotula L, 'Democracy and International Investment Law' (2017) 30(2) *Leiden Journal of International Law* 351. DOI 10.1017/S0922156517000152.

Cotula L, '(Dis)integration in Global Resource Governance: Extractivism, Human Rights, and Investment Treaties' (2020) 23 *Journal of International Economic Law* 431. DOI 10.1093/jiel/jgaa003.

Cotula L and Perrone NM 'Seeing Santurbán through ISDS: A Sociolegal Case Study of Eco Oro v. Colombia' (2024) 37 *Leiden Journal of International Law* 440. DOI 10.1017/S0922156523000730.

Cotula L and Schröder M, *Community Perspectives in Investor–State Arbitration* (IIED, 2017).

Craig P, 'Integration, Democracy, and Legitimacy' in P Craig and G de Búrca (eds), *The Evolution of EU Law* (3rd edn, Oxford University Press, 2021). DOI 10.1093/oso/9780192846556.003.0002.

Craig P, 'Institutions, Power, and Institutional Balance' in P Craig and G de Búrca (eds), *The Evolution of EU Law* (3rd edn, Oxford University Press, 2021). DOI 10.1093/oso/9780192846556.003.0003.

Craig P, 'The Rule of Law and the EU: Responsibility, Independence and Rights' in A Rosas, J Raitio, and P Pohjankoski (eds), *The Rule of Law's Anatomy in the EU Foundations and Protections* (Hart Publishing, 2023).

Craig P and de Búrca G, *EU Law: Text, Cases, and Materials* (7th edn, Oxford University Press, 2020). DOI 10.1093/he/9780198856641.001.0001.

Craig P and Harlow C, *Lawmaking in the European Union* (Kluwer Law International, 1998).

Cremona M, 'Values in EU Foreign Policy' in M Evans and P Koutrakos (eds), *Beyond the Established Orders: Policy Interconnections between the EU and the Rest of the World* (Hart Publishing, 2011) 275. DOI 10.5040/9781472565495.

Cremona M and Scott J (eds), *EU Law Beyond EU Borders: The Extraterritorial Reach of EU Law* (Oxford University Press, 2019). DOI 10.1093/oso/9780198842170.001.0001.

Curtin D, 'Challenging Executive Dominance in European Democracy' (2014) 77 *The Modern Law Review* 1. DOI 10.1111/1468-2230.12054.

Damjanovic I, *The European Union and International Investment Law Reform: Between Aspirations and Reality* (Cambridge University Press, 2023). DOI 10.1017/9781009345422.

Dashwood A, 'The Relationship between the Member States and the European Union/European Community' (2004) 41 *Common Market Law Review* 355. DOI 10.54648/cola2004007.

De Abreu Duarte F, 'But the Last Word is Ours: The Monopoly of Jurisdiction of the Court of Justice of the European Union in Light of the Investment Court System' (2019) 30 *European Journal of International Law* 1187. DOI 10.1093/ejil/chz064.

De Baere G, 'European Integration and the Rule of Law in Foreign Policy' in J Dickson and P Eleftheriadis (eds), *Philosophical Foundations of European Union Law* (Oxford University Press, 2012). DOI 10.1093/acprof:oso/9780199588770.001.0001.

De Bradandere E, 'Individuals in Advisory Proceedings Before the International Court of Justice: Equality of the Parties and the Court's Discretionary Authority' (2012) 11 *The Law & Practice of International Courts and Tribunals* 253.

De Búrca G, 'Developing Democracy Beyond the State' (2008) 46 *Columbia Journal of Transnational Law* (2008) 102.

De Búrca G, 'The European Court of Justice and the International Legal Order after Kadi' (2009) 01/09 *Jean Monnet Working Paper.*

De Búrca G, 'Europe's Raison d'Etre' in D Kochenov and F Amtenbrink (eds), *The European Union's Shaping of the International Legal Order* (Cambridge University Press, 2013).

De Búrca G, 'Is EU Supranational Governance a Challenge to Liberal Constitutionalism?' (2018) 85 *The University of Chicago Law Review* 337. DOI doi.org/10.2139/ssrn.3105238.

De Búrca, G, Kilpatrick C, and Scott J (eds), *Critical Legal Perspectives on Global Governance Liber Amicorum David M Trubek* (Hart Publishing, 2015).

Dehousse R, 'Regulation by Networks in the European Community: The Role of European Agencies' (1997) 4 *Journal of European Public Policy* 246. DOI 10.1080/13501769709696341.

Dolzer R and Schreuer C, *Principles of International Investment Law* (2nd edn, Oxford University Press, 2012). DOI 10.1093/law/9780199651795.001.0001.

Duchêne F, 'Europe's Role in World Peace' in R Mayne (ed), *Europe Tomorrow: Sixteen Europeans Look Ahead* (Fontana, 1972) 32.

Easton D, 'An Approach to the Analysis of Political Systems' (1957) 9 *World Politics* 383. DOI 10.2307/2008920.

Eckes C, *EU Powers Under External Pressure—How the EU's External Actions Alter its Internal Structures* (Oxford University Press, 2019). DOI 10.1093/oso/9780198785545.001.0001.

Eeckhout P and Ortino F, 'Towards an EU Policy on Foreign Direct Investment' in A Biondi, P Eeckhout, and S Ripley (eds), *EU Law after Lisbon* (Oxford University Press, 2012), DOI 10.1093/acprof:oso/9780199644322.001.0001.

Eeckhout P, *EU External Relations Law* (2nd edn, Oxford University Press, 2011). DOI 10.1093/acprof:oso/9780199606634.001.0001.

Fritz T, *Public Services Under Attack—TTIP, CETA, and the Secretive Collusion Between Business Lobbyists and Trade Negotiators* (2015). https://www.tni.org/en/publication/public-services-under-attack.

Gao HS, 'The EU–China Comprehensive Agreement on Investment: Between Strategic Opportunity and Strategic Autonomy' (2022) *Asian Yearbook of International Economic Law* 47.

Garcia S, *European Identity and the Search for Legitimacy* (Pinter Publishers for The Eleni Nakou Foundation and the Royal Institute of International Affairs, 1993).

Gatzert N and Kosub T, 'Determinants of Policy Risks of Renewable Energy Investments' (2015) *Department of Insurance Economics and Risk Management, Friedrich-Alexander University Erlangen-Nürnberg (FAU) Working Paper*. DOI 10.2139/ssrn.2685114.

Gehring M and Tokas M, 'Synergies and Approaches to Climate Change in International Investment Agreements: Comparative Analysis of Investment Liberalization and Investment Protection Provisions in European Union Agreements' (2022) 23 *The Journal of World Investment and Trade* 778. DOI 10.1163/22119000-12340270.

Geiger R, 'Multilateral Approaches to Investment: The Way Forward' in JE Alvarez, KG Ahmed, GP Vizcamno, and KP Sauvant (eds), *The Evolving International Investment Regime: Expectations, Realities, Options* (Oxford University Press, 2011). DOI 10.1093/acprof:oso/9780199793624.001.0001.

Gelos G and Wei S, 'Transparency and International Investor Behavior' (2002) *National Bureau of Economic Research Working Paper* 9260.

Grevi G and Vasconcelos Á (eds), *Partnerships for Effective Multilateralism—EU Relations with Brazil, China, India and Russia* (European Union Institute for Security Studies, 2008). DOI 10.2815/5533.

Gruni G and Bronckers M, 'Retooling the Sustainability Standards in EU Free Trade Agreements' (2021) 24 *Journal of International Economic Law* 25. DOI 10.1093/jiel/jgab007.

Gutmann A and Thompson D, *Democracy and Disagreement* (Harvard University Press, 1996).

Habermas J, 'Democracy in Europe: Why the Development of the EU into a Transnational Democracy is Necessary and How it is Possible' (2015) 15 *European Law Journal* 546. DOI 10.1111/eulj.12128.

Habermas J, 'On the Internal Relations between the Rule of Law and Democracy (1995) 3 *European Journal of Philosophy* 12. DOI 10.1111/j.1468-0378.1995.tb00036.x.

Harding A, 'The Legal Transplants Debate: Getting Beyond the Impasse?' in V Breda (ed), *Legal Transplants in East Asia and Oceania* (Cambridge University Press, 2019) 13. DOI 10.1017/9781108605991.002.

Harrison J, 'Recent Developments to Promote Transparency and Public Participation in Investment Treaty Arbitration' (2011) 01 *University of Edinburgh School of Law Working Paper*.

Harrow C, 'Global Administrative Law: the Quest for Principles and Values' (2006) 17 *European Journal of International Law* 196.

Henckels C, 'Justifying the Protection of Legitimate Expectations in International Investment Law: Legal Certainty and Arbitrary Conduct' (2023) 38 *ICSID Review—Foreign Investment Law Journal* 347. DOI 10.1093/icsidreview/siac027.

Henquet T, 'International Investment and the European Union: An Uneasy Relationship' in F Baetens (ed), *Investment Law within International Law* (Cambridge University Press, 2013). DOI https://doi.org/10.1017/CBO9781139855921.024.

Herlin-Karnell E, 'EU Values and the Shaping of the International Legal Context' in D Kochenov and F Amtenbrink (eds), *The European Union's Shaping of the International Legal Order* (Cambridge University Press, 2013). DOI 10.1017/CBO9781139519625.

Herlin-Karnell E, 'The EU as a Promoter of Values and the European Global Project' (2012) 13 *German Law Journal* 1225. DOI 10.1017/S207183220001782X.

Hermann, C, 'Neoliberalism in the European Union' (2007) 79 *Studies in Political Economy* 61. DOI 10.1080/19187033.2007.11675092.

Hirsch M, 'The Sociology of International Economic Law: Sociological Analysis of the Regulation of Regional Agreements in the World Trading System' (2008) 19 *European Journal of International Law* 27. DOI https://doi.org/10.1093/ejil/chn013.

Hirsch R, 'The Judicialization of Politics' in A Caldeira, R Kelemen, and KE Whittington (eds), *The Oxford Handbook of Law and Politics* (Oxford University Press, 2009). DOI 10.1093/oxfordhb/9780199208425.001.0001.

Hobér K, 'Arbitration Involving States' in LW Newman and RD Hill (eds), *Leading Arbitrators' Guide to International Arbitration* (3rd edn, JurisNet LLC, 2014).

Hofmann R and Tams CJ (eds), *International Investment Law and General International Law: From Clinical Isolation to Systemic Integration?* (Nomos, 2011).

Hoffman SJ, Baral P, Rogers Van Katwyk SR, Sritharan L, Hughsam M, Randhawa H, Lin G, Campbell S, Campus B, Dantas M, Foroughian N, Groux G, Gunn E, Guyatt G, Habibi R, Karabit M, Karir A, Kruja K, Lavis JN, Lee O, Li B, Nagi R, Naicker K, Røttingen JA, Sahar N, Srivastava A, Tejpar A, Tran M, Zhang YQ, Zhou Q, and Poirier MJP, 'International Treaties Have Mostly Failed to Produce Their Intended Effects' (2022) 119(32) *Proceedings of the National Academy of Sciences USA*. DOI 10.1073/pnas.2122854119.

Hübner K, Balik T, and Deman AS, 'CETA: the Making of the Comprehensive Economic and Trade Agreement between Canada and the EU' (2016) *Notes de L'Ifri*. https://www.ifri.org/sites/default/files/migrated_files/documents/atoms/files/notes_ifri_ceta_1.pdf.

Hull WI, *The Two Hague Conferences and Their Contributions to International Law* (1908) https://archive.org/details/twohagueconferen00hulluoft.

Hurst W, *Ruling before the Law: The Politics of Legal Regimes in China and Indonesia* (Cambridge University Press, 2018). DOI 10.1017/9781108551502.

Hyde-Price A, 'A "Tragic Actor"? A Realist Perspective on "Ethical Power Europe"' (2008) 84 *International Affairs* 29. DOI 10.1111/j.1468-2346.2008.00687.x.

Jørgensen KE, 'Intersecting Multilateralisms: The European Union and Multilateral Institutions' in KV Laatikainen and KE Smith (eds), *The European Union at the United Nations* (Palgrave Macmillan, 2006). DOI 10.1057/9780230503731_10.

Jørgensen KE and Laatikainen KV (eds), *Routledge Handbook on the European Union and International Institutions: Performance, Policy, Power* (Springer, 2012). DOI 10.4324/9780203083642.

Kaufmann-Kohler G, 'Arbitral Precedent: Dream, Necessity or Excuse? The 2006 Freshfields Lecture' (2007) 23 *Arbitration International* 357. DOI 10.1093/arbitration/23.3.357.

Kingsbury B, 'The Concept of Compliance as a Function of Competing Conceptions of International Law' (1998) 19 *Michigan Journal of International Law* 345.

Klager R, 'Fair and Equitable Treatment: A Look at the Theoretical Underpinnings of Legitimacy and Fairness' (2010) 11 *The Journal of World Investment & Trade* 435. DOI 10.1163/221190010X00121.

Kleinlein T, 'Matters of Interpretation: How to Conceptualize and Evaluate Change of Norms and Values in the International Legal Order' in H Krieger and A Liese (eds), *Tracing Value Change in the International Legal Order: Perspectives from Legal and Political Science* (Oxford University Press, 2023).

Kochenov D, 'Behind the Copenhagen Facade. The Meaning and Structure of the Copenhagen Political Criterion of Democracy and the Rule of Law' (2004) 8 *European Integration Online Papers* 1.

Kochenov D and Amtenbrink F (eds), *The EU's Shaping of the International Legal Order* (Cambridge University Press, 2014) DOI 10.1017/CBO9781139519625.

Kokott J and Sobotta C, 'The *Kadi* Case-Constitutional Core Values and International Law-Finding the Balance?' in M Cremona and A Thies (eds), *The European Court of Justice and External Relations Law—Constitutional Challenges* (Bloomsbury Publishing, 2016).

Kumm M, 'How Does European Union Law Fit into the World of Public Law? Costa, Kadi and Three Conceptions of Public Law' (2011) 11-16 *NYU School of Law Public Law Research Paper.*

Kwakwa E, 'Regulating the International Economy: What Role for the State?' in M Byers (ed), *The Role of Law in International Politics* (Oxford University Press, 2001). DOI 10.1093/acprof:oso/9780199244027.001.0001.

Lang A, *World Trade Law after Neoliberalism: Reimagining the Global Economic Order* (Oxford University Press, 2011). DOI 10.1093/acprof:oso/9780199592647.001.0001.

Lavenex S, 'EU External Governance in "Wider Europe"' (2004) 11 *Journal of European Public Policy* 680. DOI 10.1080/1350176042000248098.

Lavranos N, 'The Remaining Decisive Role of Member States in Negotiating and Concluding EU Investments Agreements' in M Bungenberg, A Reinisch, and C Tietje (eds), *EU and Investment Agreements Open Questions and Remaining Challenges* (Dike, 2013) 165.

Legrand P, 'The Impossibility of 'Legal Transplants' (1997) 4 *Maastricht Journal of European and Comparative Law* 111. DOI 10.1177/1023263X9700400202.

Lenaerts K, 'Upholding the Rule of Law through Judicial Dialogue' (2019) 38 *Yearbook of European Law* 3. DOI 10.1093/yel/yez002.

Lenaerts, K '"In the Union We Trust": Trust-enhancing Principles of Community Law' (2004) 41 *Common Market Law Review* 317. DOI 10.54648/cola2004002.

Lester S, 'Rethinking the International Investment Law System' (2015) 49 *The Journal of World Trade* 211. DOI 10.54648/trad2015009.

Lévesque C, 'The European Union Commission Proposal for the Creation of an "Investment Court System": The Q and A that the Commission Won't Be Issuing' (2016) *Kluwer Arbitration Blog.* https://arbitrationblog.kluwerarbitration.com/2016/04/06/the-european-union-commission-proposal-for-the-creation-of-an-investment-court-system-the-q-and-a-that-the-commission-wont-be-issuing/.

Limbasan N and Malintoppi L, 'Living in Glass Houses? The Debate on Transparency in International Investment Arbitration' (2015) 2 *BCDR International Arbitration Review* 31. DOI 10.54648/bcdr2015003.

Lucarelli S, 'European Political Identity, Foreign Policy and the Others' Image' in F Cerutti and S Lucarelli (eds), *The Search for a European Identity—Values, Policies and Legitimacy of the European Union* (Routledge, 2008). DOI 10.4324/9780203926772.

Lucarelli S, 'Seen from the Outside: The State of the Art on the External Image of the EU' (2014) 36 *Journal of European Integration* 1. DOI 10.1080/07036337.2012.761981.

Lucarelli S, 'The EU's Leadership in Global Governance: Perceptions from the Others' in N Chaban and M Holland (eds), *Communicating Europe in Times of Crisis* (Palgrave Macmillan, 2014). DOI 10.1057/9781137331175_3.

Lucarelli S and Manners I, *Values and Principles in European Union Foreign Policy* (Routledge, 2006). DOI 10.4324/9780203968758.

Maduro MP, *We the Court* (Bloomsbury Publishing, 1998). DOI 10.5040/9781472561893.

Magraw K, 'Investor–State Disputes and the Rise of Recourse to State Party Pleading as Subsequent Agreements or Subsequent Practice under the Vienna Convention on the Law of Treaties' (2015) 30 *ICSID Review—Foreign Investment Law Journal* 142.

Majone G, 'The rise of the regulatory state in Europe' (1994) 17 *West European Politics* 77. DOI 10.1080/01402389408425031.

Majone G, 'From the Positive to the Regulatory State: Causes and Consequences of Changes in the Mode of Governance' (1997) 17 *Journal of Public Policy* 139.

Majone G, 'The Regulatory State and its Legitimacy Problems' (1999) 22 *West European Politics* 1. DOI 10.1080/01402389908425284.

Manners I, 'Assessing the Decennial, Reassessing the Global: Understanding European Union Normative Power in Global Politics' (2013) 48 *Cooperation and Conflict* 304.

Manners I, 'Normative Power Europe: A Contradiction in Terms?' (2002) 40 *Journal of Common Market Studies* 235. DOI 10.1111/1468-5965.00353.

Manners I, 'The Normative Ethics of the European Union' (2008) 84 *International Affairs* 45.

Manners I, 'The Concept of Normative Power in World Politics' (2009) *Danish Institute for International Studies.*

Marceddu ML and Ortino F, 'Intersections Between Trade and Investment Law and Policy' in L Sachs, L Johnson, and J Coleman (eds), *Yearbook on International Investment Law and Policy 2019* (Oxford University Press, 2021).

Marceddu ML and Ortolani P, 'What Is Wrong with Investment Arbitration? Evidence from a Set of Behavioural Experiments' (2020) 31 *European Journal of International Law* 405. DOI 10.1093/ejil/chaa029.

Marceddu ML, 'Implementing Transparency and Public Participation in FTA Negotiations: Are the Times a-Changin'?' (2018) 21 *Journal of International Economic Law* 681. DOI 10.1093/jiel/jgy034.

Marín Durán G, 'Sustainable Development Chapters in EU Free Trade Agreements: Emerging Compliance Issues' (2002) 57 *Common Market Law Review* 1031. DOI 10.54648/cola2020715.

McCarthy C, *The Road* (Vintage International, 2006).

Mehranvar L and Sasma S, 'The Role of Investment Treaties and Investor–State Dispute Settlement (ISDS) in Renewable Energy Investments' (2022). DOI 10.2139/ssrn.4322511.

Mendes J, *Participation in EU Rule-Making* (Oxford University Press, 2011). DOI 10.1093/acprof:oso/9780199599769.001.0001.

Merrills JG, *International Dispute Settlement* (4th edn, Cambridge University Press, 2005). DOI 10.1017/CBO9781139165488.

Meunier S, *Trading Voices* (Princeton University Press, 2005).

Meunier S, 'Integration by Stealth: How the European Union Gained Competence over Foreign Direct Investment' (2014) 66 *EUI RSCAS Global Governance.*

Meunier S and Nicolaïdis K, 'The European Union as a Conflicted Trade Power' (2006) 13 *Journal of European Public Policy* 906. DOI 10.1080/13501760600838623.

Michalena E and Hills JM, *Renewable Energy Governance* (Springer, 2013). DOI 10.1007/978-1-4471-5595-9.

Montanaro F, *The European Union and International Investment Law – The Two Dimensions of an Uneasy Relationship* (Hart Publishing, 2023).

Morgenthau H, *Power Among Nations: The Struggle for Power and Peace* (Alfred A. Knopf, Inc., 1948).

Morlino L, 'The Two "Rules of Law" Between Transition to and Quality of Democracy' in L Morlino and G Palombella (eds), *Rule of Law and Democracy* (Brill, 2010). DOI / 10.1163/ej.9789004181694.i-215.15.

Mourre A, 'Are Amici Curiae the Proper Response to the Public's Concerns on Transparency in Investment Arbitration?' (2006) 5 *The Law & Practice of International Courts and Tribunals* 257. DOI 10.1163/157180306778150614.

Mollestad C, 'See No Evil? Procedural Transparency in International Investment Law and Dispute Settlement' (2014) No. 14-20 *PluriCourts Research Paper*.

Nicolaïdis K and Howse R, '"This is my Eutopia . . .": Narrative as Power' (2001) 40 *Journal of Common Market Studies* 767.

OECD, *International Investment Law: A Changing Landscape: A Companion Volume to International Investment Perspectives* (OECD Publishing, 2005). DOI 10.1787/ 9789264011656-en.

Ortino F, 'Transparency of Investment Awards: External and Internal Dimensions' in J Nakagawa (ed), *Transparency in International Trade and Investment Dispute Settlement* (Routledge, 2012).

Ortino F, 'Investment Treaties, Sustainable Development and Reasonableness Review: A Case Against Strict Proportionality Balancing' (2017) 30 *Leiden Journal of International Law* 71. DOI 10.1017/S0922156516000595.

Ortino F, *The Origin and Evolution of Investment Treaty Standards: Stability, Value, and Reasonableness* (Oxford University Press, 2019). DOI 10.1093/oso/9780198842637.001.0001.

Ortino F, 'The Public Interest as Part of Legitimate Expectations in Investment Arbitration: Missing in Action?' in C Brower, J Donoghue, C Murphy, C Payne, and E Shirlow (eds), *By Peaceful Means: International Adjudication and Arbitration: Essays in Honour of David D. Caron* (Oxford University Press, 2024). DOI 10.1093/oso/9780192848086.003.0021.

Paine J, 'Bear Creek Mining Corporation v Republic of Peru: Judging the Social License of Foreign Investments and Applying New Style Investment Treaties' (2018) 33 *ICSID Review—Foreign Investment Law Journal* 340. DOI 10.1093/icsidreview/siy014.

Pech L, 'A Union Founded on the Rule of Law: Meaning and Reality of the Rule of Law as a Constitutional Principle of EU Law' (2010) 6 *European Constitutional Law Review* 359. DOI 10.1017/S1574019610300034.

Pech L, 'The EU as a Global Rule of Law Promoter: The Consistency and Effectiveness Challenges' (2016) 14 *Asia Europe Journal* 7. DOI 10.1007/s10308-015-0432-z.

Peers S, '"We *aren't* the World": The CJEU Reconciles EU law with International (Investment) Law' (2019). http://eulawanalysis.blogspot.com/2019/05/we-arent-world-cjeu-reconciles-eu-law.html.

Pelc KJ, 'The Politics of Precedent in International Law: A Social Network Application' (2014) 108 *American Political Science Review* 547. DOI 10.1017/S0003055414000276.

Pelc KJ, 'What Explains the Low Success Rate of Investor–State Disputes?' (2017) 71 *International Organization* 559. DOI 10.1017/S0020818317000212.

Perezcano Díaz H, 'The WTO Appellate Body's Impending Paralysis' (Centre for International Governance Innovation, 2019).

Pernice IEA, ' The Treaty of Lisbon: Multilevel Constitutionalism in Action' (2009) 15 *Columbia Journal of European Law* 349.

Perrone NM, 'The "Invisible" Local Communities: Foreign Investor Obligations, Inclusiveness, and the International Investment Regime' (2019) *AJIL Unbound* 113. DOI 10.1017/aju.2018.92.

Petersmann E and Steinbach A (eds), *Constitutionalism and Transnational Governance Failures* (Brill, 2024). DOI 10.1163/9789004693722.

Phelan W, *Great Judgments of the European Court of Justice* (Cambridge University Press, 2019). DOI 10.1017/9781108615020.

Phol JH, 'Strategic Autonomy as a Means to Counter Protectionism' (2021) 22 *ERA Forum* 183.

Piana D, 'Beyond Judicial Independence: Rule Of Law And Judicial Accountabilities In Assessing Democratic Quality' in L Morlino and G Palombella (eds), *Rule of Law and Democracy* (Brill, 2010). DOI 10.1163/ej.9789004181694.i-215.21.

Pollack AM and Shaffer CG (eds), *Transatlantic Governance in the Global Economy* (Rowman & Littlefield Publishers, 2001).

Puig RV, 'The Scope of the New Exclusive Competence of the European Union with Regard to 'Foreign Direct Investment'' (2013) 40 *Legal Issues of Economic Integration* 133. DOI 10.54648/leie2013008.

Puig S, 'Blinding International Justice' (2016) 56 *Virginia Journal of International Law*, 647.

Puig S and Strezhnev A, 'Affiliation Bias in Arbitration: An Experimental Approach' (2016) 16-31 *Arizona Legal Studies Discussion Paper.* https://papers.ssrn.com/sol3/papers.cfm?abstract_id=2830241#

Reinisch A, 'The Division of Powers Between the EU and Its Member States in the Area of Investment Politics' in M Bungenberg, J Griebel, and S Hindelang (eds), *European Yearbook of International Economic Law* (Springer, 2011). DOI 10.1007/978-3-642-14855-2.

Reith C, 'The New UNCITRAL Rules on Transparency 2014: Significant Breakthrough or a Regime Full of Empty Formula?' (2015) 4 *Yearbook on International Arbitration* 121.

Roberts A, Moraes EC, and Ferguson V, 'Toward a Geoeconomic Order in International Trade and Investment' (2019) 22 *Journal of International Economic Law* 655. DOI 10.1093/jiel/jgz036.

Ross A, 'Schwebel Criticises EU Act of "Appeasement"' (2016) 1 *Global Arbitration Review.* https://globalarbitrationreview.com/article/schwebel-criticises-eu-act-of-appeasement.

Rubenfeld J, 'Unilateralism and Constitutionalism' (2004) 79 *New York University Law Review* 1971.

Ruggie JG, 'Continuity and Transformation in the World Polity: Toward a Neorealist Synthesis' (1983) 35 *World Politics* 261.

Ruggie JG, 'Multilateralism: The Anatomy of an Institution' (1992) 46 *International Organization* 561. DOI 10.1017/S0020818300027831.

Sandholtz W, 'Is Winter Coming? Norm Challenges and Norm Resilience' in H Krieger and A Liese (eds), *Tracing Value Change in the International Legal Order: Perspectives from Legal and Political Science* (Oxford University Press, 2023). DOI 10.1093/oso/9780192855831.003.0003.

Sartor G, 'A Sufficientist Approach to Reasonableness in Legal Decision-Making and Judicial Review' in G Bongiovanni, G Sartor, and C Valentini (eds), *Reasonableness and Law* (Springer, 2009). DOI 10.1007/978-1-4020-8500-0_2.

Sartor G, 'Doing Justice to Rights and Values: Teleological Reasoning and Proportionality' (2010) 18 *Artificial Intelligence Law* 175. DOI 10.1007/s10506-010-9095-7.

Sattorova M, 'EU Investment Law at a Crossroads: Open Strategic Autonomy in Times of Heightened Security Concerns' (2023) 60 *Common Market Law Review* 701. DOI 10.54648/cola2023049.

Scheppele KL, Kochenov DV, and Grabowska-Moroz B, 'EU Values Are Law, after All: Enforcing EU Values through Systemic Infringement Actions by the European Commission and the Member States of the European Union' (2020) 39 Yearbook of European Law 3. DOI https://doi.org/10.1093/yel/yeaa012.

Scheu J, Hofmann R, Schill S, and Tams C (eds), *Investment Protection, Human Rights, and International Arbitration in Extraordinary Times* (Nomos, 2022).

Schill S, 'Editorial: Five Times Transparency in International Investment Law' (2014) 15 *The Journal of World Investment & Trade* 363. DOI 10.1163/22119000-01504001.

Schill S, 'Editorial: US versus EU Leadership in Global Investment Governance' (2016) 17 *The Journal of World Investment & Trade* 1. DOI 10.1163/22119000-01701011.

Schneiderman D, *Resisting Economic Globalization: Critical Theory and International Investment Law* (Palgrave Socio-Legal Studies, 2013). DOI 10.1057/9781137004062.

Schønberg S, *Legitimate Expectations in Administrative Law* (Oxford University Press, 2000). DOI 10.1093/acprof:oso/9780198299479.001.0001.

Shapiro M, 'Judicial Power and Democracy' in C Landfried (ed), *Judicial Power—How Constitutional Courts Affect Political Transformations* (Cambridge University Press, 2020). DOI 10.1017/9781108348669.

Shapiro M and Stone Sweet A, *On Law, Politics, and Judicialization* (Oxford University Press, 2002). DOI 10.1093/0199256489.001.0001.

Sharpston E, 'European Community Law and the Doctrine of Legitimate Expectations: How Legitimate, and for Whom' (1990) 11 *Northwestern Journal of International Law & Business* 87.

Shirlow E, 'Dawn of a New Era? The UNCITRAL Rules and UN Convention on Transparency in Treaty-Based Investor-State Arbitration (2016) 31 *ICSID Review—Foreign Investment Law Journal*. DOI 10.1093/icsidreview/siw022.

Solana J, 'The Sound of Europe' Conference, S030/06 (Salzburg, 27 January 2006).

Sornarajah M, *Resistance and Change in the International Law on Foreign Investment* (Cambridge University Press, 2015). DOI 10.1017/CBO9781316156339.

Spieker L D, *EU Values Before the Court of Justice: Foundations, Potential, Risks* (Oxford University Press, 2023). DOI 10.1093/oso/9780198876717.001.0001.

Stern B, 'The Future of International Investment Law: A Balance Between the Protection of Investors and the States' Capacity to Regulate' in J Alvarez and K Sauvant (eds), *The Evolving International Investment Regime: Expectations, Realities, Options* (Oxford University Press, 2011). DOI 10.1093/acprof:oso/9780199793624.001.0001.

St John T, *The Rise of Investor-State Arbitration—Politics, Law, and Unintended Consequences* (Oxford University Press, 2018). DOI 10.1093/oso/9780198789918.001.0001.

Stone Sweet A, 'Judicialization and the Construction of Governance' in M Shapiro and A Stone Sweet (eds), *On Law, Politics, and Judicialization* (Oxford University Press, 2002). DOI 10.1093/0199256489.001.0001.

Stone Sweet A, 'The Juridical Coup D'État and the Problem of Authority' (2007) 8 *German Law Journal* 915. DOI 10.1017/S2071832200006064.

Stone Sweet A and Grisel F, *The Evolution of International Arbitration: Judicialization, Governance, Legitimacy* (Oxford University Press, 2017). DOI 10.1093/acprof:oso/9780198739722.001.0001.

Strang D and Soule SA, 'Diffusion in Organizations and Social Movements: From Hybrid Corn to Poison Pills' (1998) 24 *Annual Review of Sociology* 265.

Tate CN and Vallinder T (eds), *The Global Expansion of Judicial Power* (New York University Press, 1997).

Teubner G, *Constitutional Fragments: Societal Constitutionalism and Globalization* (Oxford University Press, 2012). DOI 10.1093/acprof:oso/9780199644674.001.0001.

The Holy See, 'Address of Pope Francis to the European Parliament' (Strasbourg, 25 November 2014).

Trew S, 'Correcting the Democratic Deficit in the CETA Negotiations: Civil Society Engagement in the Provinces, Municipalities, and Europe' (2013) 68 *International Journal* 568. DOI 10.1177/0020702013509313.

Tropper J and Wagner K, 'The European Union Proposal for the Modernisation of the Energy Charter Treaty—A Model for Climate-Friendly Investment Treaties?' (2022) 23 *The Journal of World Investment and Trade*. DOI 10.1163/22119000-12340271.

Twining W, 'Diffusion of Law: A Global Perspective' (2004) 36 *The Journal of Legal Pluralism and Unofficial Law* 1. DOI 10.1080/07329113.2004.10756300.

Vadi V, 'Beyond Known Worlds: Climate Change Governance by Arbitral Tribunals?' (2015) 48 *Vanderbilt Law Review* 1285.

Valenti M, 'The Protection of General Interests of Host States in the Application of the Fair and Equitable Treatment Standard' in G Sacerdoti, P Acconci, M Valenti, and A De Luca (eds), *General Interests of Host States in International Investment Law* (Cambridge University Press, 2014). DOI 10.1017/CBO9781107279360.

Van der Loo G and Wessel RA, 'The Non-ratification of Mixed Agreements: Legal Consequences and Solutions' (2017) 54 *Common Market Law Review* 735. DOI 10.54648/cola2017059.

Van Harten G, *Investment Treaty Arbitration and Public Law* (Oxford University Press, 2007). DOI 10.1093/acprof:oso/9780199552146.001.0001.

Van Harten G, A Case for an International Investment Court' (2008) Society of International Economic Law (SIEL) Inaugural Conference.

Van Harten G, 'Five Justifications for Investment Treaties: A Critical Discussion' (2010) 2 *Trade, Law & Development*. DOI 10.2139/ssrn.1622928.

Van Harten G, 'Perceived Bias in Investment Treaty Arbitration' in M Waibel, A Kaushal, K-HL Chung, and C Balchin (eds), *The Backlash Against Investment Arbitration: Perceptions and Reality* (Kluwer Law International, 2010).

Van Harten G, *Sovereign Choices and Sovereign Constraints* (Oxford University Press, 2013). DOI 10.1093/acprof:oso/9780199678648.001.0001.

Vandevelde KT, 'The Bilateral Investment Treaty Program of the United States' (1988) 21 *Cornell International Law Journal* 201.

Vidigal Puig R 'The Scope of the New Exclusive Competence of the European Union with Regard to 'Foreign Direct Investment'' (2013) 40 *Legal Issues of Economic Integration* 133. DOI /10.54648/leie2013008.

Von Bogdandy A and Venzke I, 'In Whose Name? An Investigation of International Courts' Public Authority and Its Democratic Justification' (2014) 23 *European Journal of International Law* 7. DOI 10.1093/ejil/chr106.

Waibel M, Kaushal A, Chung K-H, and Balchin C, *The Backlash Against Investment Arbitration. Perceptions and Reality* (Kluwer Law International, 2010).

Waibel M and Wu Y, 'Are Arbitrators Political?' (2012). DOI 10.2139/ssrn.2101186.

Walde T, 'Alternatives for Obtaining Greater Consistency in Investment Arbitration: An Appellate Institution after the WTO, Authoritative Treaty Arbitration or Mandatory Consolidation?' (2005) 2 *Transnational Dispute Management* 1. https://www.transnational-dispute-management.com/article.asp?key=421.

Warner H and Sheppard A (eds), 'Appeals and Challenges to Investment Treaty Awards: Is it Time for an International Appellate System?—Editorial Note' (2005) 2 *Transnational Dispute Management* 1. https://www.transnational-dispute-management.com/article.asp?key=421.

Watson A, *Legal Transplants—An Approach to Comparative Law* (Scottish Academic Press, 1974).

Watson A, 'Legal Transplants and Law Reform' (1976) 92 *Law Quarterly Review* 79.

Watson A, 'From Legal Transplants to Legal Formants' (1995) 43 *The American Journal of Comparative Law* 469. DOI 10.2307/840649.

Weatherill S, *Law and Values in the European Union* (Oxford University Press, 2016). DOI 10.1093/acprof:oso/9780199557264.001.0001.

Weber M, *Economy and Society: An Outline of Interpretive Sociology* (University of California Press, 2013).

Weiler JHH, 'The Transformation of Europe' (1991) 100 *Yale Law Journal* 2403.

Weiler JHH, *The Constitution of Europe 'Do the New Clothes Have an Emperor?' and Other Essays on European Integration* (Cambridge University Press, 1999).

Weiler JHH, 'The Geology of International Law—Governance, Democracy and Legitimacy' (2004) 64 *ZaöRV* 547.

Weiler JHH, 'The Political and Legal Culture of European Integration: An Exploratory Essay' (2011) 9 *International Journal of Constitutional Law* 678. DOI 10.1093/icon/mor054.

Weiler JHH, 'Deciphering the Political and Legal DNA of European Integration: An Exploratory Essay' in J Dickson and P Eleftheriadis, *Philosophical Foundations of European Union Law* (Oxford University Press, 2012). DOI 10.1093/acprof:oso/9780199588770.003.0006.

Weiler JHH, 'Europe in Crisis—On "Political Messianism", "Legitimacy" and the "Rule of Law"' (2012) *Singapore Journal of Legal Studies* 248.

Weiler JHH, 'In the Face of Crisis: Input Legitimacy, Output Legitimacy and the Political Messianism of European Integration' (2012) 34 *Journal of European Integration* 825. DOI 10.1080/07036337.2012.726017.

Weiler JHH, 'Europe Must Learn Quickly to Speak the Language of Power: Part I' (29 October 2020) *EJIL:Talk!* https://www.ejiltalk.org/europe-must-learn-quickly-to-speak-the-language-of-power-part-i/.

Weiler JHH, Haltern UR, and Mayer FC, 'European Democracy and its Critique' (1995) 18 *West European Politics* 4. DOI 10.1080/01402389508425089.

Wessel RA and Takács T, 'Constitutional Aspects of the EU's Global Actorness: Increased Exclusivity in Trade and Investment and the Role of the European Parliament' (2017) 28 *European Business Law Review* 103.

Williams A, *The Ethos of Europe: Values, Law and Justice in the EU* (Cambridge University Press, 2010). DOI 10.1017/CBO9780511750335.

Williams AT, 'Taking Values Seriously: Towards a Philosophy of EU Law' (2009) 29 *Oxford Journal of Legal Studies* 549. DOI 10.1093/ojls/gqp017.

Zarbiyev F, 'Judicial Activism in International Law—A Conceptual Framework for Analysis' (2012) 3 *Journal of International Dispute Settlement* 247. DOI 10.1093/jnlids/ids005.

Zarbiyev F, 'On the Judge Centredness of the International Legal Self' (2021) 32 *European Journal of International Law* 1139. DOI 10.1093/ejil/chab048.

Zielonka J, 'Europe as a Global Actor: Empire by Example?' (2008) 84 *International Affairs* 471. DOI 10.1111/j.1468-2346.2008.00718.x.

Zuleta E, 'The Challenge of Creating a Standing International Investment Court' in JE Kalicki and A Joubin-Bret (eds), *Reshaping the Investor–State Dispute Settlement System* (Brill, 2015). DOI 10.1163/9789004291102_017.

Index

For the benefit of digital users, indexed terms that span two pages (e.g., 52–53) may, on occasion, appear on only one of those pages.

Tables are indicated by an italic *t* following the page number.